FIGHTERS
AND
QUITTERS

GREAT POLITICAL RESIGNATIONS

THEO BARCLAY

\B^b\
Biteback Publishing

This new edition published in Great Britain in 2019 by
Biteback Publishing Ltd
Westminster Tower
3 Albert Embankment
London SE1 7SP
Copyright © Theo Barclay 2018, 2019

ISBN 978-1-78590-461-5

10 9 8 7 6 5 4 3 2 1

A CIP catalogue record for this book is available from the British Library.

Set in Adobe Caslon Pro

Printed and bound in Great Britain by
CPI Group (UK) Ltd, Croydon CR0 4YY

For my grandmothers, Marguerite and Clare

ACKNOWLEDGEMENTS

There are several people without whom this book could never have been written.

I would like to thank the following:

Olivia Beattie, Iain Dale, Bernadette Marron, Ellen Heaney and all the team at Biteback, for taking a punt on a first-time author writing an unusual book and for coping with my inability to keep to a deadline;

My father Johnny, for introducing me to the writing of A. A. Milne and Alan Bennett, and for his unceasing enthusiasm;

Georgie, my sister, for ferreting out the hidden fun everywhere – including polling stations;

Peter and Suzanne Thackeray, the formidable duo who nurtured my interest in politics;

Sam Carter, who fed my addiction to third-rate Blair-era political biographies;

Andrew Neil, for unwittingly keeping me company through many a day and night;

Geoff Steward and Nico Gaisman for their encouragement and meticulous editing;

Michael Crick, for kindly reading through the manuscript, pointing out errors and giving sage advice;

Victor Khadem, who has nurtured this book from the first idea to the final sentence;

Riversdale Waldegrave, for heroically editing the contents while hard at work; and

Lucy Fisher, for her endless help with this book and her constant love and support.

T. W. T. B.
November 2018

CONTENTS

'We know of no spectacle so ridiculous as the British public in one of its periodical fits of morality. In general, elopements, divorces and family quarrels pass with little notice. We read the scandal, talk about it for a day, and forget it. But once in every six or seven years our virtue becomes outrageous. We cannot suffer the laws of religion and decency to be violated. We must make a stand against vice. We must teach libertines that the English people appreciate the importance of domestic ties. Accordingly some unfortunate man, in no respect more depraved that hundreds whose offences have been treated with lenity, is singled out as an expiatory sacrifice.'

LORD MACAULAY IN *CRITICAL AND HISTORICAL ESSAYS*, 1851

'A man is not finished when he's defeated. He's finished when he quits.'

RICHARD NIXON TO EDWARD KENNEDY, 1969

'Age wrinkles the body. Quitting wrinkles the soul.'

DOUGLAS MACARTHUR

INTRODUCTION

WHEN TO FIGHT AND WHEN TO QUIT

The first rule of British politics is never to resign. High office is not, after all, easily acquired. To climb the greasy pole, MPs must serve an apprenticeship as under-secretary for paperclips, suffer countless rubber-chicken dinners and develop an expertise in potholes to rival the most qualified highway engineer. Having endured such tiresome training, senior politicians rarely give up without a fight. In nearly three centuries of Cabinet government, fewer than one hundred cabinet ministers have quit. This book tells the story of the most dramatic of those plunges, from bunglers making unwitting errors, to ministers mired in corruption and even would-be political assassins.

The government's ministerial code restates two commonly cited constitutional conventions that set out the circumstances under which resignation is mandatory. First, 'collective responsibility', which dictates that ministers must leave the government if they cannot support the Cabinet's agreed position. Second, 'individual responsibility', which forces them to take the blame for their own or their department's catastrophic mistakes. But if those conventions ever existed, both have, like the requirement for the Home Secretary to be in the room for every royal birth, been consigned to history.

A look back over the past forty years of British politics proves that the doctrine of collective responsibility has shaky foundations. Cabinet members have frequently made it clear in private and in public that their views differ from the government position. United and compliant Cabinets are not the product of a nebulous constitutional convention, but of good party management, large majorities and powerful Prime Ministers. Individual responsibility is in even worse health. It summons up an idealised image of the dutiful statesman honourably falling on their sword to prevent the faulty gears of government from being exposed. But such action is anathema to the modern politician, who clings desperately to any excuse to remain in office. Embattled ministers are only too happy to blame civil servants for their department's problems, and members of the Cabinet have survived the most catastrophic blunders. In 1983, Jim Prior remained Northern Ireland Secretary despite thirty IRA fighters breaking out of prison on his watch, and ten years later, Norman Lamont refused to quit after his decisions cost the country £3 billion in one day. The last time a minister truly took the blame for their underlings' errors was in 1954, when Sir Thomas Dugdale sacrificed himself in the convoluted Crichel Down Affair, in which the government was deemed to have broken its promise in a land dispute. Hailed at the time as the definitive example of individual responsibility, it appears, with hindsight, to have been an isolated incident.

When, then, will politicians resign? Instead of following a set of strict constitutional rules, they quit only if they are prompted by their own conscience, considerations of political expediency or if they are forced out by the Prime Minister of the day.

Modern-day resignations tend to follow three patterns:

The first is the daylight assassination – an aggressive, rather than defensive, move. A select number of Cabinet ministers have deployed their resignation as a weapon, an Exocet launched at the government they have left behind in a bid to destabilise it. These hot-headed pretenders usually find to their dismay, however, that nobody is willing to follow them over the cliff. The only effective exponent of the tactic was Geoffrey Howe, who succeeded in his mission to destroy Margaret Thatcher in 1990 by using his resignation to call for open insurrection. Yet even his victory was a pyrrhic one, ending not only the Prime Minister's career but also his own.

The second kind of resignation is the principled stand – quitting solely to publicise a strongly held point of dispute with the government, eschewing all future preferment and ending one's frontline career. This category boasts an even smaller number of quitters, despite its connotations of nobility and probity. The most celebrated is Robin Cook, whose laser-focused demolition of the case for the Iraq War in 2003 was made in one of the few speeches to the House that has outlived its maker.

Overwhelmingly, the most common route to the political scrapheap is the third type of resignation – the slow death. This undignified end follows a torrent of blows from party, press and public. The flailing minister, enmeshed in a scandal or dogged by allegations of misconduct, attempts to hold out, but eventually succumbs to the inevitable, their reputation lying in tatters.

Not all scandals result in the departure of the politician involved, but those that do tend to share certain characteristics. What is it, then, that renders an incident fatal?

Most importantly, the offence must be sufficiently grave or titillating to attract the sustained attention of the press. Ministers who are merely inept or unpopular usually manage to limp on until the next reshuffle. It is often obvious when a story will take hold, so Chris

Huhne's frontbench career was incompatible with his designation as a criminal suspect and, later, Andrew Mitchell could not survive accusations that he had called a policeman a 'pleb'. Such sagas, which straddle the boundary between tragedy and farce, are an irresistible gift for tabloid editors. Ostensibly less outrageous stories can also evolve into long-running scandals if, for example, they emerge in a slow news week and there are willing sources for follow-up stories, or even, as in the case of Stephen 'Liar' Byers, the minister has a headline-friendly name. The end is nigh when a story remains in the papers long enough to turn heads in the public at large. Former Downing Street director of communications Alastair Campbell reportedly stated as a rule of thumb that anyone who dominates the headlines for two consecutive Sundays should pack their bags. On the evidence of this book, many can survive for longer than that, but, once a beleaguered politician starts fending off unremitting attacks on all fronts, their days are numbered.

In the background of most ministerial resignations there is a canny opposition MP keeping the scandal in the news. Robin Cook carefully cultivated the controversy over opposite number Edwina Currie's controversial comments about salmonella in 1988, while Labour's backbench attack dogs Simon Danczuk and John Mann were tireless in pressing the issues that destroyed, respectively, Chris Huhne and Liam Fox. In contrast, a poor performer can allow their besieged opponent to survive. Theresa May repeatedly let Stephen Byers off the hook in 2002 with her dreary parliamentary performances, while in 2017 shadow Home Secretary Diane Abbott failed to take advantage of the news that her opposite number had deported an asylum seeker in flagrant breach of a court order.

Crucially, a minister hoping to fight off a scandal must never appear dishonest. For politicians, this is harder than it sounds. Although outright lies of the kind that terminated John Profumo's career are rare, ministers commonly tie themselves in knots when attempting to skirt around a difficult topic. This book is littered with examples, from Leon Brittan to Liam Fox, of those figures who may have survived if they had not been evasive when backed into a corner.

Sometimes it is better to quit than to fight, for there is such a thing as a good resignation. To pull off this rare feat, the minister must depart well before the incident has entered the public consciousness. There is no room for Clare Short's agonising vacillations over whether to depart over Iraq – it is critical to be decisive. To avoid further revelations fanning the flames of a scandal, the full facts must be willingly put out into the open, accompanied by a fulsome expression of support for the government and an understated resignation letter. Under these terms, rehabilitation is possible after a period on the back benches.

There is a noble tradition of tactically speedy resignations. In 1890, the Irish nationalist MP Charles Stewart Parnell lost the support of Parliament after being exposed for having an affair. His friend Cecil Rhodes, then South African Prime Minister, sent him a telegram from Cape Town reading: 'RESIGN. MARRY. RETURN.' – solid advice to this day. The most skilful quitter in recent years was Conservative MP Mark Harper, who, in 2013, managed to hire an illegal immigrant as his cleaner while serving as Minister of State for Immigration. He took the plunge and resigned before the story had fully emerged, releasing a concise statement on a Saturday night before melting into the background. After three months, he was back in government with a better job, his misdemeanour forgotten. Within the year, he had been promoted to Chief Whip.

There are irresistible patterns linking the most dramatic downfalls. Resignations prompted by a disagreement over policy have overwhelmingly concerned one subject. The UK's membership of the European Community has been the most destructive issue to seep into

British politics since the Second World War. From the moment Roy Jenkins and two colleagues quit the Labour shadow Cabinet in 1971, in protest against their leader's support for a referendum on membership of the Community, the European question has cleaved an inexorable fault line through the major political parties. Six of Margaret Thatcher's Cabinet ministers resigned over Europe, triggering the vicious war that would later cause David Cameron to lose Douglas Carswell and Mark Reckless from the Conservative benches and Iain Duncan Smith from the government, before eventually prompting his own resignation. As this book shows, his successor has fared no better. The Labour Party's split, so destructive in the 1980s, has now re-emerged with the election to the party leadership of lifelong anti-EU activist Jeremy Corbyn. His lacklustre efforts in 2016's referendum campaign triggered the departure of over 100 frontbenchers, including fifty in one weekend. As Britain continues to hurtle towards a messy exit from the bloc, there will be more resignations in which Europe plays its part.

Whether they have quit over policy or scandal, there are personality traits that link most of the politicians considered in this book. None were cautious bureaucrats or punctilious administrators; rather they were gamblers and thrill-seekers, inspired to brilliance and vulnerable to catastrophe in equal measure. Few public figures would dare to take a stand in open defiance of the popular position, as Michael Heseltine and Robin Cook did. Similarly, pursuing an unconventional sex life under a nom de plume is not an activity for the faint-hearted politician. One wonders, for instance, how Labour MP Keith Vaz convinced himself that he would stay out of the papers when hiring rent boys while pretending to be a washing machine salesman named Jim. John Profumo, John Stonehouse and Chris Huhne pushed matters yet further: all knew they were likely to be caught out, yet were brazenly dishonest and confidently backed themselves to get away with it. But it should not be any surprise that the most successful MPs have a propensity for recklessness and delusional self-belief. They have, after all, chosen a career that invariably ends in failure.

The decades following the Second World War proved a uniquely fertile breeding ground for scandal. From the late 1950s onwards, social change was in the air, and all authority fell to be questioned. The Profumo Affair in 1963 exposed a world of hidden privilege and vice, prompting a shocked public never again to grant politicians the benefit of the doubt. In response, a new class of ambitious press barons emerged to rival previously entrenched establishment figures like Lords Beaverbrook and Rothermere. These proprietors, from Rupert Murdoch to Robert Maxwell, took their chance to build business empires off the back of the public's newly found insatiable desire for scandal. Their journalists soon became experts at digging up morsels to feed the unquenchable appetite for intrigue, catching a whole generation of public figures off their guard.

The socially conservative newspaper readers of the 1960s took a prurient interest in what they deemed deviant behaviour. Many of the stories in this book explore the consequences of being a gay politician, with most of its subjects growing up at a time when homosexuality was neither legal nor openly tolerated. Liberal leader Jeremy Thorpe's actions would in any age be deemed worthy of resignation, but they were born out of the extreme lengths to which he went to hide his sexuality from public view. Although the law had shifted to decriminalise abortion and homosexuality by the late 1960s, public attitudes took far longer to change. As late as 1998, there was still no question that Ron Davies's ministerial career was over when he was apparently caught with a man on Clapham Common in a scandal that caused as progressive a figure as Tony Blair to worry that 'we could get away with Ron as a one-off aberration, but if the public start to think the whole Cabinet is indulging in gay sex we could have a bit of a political problem'.

With Blair's government, the pace of change increased sharply, and in a demonstration of how far attitudes had shifted, Thorpe's successor, Tim Farron, a staunch Christian, was heavily criticised in 2017 after giving the impression he believed gay sex was a sin. His inability to deny this overshadowed his party's entire general election campaign and eventually contributed to his own resignation. The current liberal sentiment means that the resigning matters of yesterday barely make the news in modern times. Indeed, there is perhaps today a greater respect in the media for the private lives of politicians than before.

But it is not only social change that has rendered the dramatic resignation an endangered species. Knowing how easily careers are ruined by a tenacious press and baying public, those entering politics are far more careful than their predecessors were. In an age when mobile phone cameras and social media make personal information readily accessible, there is now barely any distinction between the public and private life. As it is impossible to keep a secret for long, most prefer to keep no secrets at all, and there are, one suspects, fewer scandals waiting to be uncovered.

Commentators rightly bemoan the present shortage of great political characters. It is the threat of scandal that has nearly eliminated the reckless gambler from public life, and instead replaced them with those who remain vigilant in avoiding any risky situations. Most ministers now plot their route to power from youth, scouring their social media history for potential embarrassments and ensuring that their lives never appear too extravagant. With Britain's leading figures ever more cautious, and the public less prone to being shocked, the end may be in sight for the age of the great political resignation.

CHAPTER ONE

THE DUCHESS OF ATHOLL

Katharine Atholl was a most unusual lady, and a knot of contradictions. The woman who would become known as the 'Red Duchess' was a pioneer of the women's movement that believed her gender better suited for the home; an anti-Soviet polemicist who fought alongside socialists; and a female minister who always rejected women's right to vote. It may come as a surprise that she is most distinguished by her stubborn constancy during a protest that ended her political career. On the eve of a world war that she had foreseen before most others, the duchess took the unprecedented step of triggering a by-election that nearly destroyed Neville Chamberlain's fragile grip on power.

Born into Scotland's ancient Ramsay family on 6 November 1874, she spent a happy childhood in the artistic circles of Scottish high society. She was a talented pianist and composer, becoming one of an elite group of women to study at the Royal College of Music under Sir Hubert Parry. It was here that she met Ted Butler, the son of one of her tutors, who became the first – and enduring – love of her life. But the middle-class Butler family were not considered suitable company for the aristocratic young lady. In a move that prompted her lifelong resentment, her family ended the relationship, cut short her studies and enforced a return to Scotland. She was instructed to wait for a suitable husband, and was eventually sent off to the palatial Blair Castle to marry John, the heir to the Dukedom of Atholl.

John was a gentle man and a natural homemaker. Against his inclinations, his father pressured him to become a Conservative politician, and he was duly awarded the safe seat of West Perthshire.

The marriage to Katharine reversed customary gender roles. He preferred the confines of the home, where he was an enthusiastic host, while she took to the public sphere, gaining a reputation as a confident and effective operator who harboured little affection for domesticity. While her husband reluctantly came to terms with parliamentary procedure, she ascended to the head of the Perthshire Women's Unionist Association, edited a military history of Perthshire and became a leading voice in local government in the region.

The marriage was underscored by sadness, however, for the couple were unable to produce a child. Believing that motherhood was 'the basic fact of [women's] existence', Katharine was dogged by a pervading sense of failure. Bereft of the chance to head a family, she decided instead to devote her life to politics.

John held his seat until 1917, when he succeeded his father to become the eighth Duke of Atholl. He resigned his place in the House of Commons to take up his birthright of a seat in the House of Lords. While it was not uncommon at the time for hereditary peers to become MPs before later moving to Parliament's upper chamber, John's departure sparked a chain of events that shocked his local party. His successor as local Tory candidate in West Perthshire proceeded to lose the next election to a rival Liberal. Reeling from the surprise result, the West Perthshire Conservative Association did not select a new candidate for four years.

In 1923, the former Liberal Prime Minister David Lloyd George came to Blair Castle on a social visit. It was over dinner that he suggested to Katharine that she should become one of the first women to enter Parliament. Immediately taken with the idea, she determined to stand, ignoring the objections of her husband and also of King George V, who, naturally, was a family friend. She duly wrote to the Conservative Association to nominate herself and was unanimously adopted as their candidate in the election later that year. On defeating her Liberal opponent, she became the first female MP in Scotland. Over the next fifteen years she proved so popular that her majority soared from 150 to over 5,000 votes.

The duchess's parliamentary career was defined by conviction over ambition. Her maiden speech set out her personal priorities – the welfare of women and children, the protection of the empire and a vociferous opposition to socialism. Plainly dressed and humourless, she was caricatured as a schoolmistress. When the eight women elected in 1923 met with one another, she found the gatherings 'very friendly, but … rather an ordeal', noting that their wild divergence of opinion on a range of issues trumped any gender-based solidarity. Unlike her colleagues, she felt that 'the supreme sphere of women must remain the home', as 'we, who are incapable of taking upon ourselves the burden of national defence, should have [no] decisive voice in questions of peace and war'. Perhaps because of her opposition to the further preferment of women, she was appointed by Stanley Baldwin as the first female minister in a Conservative government.

The duchess grew into a belligerent campaigner with a penchant for unpopular causes. Her husband observed that 'if there was a breeze, she would always face it'. A notably uninspiring speaker, however, she was nicknamed the 'Begum of Blair' for her rambling and tortured interventions. Sometimes, her speeches ironically sometimes achieved the opposite of what was intended, with a vigorous defence of the Hoare–Laval Pact reported to have convinced several MPs to oppose it.

Despite her rhetorical shortcomings, the young minister was vindicated on many of the issues that she chose to make her own. The first cause she seized upon with passion was the plight of the people in Soviet Russia. With the assistance of exiled Tsarist leaders, she began to draw attention to the starvation, religious persecution and forced labour faced by millions under Stalin's rule. She then conducted a forensic study of Soviet society, publishing her findings in a book entitled *Conscription of a People*. Written at a time when Soviet dupes such as Sidney and Beatrice Webb were extolling Stalin's virtues, this stands as one of Britain's first trenchant critiques of Bolshevism.

She was also a leading advocate for the better treatment of women across the world, a cause that gave her an early taste of bipartisanship. In 1931, she led a cross-party delegation to the International Conference on African Children and called on all colonial powers to put an end to female genital mutilation – another issue on which she was well ahead of her time.

But it was the more traditional realms of foreign policy that were to dominate the duchess's political career. In 1935, Ramsay MacDonald's government responded to the growing territorial ambitions of Adolf Hitler with appeasement, a policy that was later to prove a grave misjudgement. She became alarmed by the German Chancellor's audacious remilitarisation of the Rhineland in March 1936. As with the other issues that she had made her own, she first disappeared into the library to undertake thorough research before emerging with a book of her own to release. She began by reading Hitler's *Mein Kampf* – not just in the abridged and sanitised English translation, but also in the original

German. Shocked by its contents and concerned by how little of Hitler's malice was conveyed in the English version, she noted that 'never can a modern statesman have made so startlingly clear to his reader his ambitions'. Reaching the view that it was fascism that was 'the only serious danger to Europe', rather than socialism, as the pervading orthodoxy would have it, she released her own translation of Hitler's tome in May 1936. This publication began to convince her allies and constituents of the imminent danger posed by the German dictator.

The duchess's burgeoning reputation as a maverick was reinforced by the stance she took over the Spanish Civil War; a war triggered by the attempt of the ultra-conservative General Franco to overthrow the democratically elected socialist government. Franco was backed by Mussolini, Hitler and by British and American companies that feared the spread of socialism. Soviet Russia supported the governing Republicans. The ensuing conflict became a uniting cause for the British left, portrayed as a fight for socialism against the forces of capitalism and fascism. Although Britain's government remained neutral, thousands of leftists volunteered to fight for the Republicans in the International Brigades.

The duchess declared herself a strong supporter of the Republican cause. Isolated among her Tory colleagues, who overwhelmingly backed Franco, she became close to those socialists that she had formerly despised. In 1938, she visited Spain with three female colleagues from the Labour Party to arrange the evacuation of 4,000 Basque children to London, an act that several Tory colleagues regarded as treason. She was in Madrid when it was bombed by Franco's forces and returned traumatised by what she had seen. Again, she retreated to the library before presenting her research and empirical testimony in a book: *Searchlight on Spain* sold over 300,000 copies in Britain and was soon translated into French, Spanish and German. It set out a detailed history of the events leading up to the war, outlined the humanitarian crisis and called for the British government to arm the Republicans against their fascist opponents.

Exasperating her anti-Soviet party colleagues further, the duchess began to associate with outwardly leftist Republican supporters, even addressing meetings of the International Peace Campaign at which the left-wing anthem 'The Red Flag', today the Labour Party's unofficial song, was bellowed out. It was these curious appearances that earned her the nickname 'Red Duchess'.

Her position on Spain brought her into bitter conflict with her own constituents. The significant contingent of West Perthshire Roman Catholics fiercely supported Franco, and many on the anti-Soviet right considered the rise of fascism a welcome bulwark against communism. Most importantly, middle-class electors were offended by her neglect of local issues and flagrant disloyalty to her party. She had come to rely on the continuing support of her voters and Conservative Association members without canvassing their views. In a stark warning, they declared that they had been tolerant 'almost to breaking point'. Affronted by such insolence, she declared herself 'not the delegate of the Association with a commission to act on its behalf', but 'the representative in Parliament of the constituency'.

On the morning of 12 March 1938, the Nazis left the Treaty of Versailles in tatters by invading Austria, establishing the *Anschluss* that formed the starting point for Hitler's vision of a Third Reich. This aggression took Europe a step closer to war, and further emboldened the duchess. On 22 April, she publicly criticised Prime Minister Neville Chamberlain for his naïveté and declared that Hitler must be defeated. Disregarding the growing insurrection in her constituency, she embarked on a lecture tour of the USA in a forlorn attempt to direct American attention towards the European crisis.

While she was across the Atlantic, Chamberlain signed the Munich Agreement in which he accepted Hitler's promise that Germany would not provoke a war with Britain. The duchess was implored by her embarrassed husband, her friends and parliamentary colleagues not to criticise the accord upon which Chamberlain had staked his premiership. She refused, and within weeks was distributing pamphlets castigating the agreement as a shameful surrender.

Her actions were the final straw for her constituency association members, who voted to deselect her as their parliamentary candidate. The duchess's response was characteristically bold. Ignoring the advice of her friend and fellow anti-appeasement campaigner Winston Churchill, she decided to resign as an MP, to trigger a by-election and stand on the single-issue platform of opposing the policy of appeasement. On 24 November 1938, she was appointed the Crown Steward of the Chiltern Hundreds, a ceremonial title awarded to resigning members of Parliament, and officially triggered the ballot, which was held less than a month later. Her slogan was pithy and to the point: 'Country before Party'.

In a move that demonstrated the growing level of consensus outside the Conservative Party about her views, the Liberals decided not to field a candidate against her. This left the by-election a straight fight between the duchess and her former party. The short campaign suited her, as growing scepticism about the Munich Agreement coincided with rumours of Nazi abuse of Jews in Germany.

Her Conservative opponent, William McNair Snadden, embarked on a tour of all areas of the constituency, speaking at sixty-four public meetings in three weeks and receiving strong backing from a Conservative Association united against their former MP. Chamberlain, aware that a loss would catastrophically undermine his flagship policy, despatched fifty Conservative MPs to West Perthshire. These included his own parliamentary private secretary and the Secretary of State for Scotland. All the Tories repeated the same message – a vote for them was a vote to avoid war. In contrast, a vote for the Red Duchess risked the lives of your children. This warning resonated strongly with a generation scarred by the Great War.

By all accounts the duchess ran a poor by-election campaign. She neglected the more populous towns in favour of Conservative-voting villages. Public meetings were badly advertised and ill-attended. Accepting that the gentry and middle class would stick with Chamberlain, she sensibly targeted the working class, but adopted a patronising tone that failed to win over her targets. She also continued to antagonise her former Catholic voters by speaking at length about Spain. They could not tolerate her criticism of General Franco, who sought to restore the privileged status of the church that had been eroded by the Republicans.

The few Tory colleagues who shared her views failed to come to her assistance, fearing retribution from their own constituency associations. The enigmatic Bob Boothby had promised to campaign at her side, but withdrew because his local chairman threatened to resign. He sent her a short letter admitting: 'Frankly, I cannot face this.' The only Tory to offer open support was Churchill, who wrote publicly to say:

> The fact remains that outside our island, your defeat at this moment would be relished by the enemies of Britain and of freedom in every part of the world. It would be widely accepted as another sign that Great Britain … no longer has the spirit and willpower to confront the tyrannies and cruel persecutions which have darkened this age.

But that letter was as far as Churchill was prepared to go. The Tory whips had told him that he would be expelled if he joined her campaign and he recognised the importance of remaining in a prominent position if, as he anticipated, war broke out across Europe.

The duchess did receive some endorsements, but not all were welcome. Radical Labour MPs and communist activists descended upon West Perthshire to campaign for her, significantly boosting her rival's cause. The support of suffragette Sylvia Pankhurst, who declared 'every woman who prizes her vote should vote for [Kitty]', failed to win the approval of the patrician electors of Kinross. Most disastrously of all, with only two days to go, the newspapers received a mocking telegram from Joseph Stalin himself, reading: 'Moscow is proud of Katharine the even greater.'

Although she remained dignified throughout the campaign, she was shocked at the viciousness of her former party. It was the dirtiest by-election that had ever been contested. Tory employers secured votes by increasing their workers' wages, while estate owners suspended tenants' rent in return for support and local businesses were ordered to take down her posters.

Despite the tactics deployed against her, the duchess expected to secure sufficient Liberal votes to win. It was not to be. Snadden triumphed with a majority of over 1,000 votes following a blizzard on the day of voting. The Conservatives had, unlike Kitty, arranged buses to take voters through the snow to the polls. Snadden's team were not gracious in victory, with one laird sending the duchess a telegram reading: 'Am delighted you are out. Hope my Rannoch people voted against you. Now you might find time to remove your Basque children from Suffolk.'

She was mortified by the result, writing in her autobiography that '[the loss] was a blow, and I hated to think how I had let down all those who had helped me'. She realised that she had 'forgotten the extent to which the myth of Mr Chamberlain as the saviour of peace still gripped the country'. After her defeat, she briefly considered a return as an MP. But, as she predicted, Hitler proceeded to ignore the Munich Agreement, invaded Poland and triggered the start of the Second World War. Devoting herself to the war effort, she served as the Secretary of the Scottish Invasion Committee, tasked with the responsibility of preparing for a German attack. After the war, she became founding chair of the British League for European Freedom and campaigned against the Soviets' influence in Eastern Europe.

The duchess never regretted her resignation, which stands alone as an example of a lone MP triggering a pivotal national debate on a single issue. A similar feat was attempted by David Davis in 2008, when he resigned as an MP to force a by-election about the erosion of civil liberties. Although his cause had widespread public support and he had more immediate access to journalists, he did not manage to generate significant attention. Davis's failure highlights the Duchess of Atholl's achievement. Had the by-election gone the other way, she might just have altered the course of the Second World War.

CHAPTER TWO

JOHN PROFUMO

This was the scandal that had it all. Glamorous aristocrats, gorgeous call girls, East End gangsters, Russian spies and a rank miscarriage of justice. Above all else, the resignation of the Secretary of State for War permanently broke apart British society's fusty and buttoned-up façade. For the first time, the public realised that behind their haughty exterior, members of the establishment were at it like rabbits.

Scion of a dynasty of Sardinian barons that had become enmeshed in English high society, the young John Profumo was educated at Harrow and Oxford before joining the army shortly before the start of the Second World War. Having triumphantly led his men into Normandy on D-Day, he emerged from the conflict a highly decorated brigadier. He returned to the House of Commons in 1950, having already served a stint as an MP between 1940 and 1945. Intelligent, smooth and charming, Profumo moved in bohemian circles and always had an eye for the ladies. He frequently toured Soho's topless nightclubs and remained single until the age of thirty-nine. Soon after his marriage to famous actress Valerie Hobson, he was promoted by then Prime Minister Harold Macmillan, and took his seat on the government front bench.

On a hot July weekend in 1961, the year after his elevation, Profumo and his wife made the short journey to Cliveden, Lord Astor's magnificent Buckinghamshire estate. They had been invited to spend a long weekend with Astor and other distinguished guests. On the Saturday evening, while enjoying a stroll around the grounds with his host, Profumo spied a leggy brunette standing stark naked by the swimming pool. The minister was instantly smitten with the beautiful young girl, and he and Astor chased her all around the pool, hiding her towel.

She was Christine Keeler, a nineteen-year-old model and friend of high-society osteopath Stephen Ward, the tenant of a small cottage on Astor's estate. Keeler has often been cast as a shameless temptress, but in truth she was a troubled and vulnerable teenager. Sexually abused by her stepfather in her youth, she had fled to London two years earlier after aborting her baby with a knitting needle. On reaching the big city, she became a topless dancer in a Soho nightclub where she met the 47-year-old Ward. Her distinctive beauty and easy charm made her the ideal girl for him to introduce to his influential clients.

That evening, Keeler and Ward sat down for dinner with Astor and his guests, who included the President of Pakistan and the Queen's cousin Lord Mountbatten. Profumo ended the night chasing Keeler through the upstairs bedrooms and, out of sight of his wife, gave her a surreptitious grope behind a suit of armour.

Ward, who had been asked by Astor to bring girls that would get on with his guests, observed the flirtation with considerable satisfaction. At the time, he was London's go-to osteopath, boasting a client list that included Winston Churchill, Frank Sinatra and Elizabeth Taylor. His professional success brought with it considerable social standing, enabling him to moonlight as a portrait painter to the stars. Ward's renowned parties were known for their diverse list of attendees, but always included a throng of beautiful young girls. Despite being, by his own admission, 'not handsome' and with 'no money', he considered himself 'one of the most successful men in town with girls'. One of his former girlfriends recalled that he took 'immense excitement and satisfaction' in organising orgies. He enjoyed 'watching someone else making love to a girl of whom he was fond. And the more passionate or violent the sex act, the more it seemed to satisfy him.'

One of Ward's favourite clients was Soviet naval attaché and spy Eugene Ivanov. The pair had first met over lunch at the Garrick Club, introduced by the editor of the *Daily Telegraph*, and they had struck up a close friendship. Ivanov, who had already been noted by MI5 for possessing a 'thirst for women', became a frequent attendee at Ward's parties. The Russian arrived at the Cliveden cottage the morning after Profumo met Keeler. As soon as he had unpacked his bags, the group converged by the pool. Ward later recalled that 'Ivanov and [Profumo] had a race down the pool …We started off with a countdown, "Three, two, one, fire" in Ivanov's honour. And although no legs were to be used, John Profumo shot ahead – using his legs.' Having cheated to win the race, Profumo joked that his actions should teach Ivanov a lesson about trusting the British government.

Keeler was instantly attracted to the glamorous Russian, and at the end of the day asked him to drive her home. Once they had arrived at the mews house she shared with Ward, she invited him up for a cup of coffee. He produced from his jacket a bottle of vodka and poured them both a large glass. According to Keeler, before long they were having 'good old-fashioned sex without any fuss or trimmings' on the kitchen floor.

With no idea that Keeler was involved with the Russian agent, Profumo resumed his pursuit of her after the weekend. After obtaining her telephone number from Ward, he arranged to meet up with her and soon the pair was having what Keeler described as frequent 'screws of convenience'. These occurred in a variety of locations, from Ward's flat to Profumo's Mini Cooper, his friend's Bentley and, once, his marital bed. The Secretary of State spoiled his new lover, buying her gifts and giving her money ostensibly 'for her mother'. Ward actively encouraged her to continue the affair, joking that he was able to start a world war.

Keeler always knew that her dalliance with Profumo 'was no grand romance', and that she was 'clearly not the first girl he chased'. For Keeler, their sex 'had no more meaning than a handshake or a look across a crowded room'. She was far more excited by the ursine Ivanov, whom she continued to see, apparently ignorant of the threat to national security that this presented.

The security services were not as oblivious. Aware that Ward was, in the words of one agent, 'the provider of popsies for rich people', they spied the chance to honeytrap the Soviet. After putting Keeler under surveillance, they rapidly discovered that she was also sleeping with Profumo. This realisation prompted the panicked head of MI5 to contact the Cabinet Secretary, who subtly warned the Secretary of State for War to be careful about his private life.

Profumo took the hint and soon after wrote a polite note to Keeler breaking off their month-long fling. She was not particularly disappointed and soon turned her gaze to two East End hustlers: Johnny Edgecombe and 'Lucky' Gordon. Her two-timing eventually ended with a fight at a Soho jazz club, which left Gordon with a badly slashed face. Keeler briefly moved in to Edgecombe's house in Essex but soon grew tired of him and returned to Ward.

In December 1962, the spurned Edgecombe arrived at Ward's house and attempted to shoulder the door down. When Keeler refused to let him in, he drew a handgun and fired six shots at the door before being arrested for attempted murder. Shaken by the attack and fearing that his high-society friends would abandon him if he courted publicity, Ward ordered Keeler to leave.

Seething at Ward's brutality, she sought to destroy his social standing and make herself some serious money in the process. She approached journalist Paul Mann and Labour MP John Lewis and recounted the story of her trysts with Profumo and Ivanov. Lewis tape-recorded her allegations while Mann persuaded her to go to the press. After she showed a *Sunday Pictorial* reporter a note written to her by Profumo, they offered her £1,000 for the exclusive: the largest sum that had ever been paid for a news story.

The Prime Minister was told in February 1963 that Profumo had been having an affair, but, having not been briefed about the Ivanov connection, failed to recognise the security risk it posed. To Macmillan, it seemed to be simply part of the routine escapades of Profumo's louche set and none of his business. He noted in his diary that his minister

> had behaved foolishly and indiscreetly, but not wickedly. His wife is very nice and sensible. Of course, all these people move in a selfish, theatrical, bohemian society, where no one really knows anyone and everyone is 'darling'. But Profumo does not seem to have realised that we have, in public life – to observe different standards from those prevalent today in many circles.

Johnny Edgecombe was due to stand trial in March 1963 for his attack on Ward's flat. Despite appearing as a witness in the preliminary hearings, Keeler absconded before the main trial, decamping with a journalist to a remote fishing village in Spain to prepare for the release of her story by the *Sunday Pictorial*.

Realising that his business and social lives were about to be ruined, Ward panicked. He tipped off Profumo and begged the minister to help him bury the story. Forming an unlikely team, the pair contacted Keeler, who offered to deny everything if she was paid £5,000. Neither man was prepared to submit to this extortion, knowing that she would come back for more money eventually.

Profumo instead deployed his extensive contact book to try to stop the story coming out. His first move was to persuade MI5 to impose reporting restrictions on Keeler. When that failed, he and Ward heaped pressure upon Reg Payne, the editor of the *Sunday Pictorial*. Out of deference to Profumo, and realising that he would be relying on the word of a young girl on the run from the law against a Cabinet minister of unblemished reputation, Payne agreed to drop the story. For a short time, it looked like Ward and Profumo had escaped.

Fleet Street's hacks have never been, however, renowned for their discretion. Within weeks, reporters across the world had heard rumours of Profumo's extramarital activities. The editor of the *Daily Express* decided to hint heavily at the scandal, publishing the headline 'War Minister Shock' and asserting on his front page that Profumo had offered his resignation to Harold Macmillan for mysterious reasons. Placed right next to the story on the front page was an ostensibly separate article about Christine Keeler's disappearance, and the inside pages were adorned with the now-infamous pictures of Keeler wrapping her legs around an Arne Jacobsen chair. Realising that the scandal was bound to unfold, Commander Ivanov quietly left Britain, never to return.

The Labour Party needed no excuse to spread the juicy rumours about Profumo further, but the security implications provided a good reason to keep the story going. 'Westminster Confidential', the House of Commons's internal newsletter, printed the outline of the allegations in their March edition, asking: 'Who was using the call girl to milk whom of information – the War Secretary or the Soviet military attaché?'

Profumo moved into damage-limitation mode. He called his most senior colleagues to deny his having an affair with Keeler, imploring them to believe that the allegations had been invented. For many Tory ministers, suspicion soon melted into sympathy. Their attitude must be understood in the context of the previous year's Vassall Affair, in which a young British diplomat was honeytrapped by the Soviets and forced to turn spy against his own country. As that scandal emerged, damaging rumours were spread about Conservative minister Thomas Galbraith's close relationship with the traitor. Galbraith was forced to resign, but was cleared of any impropriety in a subsequent inquiry. Since then, many MPs had taken a dim view of journalists' reliability and were prepared to give Profumo the benefit of the doubt.

Fearful of libel actions, the tabloid editors would go no further than the *Daily Express*'s insinuation. It was left to politicians to expose the affair using parliamentary privilege, an ancient right permitting MPs to speak with impunity when in the House. One Labour MP was only too happy to oblige. Colonel George Wigg harboured a long-standing grudge against Profumo, having clashed with him over military provision when he complained that the Secretary of State for War was willing to send troops into battle 'without anti-aircraft cover, with ineffective anti-tank weapons, with no ground strike force, short of long-range fighters and without any satisfactory long-distance freighters'. The colonel quipped: 'If that satisfies him then God help us if he had been disappointed.' On that occasion, Profumo loftily batted away Wigg's grievance and failed to contact him afterwards. It was to prove a fatal error.

On 21 March 1963, Wigg used an obscure parliamentary debate held at 10 p.m. to relay the rumours to the House of Commons, saying:

There is not an honourable member of this House, nor a journalist in the press gallery, nor do I believe there is a person in the public gallery, who in the last few days has not heard rumour upon rumour involving a member of the government front bench. The press has got as near as it can – it has shown itself willing to wound, but afraid to strike ... In actual fact, these great press lords, these men who control great instruments of public opinion and power, do not have the guts to discharge the duty they are now claiming for themselves. That being the case, I rightly use the privilege of the House of Commons – that is what it is given to me for – to ask the Home Secretary, who is the senior member of the government on the Treasury bench now, to go to the despatch box – he knows the rumour to which I refer relates to Miss Christine Keeler ... and a shooting by a West Indian – and, on behalf of the government, categorically deny the truth of these rumours. On the other hand, if there is anything in them, I urge him to ask the Prime Minister to do what was not done in the Vassall case – set up a select committee so that these things can be dissipated, and the honour of the minister concerned freed from the implications and innuendoes that are being spread at the present time.

Wigg's call for an inquiry was supported by prominent Labour front-benchers Richard Crossman and Barbara Castle, who asked the Home Secretary if Profumo had been sleeping with Keeler. Rising to defend Profumo, the Home Secretary was dismissive, saying: 'I do not propose to comment on rumours which have been raised under the cloak of privilege and safe from any action at law. [The Labour Party] should seek other means of making these insinuations if they are prepared to substantiate them.'

It was not just Tories that spoke in support of Profumo. Labour stalwart Reginald Paget asked the House: 'What do these rumours amount to? They amount to the fact that a minister is said to be acquainted with an extremely pretty girl. As far as I am concerned, I should have thought that was a matter for congratulation rather than an inquiry.'

The Prime Minister was deeply alarmed that the affair had become public. The newspapers were now free to print the story with impunity, and there was sufficient material for the coverage to continue for months. The Chief Whip hastily arranged an emergency summit for 2.45 a.m., attended by the Attorney General, the Leader of the House of Commons, the Solicitor General and Bill Deedes, Minister without Portfolio and later editor of the *Sunday Telegraph*. The assembled ministers were blunt, with the Attorney General getting straight to the point, saying: 'Look, Jack, the basic question is, "Did you fuck her?"' Profumo again assured them that the answer was no. He later revealed that 'I felt I couldn't tell the truth at that stage … it would have been beyond my political ability to own up to them – having got that far telling lies.'

Again, his colleagues took him at his word, using the meeting to decide how the swelling political crisis would be handled. They decided that the best response would be for Profumo to make a full statement to the House denying the allegations. As the most media-savvy among those present, Bill Deedes set about drafting a statement that might bring the affair to a swift conclusion.

On Friday 22 March 1963, Profumo stood up in the House to deliver his personal statement with the Prime Minister sat beside him. He said:

I understand that in the debate … last night, under protection of parliamentary privilege, the honourable gentlemen the members for Dudley [Wigg] and for Coventry East [Crossman] and the honourable lady the member for Blackburn [Mrs Castle], opposite, spoke of rumours connecting a minister with a Miss Keeler and a recent trial at the central criminal court. It was alleged that people in high places might have been responsible for concealing information concerning the disappearance of a witness and the perversion of justice. I understand that my name has been connected with the rumours about the disappearance of Miss Keeler. I would like to take this opportunity of making a personal statement about these matters.

I last saw Miss Keeler in December 1961, and I have not seen her since. I have no idea where she is now. Any suggestion that I was in any way connected with or responsible for her absence from the trial at the Old Bailey is wholly and completely untrue. My wife and I first met Miss Keeler at a house party in July 1961, at Cliveden. Among a number of people there was Dr Stephen Ward, whom we already knew slightly, and a Mr Ivanov, who was an attaché at the Russian embassy. The only other occasion that my wife or I met Mr Ivanov was for a moment at the official reception for Major Gagarin at the Soviet Embassy. My wife and I had a standing invitation to visit Dr Ward. Between July and December 1961, I met Miss Keeler on about half-a-dozen occasions at Dr Ward's flat, when I called to see him and his friends. Miss Keeler and I were on friendly terms. There was no impropriety whatsoever in my acquaintanceship with Miss Keeler. Mr Speaker, I have made this personal statement because of what was said in the House last evening by the three honourable members, and which, of course, was protected by privilege. I shall not hesitate to issue writs for libel and slander if scandalous allegations are made or repeated outside the House.

When Profumo sat down, Macmillan clapped him on the shoulder in a public gesture of confidence. The Secretary of State for War swiftly left the chamber to meet his wife, who had been watching from the public gallery. They departed straight away to join the Queen Mother for an afternoon at the Cheltenham races, in which fortune smiled upon Profumo when he backed the Gold Cup-winning horse at 10–1.

Only days later, Lord Astor evicted Ward from the Cliveden cottage, and, on the orders of the security services, the police began to investigate whether they could prosecute the osteopath. Realising that he was being set up as the fall guy for the whole affair, Ward responded by writing a dossier proving that Profumo had lied to the House. He sent it to Leader of the Opposition Harold Wilson and the Home Secretary before issuing a press release saying:

> I have placed before the Home Secretary … certain facts of the relationship between Miss Christine Keeler and Mr John Profumo, the War Minister, since it is obvious now that my efforts to conceal those facts in the interests of Mr Profumo and the Government made it appear that I myself have something to hide – which I have not. The result has been that I have been persecuted in a variety of ways causing damage not only to myself but to my friends and patients – a state of affairs I propose to tolerate no longer.

Refusing to believe the Secretary of State for War's denials, Colonel Wigg appeared on BBC's *Panorama* to denounce Profumo's behaviour as a risk to the security of the country. Having seen the programme and Ward's dossier, Harold Wilson raised the issue in a private meeting with the Prime Minister. He described what he had read as a

> nauseating document, taking the lid off a corner of the London underworld of vice, dope, marijuana, blackmail and counter-blackmail, violence, petty crime, together with references to Mr Profumo and

the Soviet attaché ... if it were published as a fiction paperback in America hon. Members would have thrown it away, not only for what it contained, but as being overdrawn and beyond belief even as credible fiction.

Realising that the scandal would be impossible to suppress, Macmillan acquiesced to Wilson's request to set up an inquiry chaired by the Lord Chancellor, Lord Dilhorne.

Profumo assured Dilhorne that he would be sticking to his story, then left London for a holiday in Italy with his wife. While dining in Venice that week, she finally forced him to confess the truth to her and told him that he must return home and own up to his dishonesty. The next morning, Profumo met in London with the Chief Whip. After explaining that he had lied to the House, he immediately offered his resignation both as a minister and an MP. He returned his seals of office to Buckingham Palace by courier because he was too ashamed to attend the traditional audience with the Queen.

Profumo and Macmillan exchanged unusually curt letters of resignation the next day. The Prime Minister ignored the convention of listing his former minister's achievements in office in favour of a curt three-sentence reply. Profumo had left office in total disgrace.

The scandal split the Cabinet in two. Macmillan's great rival, Enoch Powell, was critical of the deferential, trusting way in which the crisis had been handled and spied a chance to destabilise the Prime Minister. He was supported by other prominent ministers Keith Joseph, Henry Brooke and Edward Boyle. For several days it was rumoured that Powell would use the Profumo resignation to stage his own departure, which would have spelled the end of Macmillan's tired and fragile administration. The Prime Minister was incredulous and remained 'determined that no British government should be brought down by the action of tarts'. After a tense couple of days, Powell was placated, the prospect of a series of resignations temporarily receded, and Macmillan limped on.

The police arrested Ward two days after Profumo's resignation on trumped-up charges of 'having knowingly lived wholly or in part on the earnings of prostitution'. The alleged 'prostitutes' were Keeler and her friend Mandy Rice-Davies, who had each paid Ward rent.

After his arrest, the tabloids exposed the full details of Ward's activities alongside a wide variety of rumours about all manner of establishment figures, their contents ranging from the credible to the outlandish. Mandy Rice-Davies gladly joined in this very public airing of gossip, revealing that 'a number of well-known people' were involved in orgies at Ward's home, before speaking of one party 'where the host opened the door wearing nothing but his socks'. 'Then', she said, 'there was a dinner party where a naked man wearing a mask waited on the table like a slave. He had to have a mask because he was so well-known.' The identity of the man in the mask became the object of great intrigue, and the *Daily Express* quoted another guest who said:

> As the 'slave' handed cocktail snacks the guests abused and reviled him. He was obviously enjoying it. I was told by the host that the man arrived first at the party. He undressed and put on a mask before other guests arrived. The host revealed his identity to me. I could hardly believe it.

The identity of the 'man in the mask' soon became the talk of London.

A separate media storm centred on the divorcee, the Duchess of Argyll, who was revealed to have led a private life that caused a judge to refer to her as 'a highly sexed woman, who has ceased to be satisfied with normal sexual activities and has started to indulge in disgusting sexual activities to gratify a debased sexual appetite that can only be satisfied by a number of men', before adding: 'Her attitude to the sanctity of marriage was what moderns would call enlightened, but which in plain language was wholly immoral.' The tabloids then acquired and published a polaroid photograph of the Duchess fellating a man whose head was just out of shot. Public attention focused on the identity of the headless man, with strong rumours that he was Duncan Sandys, the Colonial Secretary.

Faced with a rapacious, unleashed press and knocked off guard by the relentless stream of scandals, the Cabinet agreed that a full inquiry was required. It was to be conducted by the Master of the Rolls, Lord Denning, who promised to get to the bottom of the whole affair and restore order to the rattled establishment.

Denning was particularly determined to discover the truth behind the Duchess of Argyll rumours and, in perhaps the ultimate expression of judicial authority over the executive, took the extraordinary step of ordering the Colonial Secretary to undergo a medical examination of his penis to confirm that he was not the person in the photograph. It remains, for now, the only instance of a judge forcing a minister of the Crown to have his or her genitals measured. The identity of the 'headless man' did not become clear until 2013, when the Duchess's stepdaughter revealed that it had been an American airline executive called Bill Lyons.

Denning published his 70,000-word report in October 1963. The raciest and most readable government document ever published, it sold 4,000 copies in the first hour. The full text was soon published in a *Sunday Telegraph* supplement.

Although Profumo was never able to resume his political career and an exhausted Macmillan resigned as Prime Minister on health grounds soon after receiving Denning's report, it was Stephen Ward that came out worst from the scandal. In July 1963, he faced an eight-day trial at the Old Bailey; vigorously denying the allegations that he had lived off the earnings of prostitution, he diagnosed the proceedings in his opening speech to the jury as 'a political revenge trial', adding: 'Someone had to be sacrificed, and that someone is me.'

The prosecuting barrister was Mervyn Griffith-Jones QC, a renowned social reactionary who in 1960 had fought vigorously, albeit in vain, to restrain the publication of *Lady Chatterley's Lover* for obscenity. According to Ian Crawford, a journalist observing Ward's trial, in his opening speech Griffith-Jones seemed palpably shocked by Ward's 'departures from the strictly domestic sexual code', and 'considered it his divine calling and mission to see that he was convicted'.

His cross-examination was brutal from the first question: 'Are your sexual desires absolutely insatiable?' Ward accepted that he liked to be surrounded by a coterie of young, beautiful girls, frequently used prostitutes and that he knew Christine Keeler had, at the very least, received presents in exchange for sex. He noted, however, that 'half the shops in London would close down if people did not buy their girlfriends presents', and flatly denied being a pimp.

When Keeler and Rice-Davies gave their evidence, the proceedings descended into farce. Both had negotiated substantial sums for memoirs and reflections that would be published soon after the trial and both knew that they would profit from greater publicity. Keeler staged her arrival at court to be as dramatic as possible, with the brunette pushing her way through waiting crowds that were five rows deep. Inside the courtroom, Rice-Davies played up to the press gallery. When it was put to her that Lord Astor had said he did not know her, she replied in much-celebrated fashion: 'Well he would, wouldn't he?'

On 30 July, the judge started his two-day summing-up speech to the jury. He betrayed his own innate conservatism on the first day by telling them that there are many people of high estate and low who could have come forward and testified … one would have thought from the newspapers that this country has become a sink of iniquity. But you and I know that the even tenor of family life over the overwhelming majority of the population goes quietly and decently on.

Ward was not prepared to hear the rest of the speech. After the first day of summing up he had dinner with his friend Noel Howard-Jones, with whom he was staying during the trial. When they had finished eating, Ward drove himself in his open-top Jaguar on one final trip around many of his former haunts in Soho. He then made his way back to the flat, wrote letters to his solicitor and barrister thanking them 'for their help, kindness and loyalty during the long days of the trial' and took a massive overdose of barbiturates. He left behind a note for Howard-Jones, which read:

Dear Noel,

I am sorry I had to do this here! It is really more than I can stand. The horror, day after day at the court and in the streets. It is not only fear, it is a wish not to let them get me. I would rather get myself. I do hope I have not let people down too much. I tried to do my stuff but after Marshall's summing up, I've given up all hope.

The car needs oil in the gearbox, by the way. Be happy in it.

Incidentally, it was surprisingly easy and required no guts. I am sorry to disappoint the vultures.

I only hope this has done the job. Delay resuscitation as long as possible.

Howard-Jones found Ward at 8.30 a.m. the next morning. He later said: 'I looked at Stephen and I thought he was dead. His face was blue … but then he breathed and I knew there was a chance. I dialled 999 and waited for an ambulance.'

Mere hours later, despite the objection of the barristers from both sides, the judge decided that the trial should continue in Ward's absence. While doctors were desperately trying to save his life, the jury unanimously found him guilty of the substantial majority of charges against him. He never regained consciousness and died soon after the verdict.

Since his death, many have recognised the unfairness that underlay Ward's trial. Prominent barrister Geoffrey Robertson QC has identified six principal reasons that his trial was unfair. First, Keeler had lied to the court in a previous trial but the jury was not told to treat her evidence with caution. Second, the judge failed to warn the jury against relying on Keeler and Rice-Davies's evidence to corroborate the other as they were friends and accomplices. Third, the judge should have told the jury to bear in mind Ward had no previous offences and was of 'good character'. Fourth, on Keeler's unchallenged evidence, she had not at the relevant time been a prostitute. Fifth, even if she had been a prostitute, there was no evidence that Ward knew about it. Finally, his prosecution was initiated directly by the Home Secretary, who should instead have granted the police operational independence.

In 2017, fifty-four years after the trial, the Criminal Cases Review Commission apologised to Ward's family and acknowledged that the conviction would probably be quashed if an appeal were now heard. Many still believe that he was the victim of a plot to silence him in revenge for the embarrassment he caused the establishment. If such a plot existed, there is no evidence for it in the Secret Service's files, but there is no doubt that he was set up as a scapegoat for the affair.

Profumo disappeared from political life immediately after his resignation. For the next forty years he quietly devoted himself to helping London's poor, rendering himself a role model for all disgraced politicians seeking to recover some respect. He never spoke about the affair that came to define his life, but his friend the Bishop of Stepney said that 'no one judges Jack Profumo more harshly than he does himself. He says he has never known a day since it happened when he has not felt real shame.' His wife remained loyal to him until her death in 1998, and Profumo himself died eight years later at the age of ninety-one. Shortly before his death, he told his son: 'You know, I *have* enjoyed my life!'

Aside from the considerable charitable achievements of his later years, Profumo's real legacy was a marked break in the nation's social history. The scandal that bears his name allowed the British media to bin its antiquated deference in favour of the irreverent, insatiable appetite for outrage that still defines it. From then on, politicians of all persuasions knew that, whatever their social standing, they would never be safe.

JOHN PROFUMO TO HAROLD MACMILLAN

Dear Prime Minister,

You will recollect that on 22nd March, following certain allegations made in Parliament, I made a personal statement. At that time the rumour had charged me with assisting in the disappearance of a witness and with being involved in some possible breach of security.

So serious were these charges that I allowed myself to think that my personal association with that witness, which had also been the subject of rumour, was by comparison of minor importance only. In my statement I said there had been no impropriety in this association. To my very deep regret I have to admit that this was not true, and that I misled you and my colleagues and the House.

I ask you to understand that I did this to protect, as I thought, my wife and family, who were misled, as were my professional advisers.

I have come to realise that, by this description, I have been guilty of a grave misdemeanour and despite the fact that there is no truth whatsoever in any of the other charges, I cannot remain a member of your Administration, nor of the House of Commons.

I cannot tell you of my deep remorse for the embarrassment I have caused you, to my colleagues in the Government, to my constituents and to the Party which I have served for the past twenty-five years.

Yours Sincerely,

Jack Profumo

HAROLD MACMILLAN
TO JOHN PROFUMO

Dear Profumo,

The contents of your letter of 4th June have been communicated to me, and I have heard them with deep regret. This is a great tragedy for you, your family and your friends. Nevertheless, I am sure you will understand that in the circumstances I have no alternative but to advise the Queen to accept your resignation.

Yours very sincerely,

Harold Macmillan

CHAPTER THREE

LORDS LAMBTON
AND JELLICOE

Tony Lambton was one of the rudest men ever to serve as a government minister. The son of the Earl of Durham and heir to a colossal fortune, he revelled in embarrassing those around him, once approaching an acquaintance in front of a crowd of people and asking him: 'Do you masturbate a lot?', before adding enthusiastically: 'I do!' Later in life, he punished a tiresome dinner guest by letting a young lion loose in his bedroom. He boasted an incisive brain, however – a virtue he twinned with striking looks and a troublesome taste for hedonism. Arriving on the political scene at a time when peers could not remain in the Commons without renouncing their titles, Lambton was ambitious enough to forego his in order to have a shot at reaching the top ranks of British politics. The first victim of a proper newspaper sex sting, his demise was viewed by friends as a devastating, if predictable, calamity.

At the age of twenty-nine, the young viscount, unfulfilled by his occupation as a full-time playboy, resolved to propel himself onto the political stage. He was elected in the 1951 election as Tory MP for Berwick-upon-Tweed in Northumberland. Tall, rakishly slim and a dapper dresser, he cut a fine figure in an era dominated by grey administrators. He treated the constituency duties that accrued to his role much as his grandfather would have done; his sporadic trips to Berwick were usually for shooting parties rather than opportunities to engage with local voters.

Lambton's progression to high office was frustrated by his poor choice of allies and his disdain for dour Prime Minister Harold Macmillan, who identified the aristocrat as part of 'the small group of people who really hate me'. He was unwilling to abandon his youthful indiscretion and embraced the sexual mores of the Swinging Sixties with gusto. In the lavish parties he hosted with his wife Bindy, a muse for the painter Lucian Freud, sex, alcohol and amphetamines all flowed liberally.

It was the unlikely figure of Edward Heath, a hard-working and distinctly anti-social figure, who eventually granted Lambton the role he yearned for in government, appointing him Minister for the Royal Air Force in 1970. The token of preferment came as a surprise to colleagues. The Prime Minister was as uptight and stiff as his new underling was relaxed and decadent, and Lambton's louche existence was far removed from Heath's dutiful piano practice and wholesome sailing classes. It was perhaps the Prime Minister's cosseted nature that prevented him foreseeing the dangers posed by his colleague's lifestyle.

Life became more difficult for Lambton after the ministerial appointment. Bindy suffered a dramatic go-karting accident that fractured both her legs, leading to experimental surgery and a prolonged recovery. As soon as she was back on her feet, she drove the wrong way down the A1 and veered straight into the path of a lorry. The collision shattered nearly every bone in her body, leaving her encased in plaster and confined to a wheelchair for two years. Lambton soon tired of nursing her, and began to turn his attention to a string of increasingly exotic mistresses.

In 1972, he started to visit a call girl in Maida Vale named Norma Levy. She specialised in sadomasochism and domination, so was well placed to fulfil the minister's more niche predilections. At first, Lambton was sensible enough to use the alias 'Mr Lucas', but soon grew careless, leaving his real name on his clothing and on one occasion paying with a personal cheque. Like Christine Keeler before her, Levy couldn't resist boasting to her friends about her glamorous and high-profile client.

Spying his chance to cash in on the arrangement, Levy's pimp tried to photograph Lambton naked through a gap in the prostitute's doorframe. However, when he went to flog the pictures to the *News of the World*, the paper rejected the poor quality of the prints. Instead, the tabloid sent its own staff to rig up the flat. In their first attempt at a full-throttled sex sting, they installed a tape recorder and camera in holes in the wall and inserted a second lens inside a teddy bear on the bed.

Lambton was caught by the devices reclining in bed beside two naked women – all three were smoking cannabis. The story – boasting sex, illegality and a high-society protagonist – was the stuff of a tabloid editor's dream. But the *News of the World* declined to run the story: out of deference to the aristocrat's status, fearful of reprisals and as a staunch Conservative supporter, its editor buried the tale. Levy's pimp was incandescent and desperate for money, so moved on to hawk his images to fellow tabloid the *Sunday People*, who handed the documents straight to the police.

The following day, Lambton was met by the deputy assistant commissioner of New Scotland Yard, who searched his London home. Twenty-eight grams of cannabis, several packets of amphetamine and an unlicensed gun were found. On the scene the squirming minister awkwardly acknowledged: 'I have been made a complete monkey out of.' The security services immediately demanded to interview him, fearing that he may have been compromised in an echo of the Profumo Affair. The MI5 operative who interrogated Lambton recorded that his 'behaviour … was of a man who is on the verge of collapse. He spoke very quietly as if in a daze.' The MP conceded that he may well have left himself 'open to blackmail because of his use of drugs and the fact that photographs exist of sexual practices deviating from the normal'. In justification, he explained that the sheer tedium of his ministerial job had driven him to the twin hobbies of gardening and whores.

With his political career in tatters at the hands of a newspaper story that had not even been published, Lambton attempted a dignified departure from the front bench. He sent a short letter to Heath, identifying 'personal and health reasons' as the basis for his resignation from government. Although this euphemistic excuse was accepted without fuss, a Soho pornographer had meanwhile been briefing the press about the real story, which made its way into a German gossip magazine the next day.

Realising that the details were bound to emerge, and desperate to avoid an ongoing saga, Lambton decided that the best defence was honesty. On 23 May 1973, he issued a frank and unapologetic statement:

This is a sordid story. I have a casual acquaintance with a call girl and one or two of her friends. But there has been no security risk and no blackmail and never at any time have I spoken of any aspect of my late job. All that has happened is that some sneak pimp has seen an opportunity of making money by the sale of the story and secret photographs to the papers at home and abroad. My own feelings may be imagined, but I have no excuses whatsoever to make. I behaved with incredulous stupidity. I must repeat that there has been no high life vice ring, no security leak, no blackmail and, as far as I know, no politician of any party is remotely connected to these events. Thank you.

Aware of the rumours and hearsay stoked by the Profumo Affair, and wanting to control as far as possible the release of information about his sex life, he resolved to make a full confession of his many indiscretions. To that end he went on Robin Day's flagship interview programme, claiming that he had often used 'whores for sex' because 'people sometimes like variety. It's as simple as that.' He added that 'most men would expect their wives over an incident basically unimportant like this to understand it'. Batting aside allegations that there was a risk of blackmail or the divulging of state secrets, he noted that 'people don't go to call girls to talk about … secret affairs … I mean if the call girl suddenly said to me: "Please, darling, tell me about the laser ray" or "What do you think of the new Rolls-Royce engine?" I mean I would have known that something was up…' Finally, in an interview for *Panorama*, he famously declared that he 'couldn't think what all the fuss was about. Surely all men visit whores?'

Lambton had planned to remain an MP, but the outraged Heath demanded his departure from politics altogether. Fellow Tory Nicholas Fairbairn criticised the Prime Minister's attitude, saying that 'Ted Heath handled it in his way – as a puritan and a prig': an unsurprising sentiment from a man who used his *Who's Who* entry to list 'making love' as his recreation.

Lambton's was not the only resignation over the affair. The day after his confession, rumours circulated that the press were poised to name a second minister involved in the same vice ring. The police had uncovered a document from Norma Levy with repeated references to the word 'Jellico', which in fact referred to a hotel where Levy met her clients. Robert Armstrong, then Heath's private secretary, assumed it was a reference to a second client, who he took to be the second Earl Jellicoe, Lord Privy Seal and Leader of the House of Lords. Armstrong rushed to intercept the Prime Minister as he was attending a performance at the Royal Opera House and promptly arranged a meeting with the implicated peer at No. 10.

Heath asked Jellicoe outright whether he too was a client of Levy. According to Armstrong's notes of the meeting, Jellicoe was 'not unnaturally taken aback by what the Prime Minister had to say, and asked several times to clarify the nature of the allegations'. The peer then insisted that Levy was 'completely unknown to him' and that it was impossible that there were any photographs of him in a compromising position. The next morning, however, Jellicoe returned to No. 10 uninvited. This time he confessed to Heath that while he did not know Levy, he had nonetheless 'used the services of call girls' for a string of casual affairs. Assuming – incorrectly – that the sex workers with whom he had liaised had also gathered material about him, he tendered his resignation. A failure to hold his nerve saw him own up to his indiscretions needlessly. Friends called it damn hard luck.

Lambton initially won the support of his long-suffering wife, but soon betrayed her and eloped to Italy with a new mistress. He settled in Tuscany, spending the rest of his life tending bougainvillea and hosting spectacular parties at the Villa Cetinale, the seventeenth-century palace that he had bought himself. Through throwing thirty-five years of luxurious bashes, to which he invited the likes of Mick Jagger, Tony Blair and Kate Moss, he earned himself the nickname 'the King of Chiantishire'.

The Lambton affair has now been largely forgotten, sandwiched between the larger scandals surrounding John Profumo and Jeremy Thorpe. Yet it remains an important landmark in the gradual erosion of respect for the private lives of public figures. The first time a national newspaper had stitched up a government minister so brazenly, it marked an acceleration in the move away from the conventions of class deference. Politicians of all backgrounds were, from then on, held to a higher standard than other citizens, and it seemed there was no longer a place in the political arena for hedonistic aristocrats.

CHAPTER FOUR

JOHN STONEHOUSE

Tossing his clothes, passport and wallet in a small pile on the Miami beach, the man slowly waded into the sea. He had no intention of returning to his former life. As he submerged his body deeper and deeper into the waves, he felt the sea washing away the tensions and sins of his past. It felt, to him, 'like the baptism of a new being'. The year was 1974, and the man was John Stonehouse – the only MP known to have faked his own death. He came tantalisingly close to pulling off the disappearing act, but was, in the end, foiled by bad fortune and hubris. As his plot unravelled, the backdrop of illicit affairs, fraud and espionage that he had tried to run from were swiftly uncovered. Against the odds, the discovery that he was alive paved the way for a dramatic return to the Commons and – eventually – the strangest resignation that the House has ever seen.

Stonehouse's early life provided no indication of the intrigue that was to follow. A strikingly intelligent boy with an IQ of 140, he was born into a middle-class family steeped in the Labour movement. His father was a trade union official, and his mother the socialist Mayor of Southampton. He entered Parliament in February 1957 as Labour member for Wednesbury, a seat in the Black Country, and soon developed a reputation as a gifted administrator. Handsome, urbane and a known womaniser, he pursued a string of affairs with young party employees. These indiscretions did not prevent his appointment as a junior minister in Harold Wilson's government after the 1964 general election, and he went on to hold several ministerial positions throughout the Wilson era. By 1969, he was tipped for a Cabinet post.

This rapid advance came to an abrupt halt in July 1969, when Stonehouse was accused of espionage. Josef Frolík, a Czechoslovakian defector, reported to the American authorities that he was '90 per cent sure' the minister was a Soviet agent. MI5 apprehended and interviewed him. Surprisingly calm and assured in the circumstances, he convincingly rebutted each of Frolík's allegations. The security services were wary of his intelligence and already suspicious of his business dealings. They reported to the Prime Minister that they could not be certain of his innocence. But as there was no evidence that he had given the Czechs information they should not have had, or that 'he ever consciously acted as an agent', so the matter did not officially progress any further. Nonetheless, Wilson quietly dropped him from the government and he was never again awarded a seat on the front bench. Wilson remembered that he 'never thought [Stonehouse] was a spy, but always thought he was a crook'.

When the Czech Secret Service released their Soviet-era files in 2010, over twenty years after Stonehouse's death, it was revealed that he had been both a spy and a crook. Recruited as an opposition backbencher, it transpired that he had transferred money to, and received payments from, the Czech secret police via a network of shady business interests. When he had been elevated to government he had 'provided information about government plans and policies and about technological subjects including aircraft'. He is the only British politician known to have acted as a foreign agent while serving as a minister.

Although he had avoided being unmasked as a traitor in 1969, Stonehouse realised that further promotion was unlikely while a shadow of doubt hung over him. He remained an MP but shifted his focus to making money for himself. He created a large network of companies that attempted to profit from the splitting of Bangladesh from Pakistan. But one after another they fell into financial difficulties, which Stonehouse temporarily addressed by lying to his accountants, borrowing more money and fobbing off his immediate creditors. But by January 1974, he owed more than £800,000. He had spread the debt across twenty-four separate accounts with seventeen banks, with additional liabilities in personal guarantees of a further £700,000. Under investigation by the Treasury for alleged embezzlement from a charity, the former minister entered the crosshairs of investigative journalists in the *Sunday Times*'s fearsome Insight team.

His financial woes plunged him into a spiralling depression. He realised that he was, in his words, 'increasingly engaged in a game of sham' and that 'suicide was ever near'. Refusing to face up to reality, he sought comfort from his glamorous and devoted young secretary, Sheila Buckley, and the two began an affair. Buckley was soon installed in Stonehouse's London home, while Barbara, his devoted wife of twenty-six years, remained in the countryside beyond the reach of rumour.

By mid-1974, with creditors and regulators closing in, Stonehouse vowed to pursue the most drastic of solutions to his financial, marital and psychological woes. Resolving to 'break away from the Stonehouse burden', he decided to kill off his former self and live the rest of his life as somebody new. The only person who could be trusted with the truth would be his lover and confidante, Buckley.

The planning for his disappearance was meticulous. He rifled through constituency correspondence to find two locals around his age who had recently died. Identifying Joseph Markham and Clive Mildoon, he confirmed that neither man had travelled abroad. Visiting their widows under the pretence of consoling them, he acquired sufficient information to fill out passport applications and open bank accounts in the names of their dead husbands. He then began to siphon money from his companies into those new bank accounts. Finally, he took out a £125,000 life insurance policy to be paid to his wife Barbara after his 'death' as a thank you for her twenty-six years of loyalty. All the time he avoided arousing suspicion by acting his usual self and fulfilling his regular parliamentary duties, including winning re-election to his seat in the general election of October 1974.

His plans were in place by November that year. He had decided that death by drowning would be the most convincing method. Desiring a location hundreds of miles away, he selected a beach in Miami famed for its dangerous currents and arranged to travel there on business. After a couple of failed attempts, he finally summoned the courage to follow through on his months of plotting on the morning of the twentieth. He headed down to the empty beach outside the five-star Fontainebleau Hotel and slowly entered the sea.

A strong swimmer, he braved the riptides to swim around to the next bay, pulled himself out of the water and went to collect a suitcase he had left nearby. Switching the parting of his hair from side to centre, he slipped on a pair of spectacles and dashed to the airport. Posing as Joseph Markham, he easily moved through passport control and boarded a flight to Hawaii. John Stonehouse was gone.

The Miami police found the belongings on the beach later that day. After a 48-hour manhunt involving dozens of coastguards and a helicopter, he was declared missing, presumed dead. Stonehouse's wife was said to be so distraught at the news that she had to be sedated. Buckley played her part well, confirming to the press that he 'used to go for long swims by himself', and that she had warned him of the danger.

The story was splashed across British newspapers. The *News of the World* speculated with characteristic sensitivity that 'Sharks ate John Stonehouse!' Tributes poured in from colleagues, who observed a minute's silence in the Commons. While being eulogised on the green benches, Stonehouse himself was relaxing on a Hawaiian beach flicking through his own obituaries with a wry smile. The following week he crossed the ocean again, this time arriving at his final destination: Australia. He settled as planned in a mock-Elizabethan manor called Tudor Lodge in the suburbs of Melbourne and applied to join the local jazz club.

And he very nearly pulled it off. It was a case of mistaken identification that led the authorities to find out who he truly was. At the time he had arrived in Melbourne, Australia was in the grip of a series of bank frauds. Stonehouse aroused the suspicions of a vigilant young bank clerk, who spotted the same Englishman withdrawing cash under the name of Joe Markham and then depositing it at the branch up the road as Clive Mildoon. The police received this news on the same day they were sent the uncannily similar description of another fugitive Englishman suspected to have arrived on Antipodean shores: Lord Lucan. The aristocrat had recently disappeared from the United Kingdom following the murder of his child's nanny. As a well-spoken, suave, dark-haired Englishman, Stonehouse fitted the peer's description and the Australian security services began to tail him.

Unwittingly evading their surveillance, he travelled to Copenhagen, where he enjoyed a clandestine rendezvous with Buckley. Perching on a bench in the Danish capital during their secret liaison, he read through newer accounts of his death that were provided by Buckley, who had saved the newspaper cuttings for her roguish lover. 'Envy and spite' came 'rushing out like the bursting of a boil' upon reading his old enemies settling their scores, for the papers had picked through his business and charity affairs and raised the spectre of embezzled funds. Stonehouse felt 'powerless to defend the honour of his dead twin'.

He returned to Melbourne in late December, stopping off en route in Moscow for reasons that will probably never be known. Having re-entered Australia as Clive Mildoon, he began to make new friends. The police re-established their watch, by now convinced that they had found the elusive Lucan. They made their move on Christmas Eve, arriving at his lodgings armed with the knowledge that Lucan had a six-inch scar on his inside right thigh. The dramatic arrest began with Stonehouse answering the door, being pinned to the wall and forced to pull down his trousers. Finding no scar, the chief investigating officer looked up and ordered him to reveal his real identity. Presuming he was being arrested for identity fraud, and perhaps thinking that the trouser removal was standard procedure for the Australian police, Stonehouse believed the game was up and admitted his real name.

The sensational news of his reappearance caught British news desks off guard. Unprepared for such a big story to drop on the other side of the world and in the middle of the night, editors initiated one of the great Fleet Street scrambles. Reporters from all the London papers raced each other to Melbourne. The *Daily Express* put twenty-two staff on the case, including the nearest one: a bemused cricket correspondent preparing to cover the Boxing Day Test match against England. He found himself, for the first and last time, competing for a scoop with *The Times*'s opera correspondent, who had been summoned from the stalls at Sydney Opera House. Not to be outdone, the *News of the World* flew out nine men, armed with a suitcase full of £15,000 to procure the first-person exclusive. The story dominated the news for the entire Christmas period.

In the days after his arrest, Melbourne Police allowed Stonehouse to telephone his wife, who had believed him dead. They recorded the call, in which he apologised to Barbara and told her that he wanted to remain in Australia permanently. She thought that 'his voice sounded so strange, he was like a naughty boy who had just been found out'. She thought that he must have suffered a mental breakdown and resolved to help him.

Stonehouse was also permitted to write to Wilson to explain in his own terms what he had done. He told the Prime Minister that he had 'considered, clearly wrongly, that the best action that I could take was to create a new identity and attempt to live a new life away from the pressures. I supposed this could be summed up as a brainstorm, or a mental breakdown.'

Alighting on a chance to cause further mischief, the *News of the World* sent reporters to the houses of Barbara Stonehouse and Sheila Buckley, armed with airline tickets to Melbourne. The two women arrived in Australia within days of each other. Buckley went to stay in Sydney with old friends. Barbara moved into Tudor Lodge with her husband, who had been released by the Australian authorities, having committed no crime in Australia other than entering on a false passport, then considered a minor offence. In July 1975, following a six-month legal battle and after being refused asylum by Botswana, Kenya, Mauritius, Tanzania, Bangladesh and Canada, Stonehouse was extradited back to the UK to face criminal trial. He was charged with several counts of fraud, misrepresentation and theft.

On his return, he instructed Geoffrey Robertson as his barrister. Now a leading QC with a towering reputation for human rights law, Robertson was then a young barrister building up his practice. He was chosen because he had previously defended Peter Hain against charges connected with his violent protest against a white-only South

African cricket team touring England in 1970. Stonehouse had convinced himself that, like Hain, he too had been persecuted by the British establishment. Robertson considered the acquisition of 'the most derided person in the country' as his client to be a badge of honour and began to prepare the defence with great enthusiasm.

The charges laid against Stonehouse and young Buckley, deemed his accomplice, were for the possession of two false passports, the theft of £29,000 of his company's money and the attempt to leave £125,000 life insurance proceeds to his family. Given the scale of the deceit, the value of the fraud was risibly low.

Publicly shamed as a charlatan and a cad, Stonehouse did little to help his own cause. Back from the dead, he remained the MP for Walsall North and refused point-blank to resign, leaving his constituents and local party saddled with a representative who had run away from Britain and fought every attempt to bring him back. Curiously, Parliament's archaic laws contained no provision for his party or his constituents to oust him.

The first step in the legal process was for Robertson to secure bail for his client, who had been remanded in custody since his return. Robertson argued at one hearing after another that his client was hardly able to flee as he was under constant siege from photographers, who would notice any attempted bid for freedom. Nonetheless, the magistrate repeatedly refused bail. Robertson eventually gave up and, before a court appearance on 3 August 1975, decided not to launch another attempt to secure it for his client. To his surprise, however, the magistrate proceeded to grant it. He later worked out why the magistrate had waited so long; by 3 August, Parliament was finally in recess, and the unedifying spectacle of the disgraced Stonehouse performing in the chamber had been temporarily avoided.

After that hurdle was overcome, Robertson sought to persuade his client to resign from Parliament. Stonehouse stubbornly refused. He returned to the House after the summer recess and continued to live life as if he were a prominent frontbencher. He made speeches in Parliament on a wide array of matters, but everyone on both sides of the house shunned him, deserting the House when he stood up and ignoring him in the corridors. Having convinced himself that he was the victim of an establishment stitch-up, he developed a hitherto un-disclosed interest in matters of domestic criminal justice and spotted conspiracies in every crevasse of government. After much persuasion, Stonehouse eventually promised Robertson that he would resign, but only after giving a 'personal explanation' to the House of Commons.

The speaker, Selwyn Lloyd, conscious of the damage already done to the reputation of the institution, would only allow Stonehouse to make the statement if he could approve its contents first. In contrast to previous speeches, throughout which he had been jeered, he was heard in a steely silence, broken only by the Speaker's exasperated interjections each time he strayed from the approved script. He railed at the House of Commons, accusing most members of being 'robots … voting on issues which they did not bother to understand after debates to which they had not bothered to listen'. He blamed Fleet Street for his demise, declaring press freedom

a false god to worship: it has become a weapon in the hands of callow, cynical and completely irresponsible men who delight in undermin-ing and destroying active people in politics and business who are the constructive and positive elements in society … the negativism of much contemporary journalism is a cancer in the body politic and is gradually eating away at the vitals of British democracy.

According to Bernard Donoughue, the Prime Minister's close aide, Stonehouse's statement to the commons was 'bizarre, but not mad, and crudely calculated to advance his own cause ... the House looked embarrassed.' Despite his earlier promise, Stonehouse still refused to resign, and there was no mechanism through which he could be forced out.

He was eschewed by his colleagues and booed by party delegates at the 1975 Labour conference. In a characteristically defiant move, he responded by switching political allegiance. In April 1976, two days after Wilson had handed over the premiership to Jim Callaghan, he left Labour to join an odd grouping called the English National Party. They were branded by Robertson 'a collection of fairly harmless odd-balls, who dressed up in Robin Hood costumes and held tea-parties before jousting on the green sward'. No doubt Maypole salesmen and Morris dancers throughout the land were pleased finally to have acquired an ally in high places.

Stonehouse's odd defection was of critical importance to the future of the government. It plunged Jim Callaghan's new administration into crisis, by taking his already wafer-thin majority down to one, compounding a period of extreme political volatility. Callaghan was desperate to force Stonehouse to leave Parliament, as the subsequent by-election would probably have given him an invaluable extra MP.

It was against this backdrop that Robertson and Stonehouse set about preparing the defence for the upcoming fraud trial. The defence that they proposed to run focused squarely on Stonehouse's mental health; essentially, he was to claim that he could not be held responsible for his own actions. Robertson had 'no doubt that he was mentally disordered, that his illness was triggered by mild reverses, and that it combined with a natural arrogance and self-regard to produce a state of mind which paid little or no attention to whether his behaviour was criminal'.

Robertson spent months of long days and late nights preparing for the trial. Instructed by Stonehouse to fight each charge to the bitter end, he felt that the worst-case scenario would be that his client would be sent to prison for three years.

Stonehouse, deluded and arrogant, paid back Robertson's hard work by sacking him. At the eleventh hour, he decided to reject all advice and represent himself at the Old Bailey. Firing his entire legal team the day before the hearing was set to start, he complained that they never 'gave the slightest hint that [they] thought him innocent'. This was, as Robertson has said, 'not entirely surprising'.

The trial went ahead without any defence lawyers. It lasted for sixty-eight days, then the longest fraud trial in British history. It was Stonehouse's conduct that ensured the trial took so long. Robertson, observing from the public gallery, found it a sad spectacle. Stonehouse foundered in technical legal submissions 'in front of a disgruntled judge undisposed to help him'. He asked long and irrelevant questions of each of the witnesses, before calling several psychiatrists to explain at great length why he was mentally unstable. While this may have bolstered his defence, it made his style of advocacy seem even more like the ramblings of a lunatic. He had planned to take the stand and answer questions himself, but, at the last minute, decided to make a 'dock statement': an arcane practice where a defendant who does not wish to be cross-examined by the prosecution barrister instead makes a short speech.

Stonehouse's speech was not short. It took six days of court time, and lasted over thirty hours. The judge became increasingly infuriated with him and many years later, when appointed to the Royal Commission on Criminal Procedure, orchestrated the abolition of the right to make a dock statement.

It came as no surprise that Stonehouse was found guilty on almost all the charges, and was sentenced to seven years' imprisonment. Buckley was also found guilty, and received a suspended prison sentence. As she heard the verdicts, Buckley staggered back and collapsed in tears. The judge rejected their defence outright, telling Stonehouse that he

did not simply decide to disappear because you were oppressed by business burdens. You decided to do so in comfort, and it is clear to me that self-interest has been well to the fore. You aimed to get rich quickly. You falsely accused other people of cant, conspiracy and humbug, when you must have known all the time that your defence was an embodiment of all three.

Stonehouse was whisked from the courtroom to HMP Wormwood Scrubs in west London to begin his lengthy sentence. It was only at that juncture, on 28 August 1976, nearly two years after he first faked his own death, that he finally agreed to resign as an MP. A by-election was called in his Walsall seat, in which the Conservatives shocked commentators by sweeping the constituency with a colossal swing from Labour; the local backlash against Callaghan's party presumably the result of Stonehouse's antics. The Conservative gain eliminated Callaghan's majority, and within months his government faced the vote of no confidence that triggered the Lib–Lab pact.

Stonehouse spent much of his time in prison playing chess, a game of strategy at which he excelled. Entering the Wormwood Scrubs chess league, he reportedly saw off the 'teacup poisoner', Graham Young, in an early round before losing in the final to the Moors murderer Ian Brady. The former MP found prison to be restorative, later writing that 'the opportunity to sleep nine hours a night and really relax has been extremely good for me' and asking readers to disabuse themselves of 'any idea that prison is harmful'.

He was released on compassionate grounds in August 1979 after three years of his sentence, having suffered three heart attacks and undergone invasive surgery. On his release, his wife insisted on a divorce and, in 1981, he married Buckley. She had remained by his side throughout, even supporting an unsuccessful attempt to become a published author. He died in 1988 at the age of sixty-two.

His former lawyer Robertson kept in contact with him until his death. He remembered that 'it was terribly sad … I would get a Christmas card from him every year and it was always a House of Commons Christmas card, even though he was no longer a member.'

CHAPTER FIVE

JEREMY THORPE

Jeremy Thorpe was rarely seen about town without his felt trilby and velvet-collared coat. His dandyish style set him apart in 1970s Westminster, but that element alone distinguished the politician from his establishment peers. The son and grandson of Tory MPs, he was educated at Eton, then Trinity College, Oxford, before training like his father at the Bar. Nobody was surprised to see the impressive young barrister embark upon a political career. What was shocking to his contemporaries was the depths to which he later plunged. Few could have predicted that Thorpe would stand trial for the attempted murder of his lover, the culmination of one of the most eyebrow-raising political scandals in modern British history.

Thorpe had been encouraged to follow his father and grandfather into the Tory Party, but that was not to be. He stuck to his strongly held ideology and instead joined the Liberals, despite their dwindling influence. On his twenty-first birthday, he put his name down as a parliamentary candidate and eight years later, at the 1959 election, became the MP for North Devon. At just thirty, Thorpe was one of the youngest of the new intake. Snappily dressed and well-connected, he developed a reputation for his engaging wit. He had a knack for encapsulating the story of the day with a newspaper-friendly one-liner. The House of Lords was 'proof of life after death', he once quipped, while Harold Macmillan had, in firing half his Cabinet, 'laid down his friends for his life'.

But, for some time, Thorpe remained a lightweight parliamentary figure. His contemporary Tony Benn considered him to be 'very nice, agreeable and kind', but without any great substance, treating 'the House of Commons as [if it were] the Oxford Union'.

Although a congenial man with a packed social schedule, Thorpe was never seen with a love interest on his arm or in pursuit of casual affairs. Most friends assumed him simply uninterested in women, but in fact he was gay. Since university he had been living a double life, engaging in secret liaisons with men while keeping his sexuality secret from his friends. Homosexuality remained on the statute books as a crime until 1967, making it impossible for any sort of public figure to be openly gay. Politicians were particularly easy targets for prosecution. Thorpe witnessed William Field, a Labour MP, forced out of the Commons for soliciting in a public lavatory and Ian Harvey, a junior minister, lose his seat after being caught in the bushes of St James's Park with a Coldstream Guard. Like many others at that time, he was forced to pursue clandestine relationships.

Unbeknown to him, his secret dalliances drew the attention of the security services soon after his arrival in Parliament. Following a business trip to the US, the FBI informed their British counterparts that Thorpe had stayed in a hotel with several male prostitutes. The incident was referred to the Devon Police for investigation and they opened a file on the young MP, which gradually became filled with tip-offs and rumours.

A year after his election to Parliament, Thorpe spent a fateful weekend at Kingham Stables, the Oxfordshire home of his friend Norman

Vater. While walking around the grounds, Thorpe cast his eyes on a slim, androgynous twenty-year-old. The young man introduced himself as Norman Josiffe, Vater's stable groom. He was, according to Thorpe, 'simply heaven'. The MP was smitten, and told Josiffe that he should call if he ever found himself in London.

The itinerant labourer, who had no family of which to speak, had suffered a slew of psychiatric problems. Shortly after meeting Thorpe, he had another mental breakdown and was forcibly detained in a psychiatric hospital. While sectioned, he changed his surname to Scott and convinced himself that he had enjoyed a sexual relationship with Thorpe. He had stolen several affectionate letters that Thorpe had written to Vater, which began 'Dear Norman…', and showed them to his fellow inmates as if they had been written to him.

On his release from hospital, Scott headed straight to the Houses of Parliament and, unfortunately for Thorpe, he happened to be in his office at the time. Omitting to tell Thorpe about his mental health problems, Scott instead claimed he had been sacked for attempting to steal a horse and was left unemployed and penniless. Thorpe took pity on the angelic-looking young man and decided to take him down to his family home in Surrey for dinner.

He introduced Scott to his mother as 'Peter' and said he was a cameraman on a current affairs programme with which he was collaborating. After dinner, Scott was shown to the guest room, where Thorpe gave him a copy of James Baldwin's novel *Giovanni's Room*, an account of the daring affair between a wealthy aristocrat and an Italian barman. Later that night, Thorpe returned to Scott's bedroom – this time clad only in his dressing gown. He sat on the bed and Scott later remembered that 'he seemed full of earnest endeavour' and, with 'great warmth and kindness', offered 'to be there, to be caring'. At Thorpe's instigation, the pair went on to have sex that night.

They drove back to London the next day and Thorpe gave Scott the rent for a flat near Westminster, additional pocket money and the use of his Savile Row tailor. He also instructed his solicitor to track down Scott's apparently long-lost mother. In return, Thorpe enjoyed daily romps with his new lover at the flat.

Early the next year, Scott suffered a relapse of his mental illness. Increasingly volatile, he was interviewed by the police on suspicion of stealing a suede jacket from a socialite. Thorpe requested that a further meeting with the police take place at his parliamentary office. When the detective arrived to start the interview, they narrowly missed walking in on Thorpe and Scott fondling each other behind the desk. Thorpe vouched for his lover, identifying himself as 'more or less' Scott's 'guardian'. That was sufficient for the policeman, who decided that no further action would be taken.

The experience left Thorpe shaken, however, and convinced that Scott must leave London for good. With the eventual aim of securing him a position in the south of France, Thorpe procured him a job in Somerset. Soon after Scott settled in the West Country, Thorpe wrote him a letter that was later to prompt public ridicule:

My Dear Norman,

Since my letters normally go to the House, yours arrived all by itself at my breakfast table at the Reform, and gave me tremendous pleasure.

I cannot tell you just how happy I am to feel that you're really settling down, and feeling that life has something to offer … The next thing is to solve your financial problems and this James Walters [my solicitor] and I are on to. The really important thing is that you are now a member of a family doing a useful job of work – with Tish – which you enjoy. Hooray!! Faced with all that no more bloody clinics. I think you can now take the Ann Gray incident [the stealing of the jacket] as over and done with…

Bunnies can (+ will) go to France. In haste.
Yours affectionately,
  Jeremy
  I miss you.

Two months after that letter was written, Thorpe was visited by his solicitor, who had uncovered alarming inconsistencies in Scott's account of his life. In particular, the claims that he had lost track of his parents appeared to have been an embellishment, for the pair were in south London, their location apparently known to their son.

Furious that he had been lied to and recognising the danger posed by Scott's volatility, Thorpe ended the relationship for good. Scott was devastated. He poured out his feelings to Caroline Barrington-Ward, the sister of one Thorpe's school friends, claiming that he planned to travel to the House of Commons to shoot Thorpe before turning the gun on himself. Convinced of the sincerity of his intent, Barrington-Ward immediately rang the police and urged them to intercept Scott.

He was arrested on his way to the Commons. While the police were handcuffing him, he told them that he wanted to make a statement about his illicit homosexual relationship with Thorpe. He then produced the letter the MP had written to him, alongside the earlier letters he had stolen that began 'Dear Norman'. The detective ordered a doctor's examination, which at the time was a routine intrusion that men suspected of illegal homosexual acts were subjected to. It apparently confirmed that Scott was what was euphemistically termed a passive homosexual.

Despite the available evidence to support his claims, the interviewing detective branded Scott a dangerous hysteric and decided that no action would be taken against Thorpe. Recalling the events years later, he accepted that Thorpe's elevated social status stopped the matter being taken further. He maintained: 'There was no need to interview Thorpe. We knew he would deny it. Do you think that a man of that calibre would admit that kind of conduct?'

The detective was not made aware of the previous investigations into Thorpe's sex life by the Devonshire constabulary or MI5's file on his American dalliances. There was, according to the ex-head of Devon Police, no explanation for the failure to share this information 'unless someone wanted to cover something up', suggesting that Thorpe may have been receiving help from his friends in high places.

Although no action was taken, the Metropolitan Police did file all of Scott's letters and kept a record of his statement to them. As long as this file remained separate from the other two in existence, however, Thorpe was relatively safe from prosecution.

Scott's outburst and accusations perturbed Thorpe, who knew how close he had come to being found out. Wanting Scott out of the country and a safe distance away, he arranged a job for the unpredictable young man in Switzerland. He completed the passport application, paid his travel fare and gave him ample spending money.

To Thorpe's horror, however, Scott took against his new employer, the accommodation on offer and the Swiss climate. He returned to England after three months and sought contact with the MP, but Thorpe refused to permit a meeting. Scott retreated only temporarily, attempting contact again a few months later. The MP received a letter from the owner of a stud farm in Ireland, saying that Scott, now employed on the farm, had claimed that Thorpe was his guardian and demanded money. Thorpe replied that he was not, 'but had merely tried to help him on occasions, which have at times proved hair-raising'. He firmly added that he was not able to take responsibility for Scott's actions.

In vengeful spirit, Scott then sent a spiteful letter to Thorpe's mother, telling her that 'for the last five years ... Jeremy and I have had a homosexual relationship.' Thorpe's mother forwarded the letter to her son, principally concerned about the effect it might have on his burgeoning career. Thorpe was even more enraged by the attempt to shame him than he had been by the previous attempt to blackmail him, and decided for the first time to confide in a parliamentary colleague.

His chosen confidant was Peter Bessell, the Liberal MP for Bodmin. Somewhat eccentric, Bessell was a Congregationalist lay preacher who campaigned in a Cadillac and managed a portfolio of questionable business interests. He was, like Thorpe, secretly gay, but due to a more cautious disposition had evaded suspicion by the authorities.

The situation with Scott was a 'disaster waiting to happen', Bessell surmised, but agreed to help. Hatching a plan that also relied on blackmail, he travelled to Dublin in April 1965 to meet Scott in a hotel bar. Bessell warned Scott, with barely concealed menace, that if he caused further trouble he would be charged for his multiple crimes and permanently extradited. Alternatively, Bessell offered, he could accept a deal in which he would be paid a modest but regular financial retainer in return for silence about his affair with Thorpe. Scott agreed, and over the next few years Bessell paid him £700 in £5 instalments. Carefully avoiding Thorpe, Scott lived in west London with a set of affluent young bohemians while working as a male model.

While Scott was enjoying the 'swinging London' of the late 1960s, Thorpe made a glittering rise up the political ladder. His emergence as a public figure happily coincided with an upswing in the Liberals' fortunes and, in 1967, he was elected leader of a resurgent party. A year later, by now thirty-eight, he married Caroline Allpass, an art expert and interior decorator, in a lavish ceremony over which the Archbishop of Canterbury presided. His cover was complete.

The higher he rose up the ladder, however, the more concerned he became about Scott, who he described as a 'black cloud hanging over him' that 'would never cease to be a danger'. In 1968, Thorpe joked with Bessell that he would love to 'get rid of' Scott, which would be 'no worse than shooting a sick dog'. Bessell reassured him that he need not obsess about the matter, and the threat from Scott duly appeared to be receding: the following year he voluntarily terminated his retainer from Bessell, married, moved to Lincolnshire and had a child.

Unfortunately for Thorpe, this would not be the end of the affair. Scott reappeared less than a year later, ringing Bessell to demand money to help him support his young family. Taking advantage of Thorpe's newly earned public profile, he raised for the first time the prospect of selling his sordid tale to the newspapers if his demands were not met. Bessell leapt into action to arrange a temporary stipend and hoped to hear no more of him, but, as before, Scott soon returned.

Scott had abandoned his wife and baby and moved to Wales, where he lodged with a politically engaged widow who believed his tales of the Liberal leader's betrayal. Hoping to blow the matter open, she wrote to Emlyn Hooson, Liberal MP for Montgomeryshire and a known rival of Thorpe's.

The MP seized the opportunity to gain compromising material on his party leader, and brokered a meeting between Scott and David Steel, the Liberal Chief Whip, in a bid to scope out the allegations. Meetings were scheduled for 26 and 27 May 1971. Initially, Steel considered 'the whole thing to be lies', but the turning point came when Scott produced the letters evidencing the retainer he had received from Bessell and the correspondence referring to him as 'Bunnies' that had been written by Thorpe. After rigorous cross-examination by Hooson, a distinguished barrister, Steel finally deemed the allegations to be credible. He set up an internal party investigation into Thorpe and Scott's relationship.

At Thorpe's suggestion, the party appointed Frank Byers, their leader in the Lords, to preside over the tribunal. Byers, a military man and friend of Thorpe's, was ill-disposed to Scott, self-admittedly treating him like 'a boy at school up before the headmaster'. Byers concluded that Scott gave 'an impression of pure evil', and that during their meeting he exploded with rage at Thorpe's accuser. He told Scott that he was a dirty little blackmailer that would get his comeuppance. Scott retorted that Byers was a 'pontificating old sod' before bursting into tears and fleeing the room.

Dented by the incident, but not deterred, Scott sought a new line of attack against his former lover. He contacted Gordon Winter, a freelance journalist, and told him that he had been 'deeply in love with Jeremy' but had been 'discarded like a cheap tart'. Despite Winter's best efforts, no Fleet Street editor would publish the extraordinary story, judging there to be too little proof to back it up. Unknown to all involved, however, Winter also moonlighted for the South African secret intelligence service, BOSS, to whom he passed the information. The National Party government received it with great interest, as Thorpe was a leading critic of their system of racial apartheid.

After Byers's party inquiry concluded, Thorpe's political career continued to soar. The Liberal Party rose in the polls and won a series of by-elections. His influence increased yet further after the general election in February 1974, in which the Liberals received over 6 million votes, just under 20 per cent share of all ballots cast. Thorpe had enjoyed a dazzling election campaign by touring seaside constituencies in his campaign hovercraft. Since neither the Conservatives nor Labour had won an overall majority, Thorpe's party gained huge leverage. Ted Heath's Tories sought to remain in government with Thorpe's support, despite winning fewer seats than Harold Wilson's Labour. Thorpe and Heath entered negotiations in which Thorpe was offered the role of Foreign Secretary in a coalition government. He refused the role in the absence of wide-ranging electoral reform and, as a result, Harold Wilson became Prime Minister again, running a minority government until October 1974, when a second general election granted him an overall majority of three.

In November 1974, Thorpe suffered a singular piece of bad luck. Bessell, beleaguered by struggling business interests, had stood down from his seat in Parliament. He had failed, however, to take all his possessions with him upon leaving Westminster. Builders converting his former office discovered a secret compartment hidden in the ceiling, inside which was a briefcase containing a file of documents about Scott, including a copy of the letter he had sent to Thorpe's mother in 1965. The builders sold the contents of the briefcase to the *Sunday Mirror*. By the skin of his teeth Thorpe survived the mishap unscathed yet again after Lord Jacobson, the *Mirror*'s deputy chairman, who was also a family friend of the Liberal leader, intervened. The peer forced his editor to return the papers to Thorpe.

Scott chose that moment to appear in the politician's life again, however, becoming more determined than ever to make his story public. After moving down to Thorpe's Devon constituency, he toured the local pubs regaling all who would listen with stories about their relationship. He was soon introduced to Tim Keigwin, Thorpe's Conservative rival in North Devon. Rumours started to spread back to Westminster, stoking the Liberal leader's rising sense of panic.

By late 1974, Thorpe's best friend, David Holmes, had assumed Bessell's former role of managing Scott. Taking a harder-line view than his predecessor, however, Holmes decided that Scott must be disposed of permanently. He met with two associates, John Le Mesurier (not to be confused with the *Dad's Army* actor) and a fruit-machine salesman named George Deakin.

Two initial attempts were made to intimidate Scott into disappearing for good. First he was tracked down to Barnstable, where two men posing as journalists stole from him his documents relating to Thorpe and issued a final warning. After that incident failed to convince Scott to scarper, several of Holmes's associates followed him to his local pub and beat him up. Far from winning his silence, however, the attack prompted an outburst of hysterics.

Holmes, Le Mesurier and Deakin hatched a final plot, this time apparently aiming to kill Scott. They initially recruited small-time criminal Dennis Meighan to execute the assassination, meeting him in a pub in Shepherd's Bush, west London. The petty crook later recalled that the trio offered him £13,500 upfront to despatch Scott and promised that he would be 'well looked after' for his efforts. At first Meighan was 'very cagey' about the proposed mission, but eventually agreed to take it on. He set out for Barnstable but changed his mind while driving there after realising that his London accent would make him conspicuous, passing the job to former airline pilot and fellow gun for hire Andrew Newton.

Newton was not a competent assassin. On his first attempt to find Scott he missed his target by 162 miles, driving to Dunstable instead of Barnstable. He finally caught up with Scott in October 1975. Scott was walking his newly acquired Great Dane, Rinka. Playing upon the paranoia of his would-be victim, Newton told him that he had been sent as protection to shield him from a fictional Canadian assassin. Scott readily believed him, agreeing to talk further at a second location.

Newton drove Scott and Rinka in his Ford saloon to a secluded spot on Exmoor. Feigning tiredness, he asked Scott to take over driving. He stopped the car at the side of the road and the pair got out. Drawing a Mauser handgun from his jacket, Newton shot the dog clean through the head. Scott ran over to Rinka and cradled him, before noticing that Newton was now pointing the gun at him. He later recalled that he 'got so frightened' after that he 'turned backwards and ran back' across the moors. As he was running backwards, Newton levelled the gun at him again, but no bullet emerged. 'It must have been jammed,' Scott later said, claiming that Newton 'gave up, said "I'll get you", jumped in the car and drove off'. Scott was left at the side of the road, covered in Rinka's blood. Soon after Newton had driven off, 'a car came along' and Scott 'ran up and tried to stop them'. He told the driver that his dog had been shot, and, in his nervous state, repeated: 'It's all because of Jeremy Thorpe.'

The shooting of Rinka was reported in the local newspaper under the headline 'Mystery of the Dog in the Fog'. In the article, Norman Scott was named as the owner of the dog and the victim of the attack, prompting a *Sunday Express* journalist who had heard rumours about Scott and Thorpe to contact the Liberal leader for comment. Auberon Waugh also included a piece in *Private Eye*'s diary that ended: 'My only hope is that sorrow over his friend's dog will not cause Mr Thorpe's premature retirement from public life.' Thorpe played down the relationship, telling the reporter: 'I have been aware of this man Scott … He once presented himself at the House. I did not see him.'

Newton was arrested for the shooting a few days later. He was easily tracked down since Scott had made a note of his number plate. He was released on bail and awaited his trial for the shooting of Rinka, scheduled for March 1976. Scott realised that he would at last be able to publicise his story as he was to be the key witness in the dock at Newton's trial. Aware that his career was now hanging by a thread, Thorpe made a series of increasingly desperate and anguished attempts to keep his name out of the trial and to bar Scott from giving evidence.

What he did not know, however, was that Scott was due to appear at another trial before Newton's. Scott had himself been prosecuted for benefits fraud, with the hearing scheduled for 29 January 1976. He tipped off journalists that he intended to make allegations about

Thorpe from the witness box. After pleading guilty shortly after he entered the room, he proceeded to shout to onlooking reporters:

> It has been fifteen years. I really would like to get this matter cleared up. It has been so sick. I am being hounded all the time by people just because of my sexual relationship with Jeremy Thorpe. It gets worse and worse. I am sorry but I must say it.

He followed up with detailed interviews with several newspapers, free to report the bones of the story now that the allegations had been revealed in the courtroom. Finally unshackled, Fleet Street seized on the opportunity to delve into ten years of rumours about Thorpe's sexuality. Many colleagues implored Thorpe to accept that he had been in a relationship with Scott. The idea was unbearable to Thorpe, who was not prepared to speak publicly about his sexuality and knew that the admission that he had lied repeatedly would kill his career. He was also loath to put his wife through the public humiliation that would ensue from such a confession. Panicked, but in denial about the reality of the situation, he issued a statement that asserted drily: 'There is no truth in Mr Scott's wild allegations.'

Liberal MPs gathered on 4 February 1975 to discuss their leader's fate. Of the party's twelve MPs, five entered the meeting thinking that he should stand aside immediately. Their view was at odds with the vast majority of Liberals in the country, who remained loyal supporters of their charismatic leader.

Like many politicians, Thorpe was at his best under pressure. Rising to the occasion, he delivered a rallying address at the meeting in which he repudiated Scott's allegations and simultaneously defended the right to a private life. Fellow Liberal MP and future Chief Whip Cyril Smith, sensed 'growing pleasure in the room as [the Liberal MPs'] doubts began to fade'. Thorpe's address was followed by a unanimous vote of confidence from his fellow MPs.

He also won the support of the Prime Minister. Towards the end of his period in office, Harold Wilson had begun to see conspiracy theories all around him. Soon after Scott's allegations became public, the Prime Minister asked Thorpe to meet him in his study. He informed the Liberal leader that the source of the allegations was the South African Secret Service, who, in his view, had planted them. Although Thorpe knew that this was not the case, it was not overly far-fetched, as the South Africans had known of the story many years before and tried to spread it. But Wilson's conspiracy theory was excellent cover for Thorpe, who told Cyril Smith that he was delighted, for 'it will be pushed on South Africa'. Wilson proceeded to offer Thorpe public support, openly stating that the South African government had a hand in his woes. Against the odds, he had wriggled free from Scott's clutches yet again.

However, the next challenge was fast upon him. It arrived in the form of Andrew Newton's trial in March 1975. The defending counsel, Lewis Hawser QC, was another old friend of Thorpe's. When Norman Scott came to give evidence, he was treated like a guilty man, rather than the victim of a violent crime. Hawser began his cross-examination by asking Scott whether 'anyone has ever told you that you are an incorrigible liar?' But, despite his best efforts to keep him quiet, Scott repeated the claim that Thorpe had tried to have him killed. Newton proved as inept a witness as he was an assassin. He claimed, without any evidence, that he had shot Rinka because Scott had been blackmailing him. A former girlfriend gave evidence in apparent support, but Newton was spotted prompting her replies to the barrister's questions and she was unable to identify Scott in the room. Newton was convicted and sentenced to two years in prison.

The Newton trial did not receive the press attention that was expected as it coincided with Harold Wilson's shock resignation and the announcement of Princess Margaret's divorce from Lord Snowdon. Without the pressure of constant coverage, Thorpe emerged from the trial bruised but not fatally damaged. He had printed a full rebuttal to the allegations in the *Sunday Times* under the headline 'The Lies of Norman Scott'. His account of the affair was widely accepted and, in a leader entitled 'Mr Thorpe Rides Again', the *Daily Telegraph* wrote of his 'seemingly miraculous resuscitation'.

His remarkable capacity for survival could not, however, protect him from facing the consequences of his actions in the end. The knife was wielded, ultimately, by his former ally. Bessell, who had proven an effective minder of Scott for so long, was by 1975 living in America, struggling under the weight of his debts and facing prosecution for fraud. Driven both by bitterness and a desperate need for money, he wrote a book about his involvement with Thorpe and sold his story to the *Daily Mail*. On 6 May 1974, the newspaper led with the headline 'I Told Lies to Protect Thorpe'.

Thorpe predicted that Bessell would next release the affectionate letters he had sent to Scott, which would expose his lies. In a desperate attempt to manage the crisis, Thorpe resolved to make them public himself. He gave them to the *Sunday Times* on 9 May, telling the paper: 'I am sick and tired of the mystery being whipped up around these two letters and I am therefore making them available. I have never made a secret that my family and I befriended Mr Scott fifteen years ago when these two letters were written.'

The *Sunday Times* duly printed the missive in which Thorpe referred to Scott as 'Bunnies', prompting much mirth across the land. Thorpe's enemies saw their chance to compound his humiliation and did not hesitate. Richard Wainwright, an ambitious young Liberal MP, took to BBC Radio Leeds to declare that his leader had 'not answered …

[some] very serious questions' about the relationship with Scott. He asked: 'Why does [he] not sue for libel, which is the proper way in England of clearing one's name?' His words were repeated across television and radio stations. Even Thorpe's staunchest supporters now conceded that he must go, and expressed fury that he had lied in the earlier party inquiry. Lord Byers, who had chaired that investigation, noted that Thorpe was 'at the end of his tether and faced a nervous breakdown if he did not give up'.

On the day the letters were published, Thorpe and his wife visited his old friend and fellow MP Clement Freud for Sunday lunch. Freud firmly counselled Thorpe to resign, warning him that he would be ousted by the end of the week if he attempted to cling on. Having fought tooth and nail, Thorpe finally, if reluctantly, accepted his fate. On Monday morning, he went to see David Steel, who was again acting as Liberal Chief Whip, at his London home and tendered his resignation. After the meeting, Thorpe circulated a letter to all Liberal members in which he said that he must step down for the good of the party. He stressed, however, that he did not accept the truth of Scott's allegations.

His resignation was presented in the press as a daylight assassination by his fellow Liberal MPs. *The Sun*'s leader said, with considerable sympathy, that Thorpe 'has become a broken man, destroyed by innuendo, the contempt of colleagues he should have been able to trust, and by the assassin's knife…' It concluded that 'the Liberal Party will pay dearly for this … [and] rightly so. When it comes to the dirty work they are pure Chicago.'

Although Thorpe resigned as leader, he remained an MP and a popular figure in the party. Steel, who became his successor, rehabilitated him and appointed him foreign affairs spokesman, but the scandal refused to die. When Andrew Newton was released from prison in

October 1977, he too wanted to cash in on the sorry affair. He tried to sell his story to the *Evening News*, offering full details of the plot for a proposed fee of £75,000, with a bonus agreed if his confession resulted in Thorpe's conviction. The *Evening News* did not agree to those terms, but nonetheless splashed on the story, which it headlined: 'I Was Hired to Kill Scott!' The article triggered two weeks of fresh coverage, with new revelations emerging every day. Spying his chance for further payments, Bessell gave a series of interviews that traced the murder plot back to 1968.

Thorpe addressed the allegations in a press conference in which he was supported by his wife. He accepted, contrary to his previous denials, that he had enjoyed a 'close, even affectionate' relationship with Scott, but maintained that 'no sexual activity of any kind took place'. He also strenuously denied any link to the apparent murder plot and insisted that he had no intention of resigning as MP for North Devon.

The interviews and Thorpe's press conference prompted police to begin an investigation into the affair. They found several willing sources of information. Bessell proved helpful, providing a lengthy statement in which he made a range of accusations against Thorpe. The former friend offered to act as the key witness against the MP in exchange for immunity from prosecution. The statement was drafted by the two journalists who had ghost-written his forthcoming book. They negotiated a deal with the *Sunday Telegraph* in which Bessell would receive up to £50,000 for the serialisation of the book, with half paid upfront and the balance paid if Thorpe was convicted. The would-be assassin Newton also agreed to be a witness against Thorpe in return for immunity for his role in the alleged murder plot and for giving perjured evidence in his previous trial.

On 2 August 1978, the police announced their decision to prosecute Thorpe, David Holmes, John Le Mesurier and George Deakin for conspiracy to murder Scott. Thorpe was charged with a separate count of inciting murder. They had agreed to grant immunity to both Bessell and Newton – probably the most sweeping concessions ever granted to prosecution witnesses.

Thorpe had previously told Steel that he would resign as an MP if he was charged, but, reneging on his promise, he resolved to contest the forthcoming general election. His parliamentary colleagues and election agent were mortified at Thorpe's decision, assuming that the adverse publicity would wreck their national campaign. Steel immediately sacked Thorpe as his foreign affairs spokesman and withdrew his public support.

Thorpe's candidacy at the general election was ridiculed. The unusual circumstances surrounding him prompted six fringe candidates in pursuit of press coverage to stand in the seat, including *Private Eye*'s Auberon Waugh, who proclaimed himself 'the dog lovers' candidate', declaring in his pre-election address that 'Rinka is not forgotten. Rinka lives. Woof, woof!' Thorpe lost the seat by 8,000 votes in the midst of an 8 per cent national swing to Thatcher's victorious Tories. Since he had received no support from his party, he had expected the defeat, noting later that he 'would rather have stood and lost than not stood at all'.

Court proceedings, billed as the 'trial of the century', opened five days after the election result. The judge was Sir Joseph Cantley, a notoriously gruff individual, who had a reputation for intolerance and for his sarcastic interjections during proceedings. Conscious of the unprecedented press interest in the case, he used his opening statement to warn any journalist thinking of interviewing the jurors that they 'had better bring a toothbrush with [them]'.

The strength of the case against Thorpe was undermined by the weakness of the witnesses on which it rested. They were all demonstrably partisan and unreliable: Bessell and Newton were both involved in the plot and both had already lied about the matter, in Newton's case to the police and in court while under oath. As for Scott, he was generally thought to be mentally disturbed and motivated solely by revenge. All three witnesses also stood to gain financially from a guilty verdict. Meanwhile, there was no significant incidental evidence.

Thorpe's barrister was George Carman QC, a legendary orator. He put the outcome beyond any doubt by systematically demolishing each of the prosecution witnesses. Newton, who was first in the dock, promptly admitted that he had told a 'pack of lies' in his previous hearing and accepted that he was now 'out to milk the case for all it is worth'. In the course of a long and tense cross-examination, Bessell accepted that he had a 'credibility problem', was 'a thoroughly amoral person' and 'had difficulty distinguishing between fantasy and fact'. After he agreed with Carman's allegation that he had been 'guilty of deviousness, of quite disgraceful behaviour', the judge intervened to note that he was clearly telling 'whoppers'. Carman concluded his cross-examination by announcing to a defeated Bessell that 'you seem almost unable to talk to any human being on any matter of consequence without introducing a lie'. Bessell agreed with him. His appearance was such a disaster that Thorpe later noted: 'Had the prosecution been aware of how [Bessell] would stand at the end of the trial on the question of honesty and reliability, they might well have taken a different view of the case.'

Scott fared little better; Carman reduced him to tears after half an hour of cross-examination. He too admitted telling countless lies and doing 'many wicked things'. He made no secret of his lack of mental stability, his delusions, his suicidal tendencies and his treatment in hospitals.

After the prosecution witnesses had given their evidence, Carman dramatically declared that he did not need to call any evidence for the defendant, asserting that the case was clear-cut. Thorpe's solicitor, Sir David Napley, recalled that this decision was taken 'only at the last possible moment', because the prosecution witnesses had been so unconvincing that no jury could say that it was beyond reasonable doubt that Thorpe was guilty.

Carman moved straight on to his closing speech to the jury, restating that there was no reliable evidence on which Thorpe could be convicted. Accepting that he may have had 'homosexual tendencies', a concession that had been negotiated with the prosecution to avoid evidence of other dalliances being raised, Carman reminded the jury that his client was not on trial for his sexual proclivities.

The judge summed up the case for the jury to make their decision in a manner that became notorious overnight. He began by instructing the jury to take account of Thorpe's 'untarnished reputation' and 'very distinguished public record'. Unusually, he moved on to criticise the prosecution case, describing it as 'almost entirely circumstantial'. But it was his views on the prosecution witnesses that made the speech notorious. Dismissing Bessell as a 'humbug' that had signed a 'deplorable' deal with the *Sunday Telegraph*, he noted: 'If there had been really enterprising and competitive media in those days, Judas Iscariot might have thought the thirty pieces of silver the least of his rewards.' He went on to describe Scott as a 'hysterical warped personality, [an] accomplished sponger and very skilful at exciting and exploiting sympathy'. He concluded that 'he is a crook … he is a fraud … he is a sponger … he is a whiner … he is a parasite,' before adding in a token nod to impartiality: 'But, of course, he could still be telling the truth.' As for Newton, the judge described him as 'highly incompetent', seemingly astonished that he had managed to bungle the plot, declaring: 'What a chump this man is!'

The jury agreed with the judge, returning unanimous verdicts of 'not guilty' on every charge. As the verdicts were read out by the foreman, Thorpe stood quietly. As they sunk in, his face suddenly erupted into a wide grin. Throwing his cushion into the air, he leaned over the side of the dock to hug his wife and shouted: 'Darling, we won!' Turning to Carman, a fellow Oxford alumnus, he added: 'Well rowed, Balliol!' He left the court at the head of a triumphant procession, doffing his trilby and revelling in victory salutes to the assembled press. He announced that 'the verdict of the jury, after a prolonged and careful investigation by them, I regard as totally fair, just and a complete vindication'.

When he got back to his Bayswater townhouse, he emerged onto the balcony with his wife and mother, posing for photographers and waving to the crowd. He viewed the outcome as such a triumph that he even sought re-nomination as the Liberal candidate for North Devon. This, however, was a bridge too far. Steel headed off his ambitions by publicly restating that his political career was over.

Before the end of the year, Thorpe was diagnosed with Parkinson's disease and forced to retreat from public life. Over the next thirty years, he made various attempts to persuade Liberal leaders to make him a peer, but was rebuffed on each occasion. He died on 4 December 2014, having never again spoken publicly about the strange and murky affair. In a sign of the esteem in which he was still held, however, all his successors as party leader attended his funeral, where his battered old trilby was placed upon his coffin.

Although Thorpe was exonerated in court, it is beyond dispute that he stood at the apex of a conspiracy to, at the very least, frighten Scott. Whether under Thorpe's direct orders or not, Scott was beaten up on more than one occasion due to his relationship with the politician. Furthermore, the woeful affair led to threats to the labourer's life and the murder of his dog. Thorpe escaped conviction primarily because the prosecution case was so poorly put together; it is impossible now to know the level of involvement he truly had with the plots of which he was accused. Beyond doubt is how well Thorpe was served by his establishment credentials, which snatched him multiple times from the gaping jaws of scandal. Whether a would-be murderer or not, Thorpe is one of British politics' great villains.

JEREMY THORPE TO DAVID STEEL

My dear David,

In the absence of Alan Beith, I am writing to you in your capacity as acting Chief Whip. You will recall that the Parliamentary Liberal Party having passed a unanimous vote of confidence in the leadership subsequently agreed that the Party would hold a leadership election in the autumn. This was a course which I myself had suggested to the President. Until such time it was clearly agreed that we act as a united party.

Since then two things have happened: first, sections of the press have turned a series of accusations into a sustained witch hunt and there is no indication that this will not continue; second, a parliamentary colleague has taken to the air publicly to challenge my credibility.

Although other parliamentary colleagues have come to my support, and agree that nothing has changed since our decision to hold an autumn election, I am convinced that a fixed determination to destroy the Leader could itself result in the destruction of the Party.

I have always felt that the fortunes of the Party are far more important than any individual and accordingly I want to advise you that I am herewith resigning the leadership.

You will appreciate the sadness with which I do this, but feel I owe the decision to my family, my constituents, and the many loyal Liberals who deserve better of us than the continued spectacle of a Party wrangling with itself with more concern for personality than policy.

You will know that from the very beginning I have strenuously denied the so-called Scott allegations and I categorically repeat those denials today. But I am convinced that the campaign of denigration which has already endured for over three months, should be drawn by me as an individual and not directed at the Liberals collectively through their leader.

No man can effectively lead a Party if the greater part of his time has to be devoted to answering allegations as they arise and countering continuing plots and intrigues.

To Liberals all over the country, whose loyalty and understanding has been quite superb and a source of great strength to my wife and myself, I ask that they use this period to redouble their efforts to build up the Party and to re-create the unity upon which alone we can build on our substantial and dedicated Liberal support.

Perhaps you would make this decision known to my colleagues and be responsible for making it known to my fellow Liberals in the country.

Yours affectionately,

Jeremy

CHAPTER SIX

MICHAEL HESELTINE
AND LEON BRITTAN

According to Bernard Ingham, the Westland Affair was 'the most idiotic thing that happened during the 1980s'. Margaret Thatcher's cantankerous press secretary looked on in disbelief as a routine squabble became a savage battle of wills that nearly toppled his leader. Michael Heseltine's dramatic Cabinet walkout and the subsequent defenestration of Leon Brittan transformed a small issue into a major crisis from which the Prime Minister never fully recovered.

Heseltine was one of the commanding political figures of his time and one of the most significant politicians never to become Prime Minister. After leaving university, he set about becoming a successful property developer and publishing baron by his early thirties, an ascent which has few parallels in British public life. But for Heseltine, business would always be a side-line. In 1966, he met a self-imposed deadline to be elected to Parliament by the age of thirty-three, and has remained there ever since, first as an MP and later as a Lord. In 2017, he continues to be a leader of the Conservatives' pro-European wing.

After several years as a junior minister, Heseltine was promoted to Cabinet by Margaret Thatcher after her triumph in the 1979 general election. He was never a natural Thatcherite, fervently believing that government intervention should play a key role in unlocking prosperity. As Secretary of State for the Environment, he pioneered urban renewal schemes in the inner cities and was acclaimed for his redevelopment of post-industrial Liverpool. The Thatcherites soon came to be suspicious both of his growing influence and his views, which they derided as counterproductive corporatism.

After the Falklands War, Heseltine was promoted to be Defence Secretary, which he considered a snub. Although he knew such an appointment was unlikely, he had hoped to become Industry Secretary and have the chance to put interventionist policies into practice.

Despite their political differences, Thatcher and Heseltine were in many ways similar characters. Both were highly driven without being collegiate, contemptuous of lower-flyers and both felt uncomfortable in the smoke-filled rooms of the Carlton Club.

Heseltine soon became Thatcher's most feared political enemy within the party. His popularity among Tory members, clear intention to be Prime Minister and open disagreement with her ideology fostered a mutual distrust. Their colleagues realised that his thrusting ambition would prove incompatible with Thatcher's dictatorial style, but few could have guessed that open confrontation would be triggered by the travails of a small company based in Yeovil.

Westland Helicopters fell into serious difficulties in late 1984 when a crucial order fell through. By April 1985, the company was on the brink of insolvency, threatening 1,700 jobs. This caused disproportionate concern to the government because the constituency of Yeovil had just been snatched from the Tories by Liberal Paddy Ashdown, and was a key target at the next election.

With both eyes on the political implications, Thatcher's first instinct was, unusually, to intervene. She suggested to the Foreign Secretary

Geoffrey Howe that the British overseas aid programme might pay for an order of twelve helicopters to be sent to Zambia. A stunned Howe rebuffed the suggestion, gently telling the Prime Minister that her request verged on the ludicrous.

Heseltine became involved in Westland's difficulties because the Ministry of Defence was its biggest customer. Firmly rejecting a proposal that his department might support the company by placing extra helicopter orders, he instead recommended arranging a takeover bid by European defence companies with support from the government. Thatcher swiftly rejected this state intervention: Westland was to be left to its own devices.

The chairman of Westland, former Secret Service operative Sir John Cuckney, set about trying to rescue his company without government help. He made an early breakthrough when Sikorsky, an American company, came forward with an offer to buy a minority stake. Alarm bells immediately sounded in the Ministry of Defence, who feared Sikorsky would abuse their position to force the British armed forces to buy their new Black Hawk helicopter. Heseltine remembers 'the word was around that America was trying to persuade us to buy the Black Hawk. This was no secret.' Heseltine was 'at the receiving end of a submission from the military saying they didn't want this helicopter and weren't going to buy it'. He resolved that he 'wasn't going to be forced to buy a helicopter the military didn't want'.

Heseltine's opposition to Sikorsky's bid went beyond issues of defence procurement. He was suspicious of the close relationship Thatcher had built with Ronald Reagan and his allies, instinctively preferring joint European projects such as Concorde and the European Fighter Aircraft. For Heseltine, the future of British global influence and prosperity lay within Europe, not with the USA. The pair had taken up positions on either side of the fault line that still runs through the Conservative Party.

After a Cabinet reshuffle in September 1985, Leon Brittan took over the role of Secretary of State for Trade and Industry, the job Heseltine coveted. Brittan had been demoted from his previous position of Home Secretary because of his awkward television manner and lack of political dexterity. A dogged, loyal Thatcherite, he was affable but inflexible. One of his parliamentary colleagues noted that if he had been captain of the *Titanic*, 'you'd have heard reassuring messages over the Tannoy about the time of arrival in New York even as the ice was crashing into the hull'.

One of Brittan's first tasks was to co-ordinate the government's efforts to assist Westland. Heseltine, determined to stave off the Sikorsky bid, sought the new Secretary of State's support. He proposed putting together an alternative rescue bid for Westland made up of European defence companies. Heseltine remembered Brittan gladly accepting his offer of help, for 'Leon was a European. He was as committed as I was to Britain's future in Europe.' Brittan's recollection of the meeting was very different; an imperious Heseltine had ordered him to support the putative European takeover bid, treating him like a 'jumped-up minor person'.

The two options for Westland began to take shape. Sikorsky's offer was open for acceptance by the company's shareholders, and the rival European bid was gradually emerging, kick-started by Heseltine. Brittan's recommendation was that both options be explored by Westland, but the government must not force the issue. The market would decide.

Thatcher's private secretary and chief advisor, Charles Powell, soon realised that Heseltine was spoiling for a fight. He remembers a chance encounter with the Defence Secretary early in the standoff. Heseltine took Powell to one side, looked him straight in the eye and said: 'She's not going to beat me on this one.' Heseltine confirms that this encounter took place.

With characteristic dynamism, the Defence Secretary set to work bringing together European defence companies and their financial supporters. Ignoring the government's preference for a market solution, he sought a commitment from European ministers that they would only buy helicopters from predominantly European-owned companies, knowing that such an arrangement would doom Sikorsky's bid.

Sir John Cuckney and the rest of the Westland board grew increasingly alarmed, fearing that Heseltine's antics would alienate Sikorsky. Cuckney appealed directly to Thatcher's policy team, who were unaware that her Defence Secretary was attempting to stitch up victory for his preferred solution. The policy team considered his behaviour tantamount to sabotage and, in a briefing note to Thatcher, they stated that 'Michael Heseltine is proposing that a Conservative government should intervene to kill a private sector rescue of Westlands – which amazingly costs the government nothing – in order to promote a European deal that will reduce competition and result in the stripping of Westlands [*sic*], such that it will only survive long term with state subsidy. This surely isn't on.'

On 6 December 1985, the Prime Minister chaired a meeting of all ministers with an interest in Westland's problems. She proposed that the government should rule out Heseltine's proposed European-only helicopter procurement programme. But, in the face of his vehement disagreement, she agreed to delay any final decision on the matter. The Defence Secretary had won the first round.

Buoyed by victory, Heseltine redoubled his efforts. He introduced new elements to the European bid, including the involvement of several British companies, which laid the ground for arguing that a Sikorsky takeover was the worse option for Britain. Powell grew increasingly worried that the matter would be raised in full Cabinet, where Heseltine might receive heavyweight support. He decided this was a battle in which he had to take personal command.

Powell believed that the conflict had been earmarked by Heseltine as a potential resigning issue, and became determined not to let him stage a 'good resignation'. Heseltine accepts that leaving Cabinet was on his mind, remembering that at the beginning of December – over a month before he walked out – he had resolved to quit if Thatcher suppressed discussion of his proposals.

On 9 December, Heseltine notched up a second victory. He managed to convince members of the powerful economic committee of the Cabinet, chaired by Thatcher, to allow the European bid further time to come together. Leaving the meeting triumphant and armed with sympathetic comments from several Cabinet members, he was later handed a personal note from Foreign Secretary Geoffrey Howe promising his full support and assistance. Heseltine remembers throwing this note into the bin rather than accepting Howe's offer, an action he struggles to explain and regrets to this day.

A flustered and humiliated Thatcher feigned exasperation, complaining to colleagues after the meeting that 'we have just spent three hours of precious time discussing a company with a capitalisation of only £30 million' and asking: 'What is the world coming to?'

Thatcher and Heseltine left the economic committee meeting with different views on what had been agreed at it. The Defence Secretary believed that he had been promised a further meeting, the civil servants taking minutes agreed with him and the Cabinet Office duly began to ring around ministers to arrange the follow-up. In Thatcher's view, however, a further meeting would only be scheduled if she deemed the European bid sufficiently changed to warrant further discussion.

Powell promptly ordered the Cabinet Office to cancel the plans. This was the moment Heseltine realised that 'the disaster was cast in steel', for he realised that Downing Street would not play fair. In the House of Commons bar, he met with allies to discuss whether to resign in protest there and then. His friends thought that he had taken leave of his senses and told him that he must stay to fight his corner. Heseltine relented, but informed Downing Street 'that if [Thatcher] refused to allow matters to be discussed, ventilated and explored at full Cabinet, I would resign.'

On 12 December, he tried to raise the issue in full Cabinet, exactly as Powell had feared. Thatcher cut him off, ruling his actions out of order for not giving notice. She refused to discuss the matter further, prompting an exchange of unprecedented hostility. Environment Secretary Kenneth Baker, sitting between the pair, was shocked at what he saw. He remembered Heseltine insisting that the government's approach was a matter for the Cabinet. Thatcher interrupted him again, this time telling him to be quiet. Heseltine turned his head around slowly, glared at the Prime Minister across the table and hissed: 'Don't interrupt me.' She retorted that, as chair, she was entitled to decide what topics would be raised, adding: 'That's the position. I'm sorry.' Heseltine scoffed, muttering under his breath: 'You're not in the least sorry.' Baker had 'never seen such a bitter exchange between colleagues, and certainly not in front of a full Cabinet'.

Many Cabinet members sympathised with the Defence Secretary's position. Leon Brittan recalled that 'there was some force in Michael's claim that there wasn't a full Cabinet discussion … he had the right to refer it to the Cabinet'. Deputy Prime Minister Willie Whitelaw agreed, and tried to convince Thatcher to reconvene the Cabinet economic committee meeting. Heseltine later regretted making no effort to co-ordinate his would-be allies.

By 16 December, the escalating tension had entered the public domain. The newspapers had begun to report a split between Brittan and Heseltine, prompting the latter to eschew all pretence of neutrality. When Brittan told the House of Commons that the government did not favour either takeover bid, parliamentary sketch writers spotted the Defence Secretary sitting next to him shaking his head vigorously in disgust.

Two days later, Thatcher convened a meeting of her closest allies, including Charles Powell, Willie Whitelaw and Leon Brittan. Brittan urged Thatcher to sack Heseltine immediately, but the others recommended caution, together drafting an ultimatum to the Defence Secretary that read:

You were on the front bench in the House yesterday when I made clear the government's position concerning the future of Westlands – namely that it is a matter for the company to decide. The company's decision is a matter of commercial judgement for its directors and ultimately its shareholders. That was the basis of the decisions reached by the economic committee of the Cabinet on 9 December. In this situation, no minister should use his position to promote one commercial option in preference to another – so long as he remains in government.

Thatcher could not decide whether to send the missive, or simply to sack her minister for his insolence. She chose to do neither – a decision that she later identified as one of the few mistakes during her premiership.

Cabinet convened the next day, 19 December, with Heseltine surprised still to be in position. Brittan informed ministers that Westland's shareholders would be deciding on its future in the next month, and the government's position was to remain neutral until then. Thatcher took her chance to stress that the doctrine of collective responsibility meant that no minister could make a public statement favouring either bid. She added, in a direct challenge to Heseltine: 'Is that clear? Is that accepted?' He nodded in acquiescence.

Despite his promise, Heseltine continued to lobby against Sikorsky, and to brief his press contacts in favour of the European bid. He also contacted Sir John Cuckney directly, ringing him at home on 23 December. Cuckney did not appreciate this disturbance during his Christmas holiday and flatly refused Heseltine's offer of a meeting.

Later that evening, Heseltine, who had cancelled a planned holiday in Nepal to keep up the fight, sent a memo to Thatcher. He first insisted that he had, as promised, expressed no public preference since the Cabinet meeting. Here, Thatcher's copy is scrawled with 'NO' in angry letters. He then outlined a 'significant development' in the affair that warranted further collective discussion. It had been discovered that Sikorsky's bid was indirectly financed by Fiat, a conglomerate partly owned by Muammar Gaddafi's Libyan regime. This risked, he argued, causing the government 'grave embarrassment'. He concluded that Brittan should announce that 'subject to the commercial interests of the parties being protected, it would prefer a British/European solution.'

The memo was accompanied by a handwritten note, in which he added: 'I know that [a rethink] will not be an easy one for you. I know also that you will understand the depths of my convictions in the matter.' Thatcher ignored the memo, instead letting Powell brief the press that she was so frustrated with Heseltine that she was considering removing him from his post.

Early in the New Year, Heseltine unearthed a new argument: if Sikorsky was to hold even a minority stake of Westland, the company may no longer be considered 'European' for the purposes of esoteric common market rules. The consequent tariffs would, it was argued, cripple the company overnight. On seeing this position in the press, a rattled Charles Powell ordered an opinion from the Solicitor General, Sir Patrick Mayhew.

In his advice, Mayhew warned Powell that the risk was a real one, and must be publicly disclosed, as the government fell 'under a duty not to withhold any information it knows to be relevant and would be a serious risk'. They therefore needed to convey that some 'take the view that a number of projects in which Westland are currently expecting to participate in ... may be lost ... if the Sikorsky offer is accepted'. Powell was furious with this advice, detecting Heseltine's influence over the law officer.

Powell's response was to counter-attack by taking advantage of a minor error in one of Heseltine's recent public letters. The Defence Secretary had written to David Horne of Lloyd's Bank, who was co-ordinating the European consortium. That letter had been published in *The Times*, and claimed that all governments involved in the European bid had confirmed that they would bar a Sikorsky-owned Westland from the new European battlefield helicopter project. In fact, only a majority of governments had said this.

Powell had decided that underhand tactics were now justified. In his view, Heseltine had been the first to deploy the law officers and deserved to 'get it right between the eyes'. He proposed to ask Mayhew, as the top-ranking government law officer, to force Heseltine into issuing an embarrassing public correction. He wrote up the plan in a memo to Thatcher that appears in her files, but is surprisingly unannotated: she must have wanted to maintain deniability over what was about to be done.

Powell's memo read:

I am proposing to suggest to the Solicitor that he should write to Mr Heseltine to say that he has read a copy of his letter to Lloyds Bank International in the Times; that he regrets that it was not cleared with him in advance; that it contains a material inaccuracy; that Mr Heseltine ought to issue a letter of correction; and that since he gave the first letter to the press he should give the second one also. I think this is worth doing but don't place great reliance on it. Mr Heseltine will all too easily obtain statements from other Ministers to give substance to the assertions in his letter…

I think the most important issue is how to handle MH next week. Nigel Wicks is inclined, I think, to suggest there should be a full discussion in Cabinet with papers from Ministers concerned. I am not sure that this is really relevant since nothing Cabinet decides at this stage will affect the outcome, though a repeat of the sort of discussion in Cabinet on 19 December could be useful.

Powell despatched the hapless Brittan to collar Mayhew, who, on Monday 6 January, sent his letter to Heseltine as instructed. That confidential missive noted that Heseltine's earlier letter had contained a material inaccuracy which ought to be corrected. Mayhew's tone was gentle and uncondemning, doing his level best to remain neutral. Later, he would describe his involvement in the Westland Affair as like 'being the family solicitor to both the Montagues and the Capulets'.

Heseltine ignored Mayhew's criticism, dismissing the letter as 'an astonishing piece of legal pedantry'.

The events that followed still today prompt vitriolic reactions from those involved. Brittan arranged for part of Mayhew's letter to be leaked to the press in order to portray Heseltine as a liar. In a doomed attempt to keep his hands clean, he delegated the deed to Colette Bowe, the chief information officer at his department.

Downing Street became involved in the leak as Bowe approached Bernard Ingham, seeking his approval. Careful not to endorse the move directly, Ingham nonetheless turned a blind eye to Bowe's proposed actions. He remembered realising 'that I had to keep the Prime Minister above that sort of thing' and insists that he could not personally have approved the leak 'without seeking Mrs Thatcher's specific permission, and I would not have been prepared to put such an idea to her'. But Ingham did not try to stop Bowe, and indeed gave her practical advice on how to get the news out. In all but name, he authorised the leak.

Bowe duly called Chris Moncrieff of the Press Association and dictated parts of the Mayhew letter down the phone. The only direct quote given to Moncrieff was the sentence that accused Heseltine of reporting 'material inaccuracies'. The newspapers took the bait, with *The Sun* splashing with the headline 'You Liar! Tarzan Gets Rocket From Top Law Man'; the *Sunday Telegraph* concluding that Heseltine had caused a 'national scandal' that left the government 'pitifully divided'.

The leak was not Brittan's personal idea. The precise source is a secret that he took to his grave, but he did go so far as to admit that Thatcher 'and her entourage were extremely keen for [the letter] to be in the public domain'. As Powell has himself accepted, Thatcher's hands 'were not entirely clean'.

The most likely explanation is that, with or without Thatcher's direct knowledge, her entourage ordered Brittan misrepresent Mayhew's letter by releasing the 'material inaccuracies' phrase. Heseltine remains furious, protesting that the attack on him 'wasn't just unfair. It was dishonest. Downright dishonest.'

Mayhew agreed, furious that his carefully worded and confidential letter had been selectively leaked. He contacted Heseltine at once to apologise, explaining that although he had 'no interest in the outcome of the row', he had 'a substantial interest in Law Officers not being perceived to be used for tendentious purposes'. He then called Downing Street and threatened to resign unless given an apology. His immediate superior, the Attorney General Michael Havers, was so incensed that he returned prematurely from sick leave to investigate the matter, soon echoing Mayhew's threat to resign.

Two days passed between the leak and the next Cabinet meeting. Both Thatcher and Heseltine knew that this summit would be pivotal to the continuing power struggle. The tension between the pair had reached record heights. Powell carefully planned Thatcher's approach, drafting her a speaking note to read out. She planned to state that she had 'never seen a clearer demonstration of damaging consequences that ensue for the coherence and standing of a [government] when the principle of collective responsibility is not respected'. Powell suggested that she should conclude: 'Anyone who does not feel able to accept [her conclusion] and act in accordance with [it] and who continues to campaign on behalf of one or other proposal, cannot do so as a minister and should do so from outside the government.'

Surprisingly reticent, Thatcher felt the last paragraph was too aggressive, and she edited the note personally to remove the explicit threat. Cabinet began at 10 a.m. with Brittan briefing colleagues on Westland's upcoming shareholder meeting at which the rival bids would be considered. Heseltine took a conciliatory approach, having 'very little to add' to Brittan's summary. He said that he would adopt 'an absolutely neutral stance' as previously promised.

Thatcher then stressed the need for absolute unity, given the chaos that had gone before. There was to be no further ambiguity about how questions on Westland were to be handled by the government. Accordingly, all public statements on the issue would be cleared through the Cabinet Office to ensure collective responsibility was maintained. Norman Fowler, the Social Services Secretary, scribbled 'Heseltine silenced!' on the pad of paper in front of him.

Heseltine smelled a rat immediately, spotting a plan to muzzle him. He 'instantly knew that this was a trap', and asked Thatcher: 'Do you mean that if I am asked the identical question tomorrow to one that I was asked a week ago, I will have to refer the reply to the Cabinet

Secretary?' The answer was yes. He immediately 'knew exactly what that would mean – Ingham would have been onto the lobby to tell the press: "The guy's a busted flush! You can ask him any question you like, about anything he has said, and he'll say he's got to refer to the Cabinet Office." Fleet Street would have laughed themselves silly.' He insisted that he must at least be able to confirm the statements that he had already made on the matter.

The atmosphere in the room suddenly became extremely tense. Although Thatcher declared in her memoirs that 'no one sided with Michael' and 'he was quite isolated', her view was not shared by others present. Even Thatcher's staunch ally Norman Tebbit agreed that Heseltine's position had merit, while Geoffrey Howe remembers intervening in support of him. He also received a show of sympathy from Norman Fowler, who felt that it was 'not surprising that Michael indignantly refused to accept [the] humiliating instructions'.

As the argument progressed, Heseltine became increasingly animated, gradually alienating supportive colleagues, who were not prepared to go out on a limb for him over this relatively minor issue. For Howe, 'the earlier validity of his argument … seemed to grow less and less as Michael's presentation became more apparently obsessive. The more he seemed faintly reminiscent of Tony Benn, and occasionally he did, the less he commanded our sympathy.' But for Heseltine, backing down was not an option. If he did, all 'would know that I was a man of straw, a man who threatens but who has not the steel to stand by his word'.

Thatcher maintained her position in the face of Heseltine's resistance. In Nigel Lawson's view, she had 'set out to humiliate Michael, in the full knowledge that this would almost certainly lead to his resignation'. She moved to end the debate abruptly, purporting to summarise the discussion by reading out a prepared speech, but the scrap of paper produced from her handbag could only have been the product of a political discussion with her close confidants, rather than a genuine summing-up. She reiterated that all statements concerning Westland had to be cleared with the Cabinet Office.

As soon as Thatcher had finished reading this speech, Heseltine took to his feet and calmly declared that 'there has been no collective responsibility in the discussion of these matters. There has been a breakdown of the propriety of Cabinet discussions. I cannot accept this decision. I must therefore leave this Cabinet.' He swept up his papers and stormed out of the room, the first Cabinet minister to walk out in the middle of a session since his hero Joseph Chamberlain nearly 100 years earlier. After stopping briefly in the bathroom to coiffeur his luxuriant mane, he swept out of the front door and into Downing Street. Striding across the road to an awaiting photographer, he announced calmly that he had resigned from the government.

For a few moments, the Cabinet sat in stunned silence. They were interrupted by a panicked official, who put his head around the door to tell them that Heseltine appeared to be giving some sort of press conference in the street. Thatcher adjourned the meeting to deal with the crisis.

Heseltine maintains that he resigned on the spur of the moment, in reaction to the attempt to humiliate him. His Permanent Secretary, Sir Richard Mottram, confirmed this, having dined with him the night before and detected no intention to stage such a sensational *coup de théâtre*. Thatcher and her team were, however, convinced that he had engineered the whole debate to create an excuse for his dramatic resignation.

The truth must lie between these two extremes. There was little for Heseltine to gain from staging a resignation. Westland was too complex a pretext for a head-on leadership challenge, and he would certainly have lost to Thatcher. However, his myopic focus on a comparatively minor issue, failure to cultivate Cabinet allies and refusal to back down rendered his position so precarious that he must have known what the likely outcome would be.

On arriving back at the Ministry of Defence, Heseltine remembers feeling 'remarkably calm … ice cold calm'. A few hours later, he had prepared a resignation statement so lengthy and detailed that the parliamentary reporter Anthony Howard mischievously suggested that it must have been drafted in advance. Heseltine, determined to make his position public as quickly as possible, shunned the conventional resignation letter and statement to the House of Commons. Instead, he arranged to hold a press conference in the foyer of the Ministry of Defence. He read out the long statement, ending with a shot across the boughs to Thatcher: 'To serve as a member of a Tory Cabinet within the constitutional understandings and practices of a system under which the Prime Minister is *primus inter pares* [first among equals] is a memory I will always treasure. But if the basis of trust between the Prime Minister and her Defence Secretary no longer exists, there is no place for me with honour in such a Cabinet.'

He spent the rest of the day touring the television and radio studios, making sure that every journalist had his side of the story before Powell and Ingham could reach them. Exploiting the occasion for every ounce of theatre it could produce, the image-conscious Heseltine reportedly wore six different ties throughout the day, each co-ordinated to the tone of the appearance.

Aware that they were on dangerous ground, Downing Street took some time to respond. Thatcher's political secretary Stephen Sherbourne wrote her a memo stating:

The most damaging effect of the Heseltine Affair has been to show the Government in serious disarray and you looking, uncharacteristically, as though you are not in control. This is bound to show itself in the polls for a bit. But it will blow over because he did not resign on a clear-cut issue. It will be seen much more as a personality clash. The opposition tactics next week will be uncertain: they will not know whether to attack you for being too tough or too weak. David Owen will probably have a go at both … Longer term you will have to consider Mr Heseltine's tactics on the backbenches.

Those tactics were to prove ingenious. Four days after Heseltine's resignation, Brittan was due to make a House of Commons statement on Westland. With Heseltine's approval, the chairman of BAE wrote a letter to Downing Street to complain about Brittan's attempts to force them out of the European consortium in flagrant breach of his supposed neutrality. Charles Powell had instructed Brittan not to mention this letter, but Heseltine ambushed him at the despatch box. Rising from the back benches for the first time in fourteen years, he asked Brittan whether the government had received any letters of complaint from BAE. Putting his training as a QC to use, Brittan replied in a manner that was both truthful and wholly misleading: he stated that *he* had not received any such letter.

The veteran Labour MP Dennis Skinner deftly spotted his chance to attack. He asked Brittan whether *the government* had received any letter from BAE, reminding Brittan that 'it is your job to answer for the whole of the government'. Brittan replied: 'I am not aware of any letter from [BAE] to anyone else either.' Unlike his previous response, this was demonstrably untrue. He had fallen head first into Heseltine's trap.

A minister that has misled Parliament is in grave danger, and Brittan was forced to return late that night to apologise. He approached the despatch box white-faced and fearful, offering the weakest of excuses. He unconvincingly claimed to have been unable to acknowledge receipt of the letter because it had been marked 'private and confidential'. Labour MPs began a slow chant of 'Resign! Resign! Resign!'

Brittan's woes were not Thatcher's only concern. The Attorney General and Solicitor General had demanded, on pain of their own resignations, an inquiry into the leak of Mayhew's letter. The Prime Minister could not afford to lose two further ministers, and was forced to announce an official investigation into the leak headed by Cabinet Secretary Sir Robert Armstrong.

That leak inquiry was quickly superseded by Labour's Tam Dalyell, who used parliamentary privilege to name Colette Bowe as the culprit. The newspapers latched onto the story, rapidly reducing it to the key question of whether Thatcher knew about the leak. To this day, Heseltine remains uncertain of the answer, concluding: 'That it was deliberately leaked is beyond question. That it was leaked in part is beyond question. That Ingham and Powell knew exactly what they were doing is beyond question. What I do not know is what Margaret knew...'

Thatcher came to the House of Commons on 23 January to set out the findings of the leak inquiry. The blame was placed squarely at Brittan's door. He had been told of the contents of the letter, wanted it leaked and gave 'authority for the disclosure to be made from the DTI if it was not made by 10 Downing Street'. Thatcher said that members of her office had been approached and refused to assist with the leak, adding: 'Had I been consulted, I should have said that a different way must be found of making the relevant facts known.' Her brazen abrogation of responsibility failed to convince her own MPs, with Alan Clark asking in his diary: 'How can she say these things without faltering?'

The influential 1922 Committee of Tory backbenchers met that evening to decide whether to back Brittan. Jonathan Aitken recalled that the meeting 'was a combination of a witch hunt and a search for a scapegoat'. It was also tainted by an undercurrent of anti-Semitism, with several members of the committee commenting that there were too many Jews in the Cabinet. They withdrew their support for Brittan.

The newspapers agreed that he was finished, with *The Sun*, *Mirror* and *Express* all calling for his head. The next day he was duly approached by the Chief Whip and curtly told that he had lost the support of his party. Although his friends Geoffrey Howe and Willie Whitelaw urged him not to resign, they pointedly did not ring Thatcher to lobby for him.

Later in the afternoon, he visited Thatcher to hand over his resignation letter. She accepted the decision with some reluctance, no doubt feeling a pang of guilt for her part in his demise. She stated in her reply to his letter: 'I hope it will not be long before you return to high office to continue your ministerial career.' It was not to be. Looking back thirty years later, Brittan remained disappointed in Thatcher, arguing that 'if she'd really defended me, I think it would have blown over.'

His resignation was at least as damaging to her as Heseltine's had been. Many Tory MPs felt that Heseltine had resigned opportunistically, intent on establishing himself as the Prime Minister in exile. But Brittan was different, as he had dutifully followed Downing Street's orders and had taken a bullet for his troubles.

The Prime Minister's authority was badly undermined. Briefings against her staff and her allies begin to appear in the newspapers. Rumours circulated that she would not survive the affair, which was cast as 'Whitehall's Watergate' by Labour's former communications supremo Joe Haines. Howe let his friends in the press know that he would be the natural replacement if Thatcher fell. Douglas Hurd was on manoeuvres, tacitly supported by a coalition of disaffected 'wets', from Chris Patten and William Waldegrave to the embittered Brittan. Inevitably, rumours abounded that Heseltine would himself issue a challenge.

Thatcher's key test was the upcoming major parliamentary debate on Brittan's leak. According to Lawson, in the run-up to the debate she entered a 'period of acute weakness'. For the first time in her premiership, the steely façade buckled. Admitting to her friends that she was in 'rough waters', her hair, usually immaculately arranged, seemed awry, and her clothes became crumpled. Alan Clark remembered that 'you could see the fear in those blue eyes', and another of her friends saw that, 'for the first time, she looked like an old lady'.

The debate presented a major political challenge. Thatcher knew that she could be skewered by a series of forensic questions about her involvement in the leak. The Leader of the Opposition, Neil Kinnock, usually an enthusiastic and talented despatch box performer, recognised this to be a moment of defining importance. The axe was his to wield.

In one of the biggest let-downs in parliamentary memory, Kinnock failed to land a single blow. Heseltine looked on, unable to believe the mediocrity of the Labour leader's effort – the worst parliamentary performance he had ever witnessed. Kinnock 'only had to get up and ask the simple question – "Prime Minister, did you know?" and sit down'. Instead, 'he rumbled on all round the subject, waffling here, waffling there. You could just feel it falling apart.' Tony Blair, then a recently elected MP, recalled that 'as Neil went on, I could see the wave of relief pass over the Tories. She thought the guillotine was going to come. Instead, she got the reprieve. She was vulnerable to a forensic dissection. It needed a scalpel. All she got was a rather floppy baseball bat.' Kinnock admits culpability, attributing his dismal showing to nerves and over-preparation, acknowledging that 'it was stupid. Entirely my own bloody fault.'

Observing Kinnock's failure, Heseltine made the quick decision to beat a tactical retreat. He rose to give a short speech declaring that Thatcher's expression of regret was 'a difficult and very brave thing for a Prime Minister to say in such circumstances'. He added that he had his own regrets about what had been done, but he considered that the debate had 'brought the politics of this matter to an end'.

This was not a sudden act of benevolence. Rather, he knew that a challenge was not viable and decided to call off the dogs for the time being. Anything else would have amounted to political suicide. As he recently recalled: 'I had made up my mind to survive.'

Thatcher was damaged irreparably by the Westland Affair. She had lost two senior Cabinet ministers, been humiliated by the law officers, revealed the dark side of Downing Street's operations and given birth to a king over the water. Spared a leadership challenge only by Neil Kinnock's incompetence, she had sowed the seeds of her later destruction. It was a heavy price to pay for victory in a petty dispute about the ownership of a helicopter company.

MARGARET THATCHER TO MICHAEL HESELTINE

Dear Michael,

It was with great regret that I accepted your decision to leave the Cabinet and the Government.

I was very glad that you supported this morning our decision to reaffirm the policy that it is for the Westland company to decide the course to follow in the best interest of the company and its employees. It was therefore a matter for regret that you were alone in being unable to accept the Cabinet's decision on how to give practical effect to that policy by inter-departmental clearance of all answers to questions addressed to Ministers during this period of sensitive commercial negotiations and decisions.

I want to thank you for your contribution to the work of Conservative Governments over the years. Your career in Government has been one of distinction from the time when you joined the Ministry of Transport in 1970 and subsequently became a Minister for Aerospace and Shipping. While you were Secretary of State for the Environment between 1979 and 1983, you pioneered radical changes in the effective management of departmental business. You carried through our policy on the Right to Buy local authority housing which has greatly expanded home ownership. You launched the Development Corporations in Merseyside and London Docklands. As Secretary of State for Defence you have presided over an historic reorganisation of the Ministry itself. You have set us on the path to achieve better value for money from defence procurement, and in the Dockyard Services Bill you have shaped the policy for the radical reform of the naval dockyards.

I am therefore very sorry about the decision that you took this morning.

Yours ever,

   Margaret

LEON BRITTAN TO MARGARET THATCHER

My dear Prime Minister,

Since your statement in the House yesterday it has become clear to me that I no longer command the full confidence of my colleagues.

In these circumstances my continued membership of your Government would be a source of weakness rather than strength and, as I have explained to you, it is for this reason that I have tendered my resignation.

It has been an honour and a privilege to serve in your Government successively as Minister of State at the Home Office, as Chief Secretary to the Treasury, as Home Secretary and as Secretary of State for Trade and Industry.

I shall of course continue to give the Government my full support from the backbenches.

It is above all vital that the crucial work of national regeneration which we were all elected to achieve should continue unimpeded.

Yours ever,

Leon

MARGARET THATCHER
TO LEON BRITTAN

My dear Leon,

I am very sorry that despite all the arguments I could use I was unable to dissuade you this afternoon from resigning. As I told you, I have received in recent hours many messages of support for you from Parliamentary colleagues. It was my wish that you should remain as a member of the Cabinet. But I have to respect your decision.

I have greatly valued you as a Cabinet colleague, as Chief Secretary of the Treasury, Home Secretary and as Secretary of State for Trade and Industry. We shall all miss you. You have been a steadfast exponent of Government policy and I have admired the dedication and loyalty with which you have carried our your duties. I hope that it will not be long before you return to high office to continue your Ministerial career.

Yours ever,

Margaret

CHAPTER SEVEN

EDWINA CURRIE

According to Edwina Currie, life as a Tory MP from Liverpool was like 'being the only gay in the village'. Fiery, attention-seeking and never afraid to make an enemy, she is now chiefly remembered for her salacious affair with former Prime Minister John Major, but was once tipped as a rising star of the Conservative Party. That burgeoning career in frontline Tory politics came to an abrupt halt in 1988, because of her chronic tendency to pick a fight.

First elected as South Derbyshire's MP in 1983, Currie twinned a fanatical commitment to Thatcherism with an insatiable appetite for publicity. Always at her most confident in front of the camera, from her first entry into the Commons she never turned down an opportunity for media exposure. Her captivating persona and biting wit soon provoked the Labour ranks, polarised her colleagues and piqued the attention of the wider public. At the same time, she was a courageous advocate for the people of South Derbyshire, never afraid to roll up her sleeves and plunge into a difficult battle on their behalf.

It was her mastery of detail and clarity of thought that drew the attention of the Prime Minister. From the outset, Thatcher saw something of herself in Currie. Both were outspoken women from modest backgrounds with a desire to prove themselves, although Thatcher never allowed a taste for the spotlight to trump her inner convictions. In an early demonstration of trust, Currie was brought into government in 1986 as a junior Minister for Public Health. She became one of the few women in the administration, reporting to the new Secretary of State for Health, a young Kenneth Clarke.

Currie swiftly courted controversy in her role by declaring that lower life expectancy among northerners was caused by 'ignorance and chips', encouraging pensioners to buy a pair of long johns to combat fuel poverty and claiming that 'good Christian people who would not dream of misbehaving will not catch AIDS'. Every pithy sound bite or outrageous quote prompted further requests for comment, and she soon cemented her status as one of the government's most outspoken personalities. By 1988, she was reported to be the government's best-known minister, save for the Prime Minister herself. When she spoke, the people listened.

Her demise played out against the background of a serious public health crisis. In the mid-1980s, hospitals began to notice a significant rise in cases of the dangerous stomach bug salmonella. Previous variants of the bacteria had not been able to spread to humans, and while it had caused economic damage to farmers by killing a significant number of hens, the bug posed no threat to the wider population. But the bacteria mutated after farmers fed their hens a protein supplement which, unknown to them, contained ground-up chicken meat. This spawned a strain that could be transferred from hens to their eggs. There were no longer any signs of illness in the hens nor any noticeable cracks on infected eggs, making it impossible to know whether an egg was safe to eat until it was too late. In humans, the new strain brought on particularly violent food poisoning that was highly contagious.

Major outbreaks started to occur across the country, including at the Lord Mayor's Mansion House banquet, where a rogue soufflé despatched a good proportion of the nation's financiers. By November 1988, the epidemic was taking hold, with a suspected 500 new cases reported each week. The last straw was a dinner in the House of Lords that afflicted bouts of violent diarrhoea upon a plethora of unsuspecting aristocrats.

Currie was shown studies concluding that twenty-eight people had died from salmonella so far, and was warned that without immediate action a hot summer would condemn many more. The management of the crisis brought the Department of Health into fierce conflict with the Ministry of Agriculture, which sought to protect the egg producers. Clandestine discussions focused on how consumers could be warned without decimating the British egg industry.

The egg producers' response was sluggish. They initially denied that there was any problem at all, then denied its extent, and finally entered interminable discussions about the appropriate response. John MacGregor, the Minister for Agriculture, Fisheries and Food (MAFF), was rendered impotent under pressure from the National Farmers' Union (NFU) and the egg producers, who blocked public announcements for fear that they would destroy the egg market.

Detecting the distinctive whiff of corporatism, Currie refused to countenance the attempt to play down a public health crisis that was killing consumers. She knew that when the truth inevitably emerged, the Ministry of Agriculture would blame her for not warning people and she would undoubtedly be sacked. Unwilling to present herself for slaughter to appease a trade union, she decided to take the initiative in the only way she knew – by making a unilateral statement. But her intervention 'was not going to be on a radio phone-in in Norwich'.

Refusing to offer any comment to a regional paper or television station from a local area, she bided her time for a better opportunity. After two weeks of turning down approaches from smaller broadcasters, ITN asked if she would make a statement about the Plymouth Health Authority's decision to use only pasteurised eggs in their hospitals. Detecting her opportunity to lead the news, she leapt at the chance.

The third of December 1988 dawned crisp and bitterly cold. Currie spent her morning visiting a council estate in Derby to promote an insulation scheme for pensioners' homes. ITN's camera crew found her halfway up a ladder stuffing foam into the roof of a council house. Once she had descended, she gave a long and considered interview that eventually provided the sensational clip the reporter had wanted. Millions watching the lunchtime news saw her warn them that 'most of the egg production in this country, sadly, is now affected with salmonella. If, however, they have use of a good source of eggs, a good shop that they know and they are content, then there seems no reason for them to stop. But we would advise strongly against using raw eggs – mayonnaise and dressings and Bloody Marys and that sort of thing.'

As she admitted much later, she had intended to say that 'much' of British egg production was infected, not 'most'. The newspapers further blurred the message by misreporting that she had claimed salmonella was present in most of the individual *eggs* in circulation, rather than most production facilities. In the ensuing storm, it was impossible to correct the false impression that had been given. Her statement had a catastrophic effect on the British egg industry. Sales dropped by 60 per cent overnight, farmers were forced to slaughter 4 million hens and 400 million eggs were destroyed. As the producers had been given no warning, they had made no preparations for the fall in demand, and were left holding vast quantities of perishable products that nobody was willing to buy.

Currie was faced with a clear choice: she could either retract her statement or double down on her position. The answer was obvious to her: she refused to retreat in the face of her critics and resolved to stand by the statement. She then returned to the airwaves and repeated the comments, because 'to back off would have permitted the [egg producers'] total denial to predominate, and the public health risk to continue'.

Kenneth Clarke now had a major interdepartmental fight on his hands. He decided to take personal control of the situation. Although he admired Currie's talent and flair, he was acutely aware of her proclivity to throw fuel on the fire and ordered her to remain quiet. In her place, he instructed the apolitical Chief Medical Officer to handle the crisis, and measured guidance on egg use was duly issued. Clarke's aim was to depersonalise the developing story and avoid any permanent stain to his junior minister's reputation.

The fight to assign blame presented the government with a tricky political problem. Accepting that Currie's comments were even partially correct would be an admission that the public had been put at risk to protect the egg producers. Conversely, if the government distanced itself from her, the producers could claim to have been needlessly traduced and would deserve compensation. The result would be both embarrassing and expensive.

Currie was unlucky that the responsible shadow minister was the incisive Robin Cook, who spotted his chance to claim a prominent scalp. Within two days of her statement, he had identified inconsistencies between her statements and previous guidance issued by the Department of Health that stated the likelihood of any egg being infected was small. He asked Clarke in the House of Commons:

Which of the statements reflects the Department's view? Is the Right Honourable and learned gentlemen content to preside over a

Department that issues two totally and utterly contradictory views in the space of two weeks? … Surely it must be clear that the Honourable Lady's embarrassment quotient exceeds her entertainment value? Is it not about time he removed such a major obstacle to our taking his Department seriously?

The former Liberal leader David Steel keenly joined in the attack, accusing her of destroying businesses and killing chickens with her 'careless talk'. He concluded that 'on any basis of the doctrine of ministerial responsibility, the Hon. Lady should, by now, have been relieved of her job.'

A more vicious campaign had been organised by Conservative MPs and trade unions who had long despised her. The NFU began to apply pressure to around fifty rural MPs with whom they had commanding influence. In most cases, these MPs – ridiculed by Currie as the 'crusty old knights of the shires' – owed their seats to the patronage of the NFU. They were only too happy to attack her in public, for several already loathed her for her feminism and, in some cases, her Jewish background. Paul Marland, MP for the honey-coloured, picture-postcard villages of West Gloucestershire, publicly denounced his Liverpudlian colleague's 'ill-considered and negligent remarks', suggesting that 'one more redundancy should be added to the list'. Likewise, Robin Maxwell-Hyslop spoke of the harm done to the poultry industry by 'a junior minister with an uncontrollable tongue and insatiable desire for self-advertisement'.

Clarke robustly defended his junior minister, endorsing her as 'an extremely valuable member of the team' and noting that 'it may be that many Hon. Members are a little envious of her natural gift for obtaining publicity.' But in private he suspected that she was fatally wounded.

Other MPs began to lobby Thatcher, with four cornering her in the division lobby – 'turds all', according to Currie. At first, the Prime Minister did not see her comments as a resignation issue. Keen to retain the talented minister, she remained publicly and privately neutral, calming nerves by declaring that having read the Chief Medical Officer's advice, she was happy to have scrambled eggs on toast for lunch.

The conspirators' argument had the advantage of simplicity. They claimed that her statement had scuppered their attempts to deal with the crisis quietly, and, in turn, destroyed the livelihoods both of farmers and producers. In Currie's view, that was 'crap, frankly' – the egg producers had prompted her remarks through their own wilful blindness. But she was unable to enter the fray, remaining muzzled on Kenneth Clarke's orders. Forced to watch from the side-lines, she was powerless to prevent her own political lynching.

The row was played out across the front pages, with Currie's enforced silence serving to prolong the story rather than kill it. Sales of eggs continued to plummet, more businesses collapsed and the numbers of redundancies threatened to enter the tens of thousands. After a week, the government needed to decide which side to take.

Currie tried to outlast the frenzy by getting on with her work, but, like other ministers who have found themselves stuck in the eye of the storm, she could not focus. On Wednesday 14 December she was due to address a lunch at the Institute of Directors, but, while making her way to Piccadilly from Whitehall, she realised that she 'could hardly string two words together'. Skipping the lunch, she boarded the 1.30 p.m. train back to her family home in Liverpool and hid away there until Thursday night. She returned to Westminster despite 'profoundly and persistently' wishing that she didn't have to.

She did not last until the weekend. Thatcher, fearful of a collapse in the rural vote, decided that she must support the Minister of Agriculture. John MacGregor obtained her permission to make a statement to the House accepting the egg producers' request for financial assistance. The government promised to release a £19 million compensation package to them, buy up eggs for destruction and then pay for the cost of culling chickens. That Thatcher was prepared to jettison her objections to state intervention is testament to the pressure she faced. MacGregor's final demand spelled the end of Currie's ministerial career. He insisted that he must state in his speech that 'it was not the case that most eggs are infected' with salmonella, an overt rebuttal to the position Currie was perceived to have taken. The Prime Minister agreed reluctantly.

That evening, the executive of the 1922 Committee of Tory backbenchers met to decide whether to call for Currie's resignation. Composed of an eighteen-member panel that few Tories would dare defy, they convened in Committee Room 13 of the House of Commons. A vociferous minority of them were baying for blood. They prevailed, chiefly because the executive was dominated by MPs with farming constituencies. The committee duly relayed to the Chief Whip that its members would begin openly calling for her resignation.

The final blow was dealt the next day. In a co-ordinated attack, the major egg producers filed writs for defamation in the High Court and served them on the Department of Health on the morning of 16 December. They claimed for damages from Currie personally for malicious falsehood, slander and negligent misstatement. The newspapers had, of course, been tipped off in advance, and she had to deploy diversionary tactics to avoid being personally served in the streets or accosted by cameras.

The legal actions had no merit. Her statements could not be proved false and she owed no duty of care to any individual farmer. But that did not matter, because the purpose of the writs was not to win in the courts but to force her departure. The NFU knew that the government would not fight protracted court proceedings against the people it was intervening to protect. John MacGregor's package of financial assistance, cleared the day before, had confirmed to them that Thatcher would stand by the Ministry of Agriculture rather than the Department of Health. The inevitable consequence was that Currie had to be thrown to the wolves. As she later quipped, in the end 'it was easier to slaughter the minister than the hens'.

As soon as he was told about the legal claims, Kenneth Clarke went to see his junior minister, planning to tell her that there was no longer any hope of retaining her position. Currie did not need to be convinced. She had already decided to resign and had been granted an audience with the Prime Minister that lunchtime. Currie and Thatcher spoke for half an hour, principally about the salmonella crisis on which the Prime Minister was now well briefed. There was no attempt to defend the egg producers, the NFU or the Ministry of Agriculture. Instead, the Prime Minister apologetically confirmed that she had been strong-armed – the resignation was a political necessity. Although Currie entered the meeting with a lump in her throat and fighting back tears, she kept herself together until the moment she was due to leave, when Thatcher uncharacteristically gave her a little hug and she finally did begin to sob. All that remained was for her to be unceremoniously ushered through the back door of Downing Street, into a waiting taxi, and out of frontline politics for good.

In her resignation letter, she refused to explain her remarks or apologise for them. The only reason she gave was that 'in all the circumstances this is the best course'. In turn, Thatcher's reply criticised neither her decision to resign nor her initial comments. Both women understood that it had been a grubby sacrifice made for political convenience.

Currie was surprised to find that her departure came as more of a relief than a disappointment. She claimed to have realised that she had not been cut out for ministerial life, noting in her diary that 'I don't want any of it … I've enjoyed not having to do sodding boxes, or adjournment debates late into the night. I've enjoyed not dining with boring old farts in the Commons, or listening to delegations [of] smarmy MPs, who then say something different in the lobby later that night.'

Although in part pleased to return to the back benches, she was bitterly disappointed with the sudden termination of her long-held ambitions, and still harbours regrets about her treatment. Frustrated at being martyred for something she did not say, Kenneth Clarke's decision to gag her still annoys her to this day. Most of all, she resented resigning over an issue on which she knew that she was correct. Study after study later proved that her statements, far from being exaggerated, were probably underplayed. The three bodies that conspired to destroy her career – the Ministry of Agriculture, the National Farmers' Union and the British Egg Industry Council – later concluded that Britain had faced a 'salmonella epidemic of considerable proportions'. Currie had been the victim of a corporatist stitch-up, but it arose out of a crisis created by her own big mouth.

EDWINA CURRIE TO MARGARET THATCHER

Dear Margaret,

When I asked to see you this morning I told you that, having considered the matter very carefully, I had concluded that I should offer my resignation from the Government. I think that in all the circumstances this is the best course.

It has been both a privilege and a pleasure to be a Minister in the Department of Health under your leadership. Your immensely successful efforts to improve the economy have made possible record funding for the National Health Service, producing standards of health care for all our people, especially women, unrivalled in the world. Greater prosperity has also made people far more interested in the promotion and preservation of good health, a movement in which I am proud to have played a part.

You first appointed me as Parliamentary Private Secretary to Sir Keith (now Lord) Joseph at the Department of Education and Science. Since then I have served as a Minister under three Secretaries of State – Norman Fowler, John Moore and Kenneth Clarke – and would like to put on record my admiration for all of them, and appreciation of their help and guidance.

Finally my thanks to you personally, for your encouragement, for your wisdom and courage, and for all you are doing for our country. I remain a firm and committed supporter of the Conservative Party and this Government and look forward to further successes in the years to come.

Yours ever,

Edwina

MARGARET THATCHER
TO EDWINA CURRIE

Dear Edwina,

I have received your letter today with great personal sadness. It has, I know, been a very difficult time and I fully understand your reasons for resigning.

We shall miss the great energy and enthusiasm you have brought to all your work both for the Government and for the Party in the country. No one could have worked harder or more loyally, not only for your own department but in support of Government policy as a whole.

At the Department of Health you have made a tremendous contribution, among other things, in making all of us realise that better health is not just the responsibility of doctors and nurses but that so much depends on the way we look after ourselves and our families.

In the country you have been tireless in promoting our cause. Locally you helped to achieve notable successes in Derbyshire where most recently we won control of Derby City Council.

I know that you will remain a staunch supporter for everything we are trying to do. We shall continue to work together for what we both believe in.

Yours,

Margaret

CHAPTER EIGHT

NIGEL LAWSON AND GEOFFREY HOWE

Margaret Thatcher's transformation of the United Kingdom was not achieved by consensus. There was never a majority of true believers in the country, the Conservative Party or even the Cabinet. It was instead a political coup executed by a small vanguard of supporters. Two of her most committed acolytes were her long-serving Chancellors, Geoffrey Howe and Nigel Lawson, who over the decade they successively served at No. 11 were architects of the economic model now vacuously dubbed 'neoliberalism'. Together, Howe and Lawson helped their leader take over the Conservative Party, dismantle vested interests in the economy and roll back the reach of the state in a manner that had never been imagined. Yet ten years after their dramatic seizure of power, these most fervent of disciples sunk a knife into their leader's chest by deploying the deadliest weapon in their arsenal: the most aggressive of resignations.

Howe was a quiet and patient man. A meticulous, long-winded lawyer, his circumspect manner contrasted with his leader's aggressive conviction. Chronically underestimated by his colleagues, his turgid speeches and owlish manner belied a dogged radicalism. Upon becoming

Chancellor in 1979, he immediately cut taxation, slashed regulation and abolished Labour's exchange controls. Responding to the recession of the early 1980s, he violated the prevailing Keynesian orthodoxy by refusing to invest his way out of the slump, instead cutting the deficit to curb inflation at the cost of thousands of jobs. He maintained his resolve in the face of pervasive condemnation while the government sank in the polls. Over 350 economists wrote a letter to *The Times* rubbishing his Budget as a document 'with no basis in theory or supporting evidence'. Despite the experts' fury, he was wholly vindicated. His transformation of Britain's economic model took the country out of recession, laid the groundwork for the great boom of the 1980s and nearly destroyed the Labour Party, which descended into internecine self-flagellation.

After Thatcher's landslide victory in the 1983 general election, Howe was shifted sideways to the Foreign Office. As Foreign Secretary for six years, he led Britain's move towards further European integration, supported at that stage by an enthusiastic Prime Minister. Thatcher replaced him as Chancellor with the thrusting golden boy, Nigel Lawson. He could not have been more different in character, embodying the bolshie swagger that characterised the boom years of the 1980s. Revered throughout Westminster for having the quickest mind in the Cabinet, he radiated authority and self-confidence. His tenure as Chancellor was defined by the 'Big Bang' of 1986, in which the City of London was deregulated, bringing enormous wealth to the capital. He prioritised further cuts to taxation, drastically reducing the top rate for investment income from the high of 98 per cent in the late 1970s that had scattered prosperous Brits across the globe. At the same time, he converted a budget deficit of £10 billion to a surplus of £4 billion. Colleagues thought that he had presided over a miracle, and Thatcher referred to him as 'my brilliant, brilliant Chancellor'. He willingly accepted the praise, which slowly inflated his already formidable ego.

By the late 1980s, however, the Lawson boom had come to an end. Inflation, thought permanently curbed, was on the rise again. Seeking to distance Thatcher from the economic troubles, Downing Street began to brief the broadsheets that Lawson had grown complacent, with his mismanagement responsible for the decline.

Thatcher's own political position had also eroded. Cabinet members had been emboldened by the glimpse of her regime's fragile underbelly presented by Michael Heseltine's dramatic resignation in 1986. She misjudged her response, and, instead of embracing potential dissenters into her circle, began to adopt a more regal tone and appearance. Gazing out across the Cabinet with increasingly wild and furious eyes, she saw enemies all around her. Having grown intolerant of the opinions of her inexperienced underlings, she governed in a more dictatorial style and began to make decisions on instinct alone.

The principal battle line with her colleagues was the perennially destructive issue of Britain's relationship with Europe. Thatcher saw in the European Community a power-hungry behemoth, controlled by socialists determined on imposing a statist hell upon an unwilling nation. By contrast, many of her closest allies saw European integration as the key to prosperity in a post-Cold War world. Howe, in particular, strongly believed that Britain could not 'opt out emotionally from the club'.

Both Howe and Lawson argued that British businesses could benefit immeasurably from further economic integration with the Continent, and dismissed Thatcher's protestations about sovereignty as oversimplified and irrelevant. They advocated joining the European Exchange Rate Mechanism (ERM), which, they argued, would remove uncertainty in the foreign exchange markets. Thatcher instinctively opposed such a move, ever-suspicious of another European power grab.

In June 1989, Lawson and Howe hatched a plan to force their leader to commit to the ERM by ambushing her on the eve of a European summit. Going together to her office just before she was due to depart, they demanded that she must agree to a date that Britain would enter. It would not be sufficient to say entry would happen 'when the time is right': she had to announce a specific date at the summit. If she did not agree to this, then they would both resign. Thatcher was incandescent at this flagrant defiance of her authority, but had little option but to concede to their demands. They would not back down, and their joint resignation would certainly prompt Heseltine to fire the starting gun on his brewing leadership challenge.

In accordance with her ministers' demands, she announced Britain's intention to enter the ERM at the summit. She made sure, however, to call their bluff by refusing to set out a date for doing so. Neither kept their promise to resign, and on her return, she taunted them in the corridor prior to Cabinet with a glare in her eye and a *sotto voce* hiss of 'No date!' Furious at their attempt to strong-arm her, she resolved that Howe, the weaker of the two, must be punished. He was duly humiliated with a shunt down the ministerial ladder to Leader of the House of Commons, losing the plumb job of Foreign Secretary and the use of Chevening House, the grace-and-favour pile that came with it. Publicly, he bore his sudden demotion with dignity. In private, however, he resolved with Lawson that he would stay in government solely to promote the European cause and protect it from Thatcher's jingoism.

Lawson resigned first, having become progressively infuriated with the conduct of one of Thatcher's special advisors, economics professor Sir Alan Walters. Walters blamed the Chancellor for creeping inflation, mocked his advocacy of the ERM and was critical of the refusal to devalue the pound. Repeating his views to chief executives across the City of London, he cast doubts on Lawson's abilities over a series of alcohol-fuelled lunches. Despite spending most of his time in Washington DC, he also fostered close relationships with the broadsheets, mischievously drip-feeding them critical quotes from 'anonymous Downing Street sources'. His activities concerned Thatcher's chief advisors, prompting Charles Powell to suggest to him that he could not be a provocative public figure and a private advisor at the same time, while Bernard Ingham, with characteristic bluntness, ordered Walters to keep quiet for his own good. He ignored their warnings.

The Prime Minister found Walters's activities useful in her battle to avoid any blame for declining living standards. After Lawson was forced to raise interest rates to an eye-watering 15 per cent on the eve of the October 1989 party conference, the *Sunday Times* was briefed that the Prime Minister had reluctantly sided with her Chancellor against the advice of Alan Walters. The paper went on to describe the split as 'another damaging disagreement on policy' between the 'two Chancellors', Lawson and Walters. The focus pivoted away from the Prime Minister.

After struggling through a stage-managed show of unity at a black-tie dinner at conference, relations between Thatcher and Lawson subsequently reached an all-time low. With her blessing, her supporters were unleashed against Lawson, as the *Daily Mail* launched a fierce attack that dubbed him 'the bankrupt Chancellor', blamed him for economic decline and speculated that his position had become untenable.

After the conference, Thatcher left Britain for a trade mission to Kuala Lumpur. In her absence, the public spat between Lawson and Walters broke into the public domain. The *Financial Times* ran extracts from an article by Walters that derided Lawson's policy on the ERM and claimed that Thatcher disagreed with his economic programme. As well as providing further negative comments in the press, Walters continued to speak at meetings of international financiers and openly criticised Lawson's commitment to maintain the value of the pound.

The Chancellor saw these challenges to his authority to be nothing short of insurrection.

Thatcher later argued that the press 'dragged [Walters's comments] out of the past and they were often torn out of context', saying that there was 'very little my staff or Alan could do' to prevent the press publishing his views. This was not quite true, for it was Walters who had sent the *Financial Times* a copy of his article and had given them permission to quote from any part of it. He could easily have issued a statement denying any rift with the Chancellor, but repeatedly refused to do so even at Lawson's direct request.

Unsurprisingly, the opposition seized upon the opportunity to attack the government. Neil Kinnock used Prime Minister's Questions on Thursday 19 October to expose the rift. Geoffrey Howe, responding to Kinnock in Thatcher's absence, robustly defended his close ally. But over the next week the Labour Party upped the pressure further and, eventually, Lawson cracked. He described Walters in the House of Commons as a 'part-time advisor' whose 'views were not those of the government', before adding: 'I think it is right that advisors do not talk or write in public. It is a good convention that should be adhered to.'

For Lawson, 'the problem was not Walters as such; nor was it even the difference between Margaret and myself ... it was her persistent public exposure of that difference, of which Walters was the most obvious outward and visible symbol'. He decided that enough was enough, telling Thatcher's parliamentary private secretary that he would no longer tolerate Walters's antics. The message that reached No. 10 was garbled, however. Thatcher was told that Lawson was irritated with Walters and concluded that he was having a tantrum.

She returned from Kuala Lumpur on Wednesday 25 October, wholly unprepared for the trouble that awaited her. Lawson saw her at 3.30 p.m. that day, but immediately noticed that 'she was absolutely exhausted'. He restricted himself to saying: 'I do not want to talk about Alan Walters now, but we must have a talk about him very soon. There is a problem there.' Her reply was curt: she simply said that she saw no problem and dismissed him.

Upon his return to No. 11 that night, Lawson resolved that he must resign unless Thatcher sacked Walters. Although he knew that she was unlikely to oblige, he 'saw no other course that I could with integrity, and sensibly, pursue'. He drafted a short resignation letter overnight. The next morning he demanded an urgent meeting and saw the Prime Minister at 9 a.m. He told her that Walters had to be dismissed for the sake of the government. As he understood this would be politically embarrassing, he would accept Walters's quiet departure in the New Year, but, if the Prime Minister refused to agree, he would resign.

Lawson's recollection was that Thatcher listened to him intently before trying to convince him to stay. She mentioned that he was on the cusp of being the longest-serving Chancellor in the twentieth century and should consider whether he intended to throw away that opportunity over such a minor issue. She remained, however, adamant that Walters would not be dismissed, as 'that would destroy my authority'. His reply was that such a suggestion was absurd, for her authority owed nothing to Alan Walters.

Thatcher remembered the meeting differently. She thought his position to be born purely of vanity and refused to take it seriously, later recalling: 'You could have knocked me down with a feather. For a Chancellor of the Exchequer, with all the importance and reputation of that position, to come to me and say: "Unless you sack one of your most loyal advisors, *I* will resign." I couldn't believe it!'

The meeting ended inconclusively and Lawson returned to Thatcher's office shortly after 2 p.m. He told her straight away that he had not changed his mind and handed her a resignation letter. Thatcher refused to accept it, again trying to prevent his departure. This time she heaped 'extravagant praise and flattery' upon him, dangling before him the chance to replace Robin Leigh-Pemberton as Governor of the Bank of England. She offered him everything she possibly could, save for the one indulgence that would have persuaded him to stay. Playing for time again, she agreed to reconvene with him after Prime Minister's Questions.

When a triumphant Kinnock asked her to choose between her 'two Chancellors', Thatcher winced at the despatch box. After limping through a difficult set of questions, she met Lawson for the final time. Both now realised that the die was cast, and there was no further attempt to persuade him to stay. After a terse discussion about their joint achievements, the Prime Minister parted ways with her most senior minister in an atmosphere of suppressed emotion. Her one request was that he should delay the announcement of the resignation until after the House of Commons stopped sitting and the markets had shut.

Although Lawson promised to do this, those working for him had other ideas. A resignation statement was immediately leaked to Chris Moncrieff at the Press Association, identifying Walters's behaviour as the sole cause of the resignation. Lawson was dictating the narrative before Downing Street had the chance to respond to it.

The House of Commons was still sitting when the Press Association relayed the news. Geoffrey Howe confirmed his friend's departure to the House, promoting scenes of jubilation across the opposition benches. According to Edwina Currie, 'the chamber, pottering through some boring legislation, suddenly erupt[ed] with a huge roar ... Labour MPs dancing in the gangways and singing 'The Red Flag'. Ours standing around dumbfounded and conversing in whispers ... [There were] some angry faces, many very upset.'

Later that day, Thatcher called Walters to tell him what had happened. He realised that his position was also untenable, and insisted, against Thatcher's advice, on resigning as well. The Prime Minister with 'two Chancellors' had managed to lose both in one day.

Looking back at Lawson's resignation, Thatcher saw only one explanation. He 'was looking for an excuse to resign because of the inflation he had created'. She felt that the reason for his rush to announce it was that he feared that she 'might telephone Alan Walters ... and that Alan would resign. That would have deprived him of the excuse he wanted.' Lawson maintains that this is 'grotesquely wrong', insisting that he hated having to resign. But by allowing his authority to be repeatedly undermined and refusing to call off the dogs, Thatcher had ensured his exit.

The resignation destabilised the Prime Minister at an already difficult time. There were now two big beasts waiting on the back benches for their chance to destroy her – Lawson and Heseltine. Geoffrey Howe used Lawson's departure as an opportunity to chip away at her fragile authority, describing him in public as a 'Chancellor of great courage'.

By that stage, Howe's personal relationship with Thatcher had broken down. She found him 'insufferably smug' with an 'insatiable appetite for compromise': a 'force for obstruction', 'the focus of resentment' and 'a source of division'. She even found being in his presence 'almost intolerable'. Her reaction was to become astoundingly rude, constantly interrupting him in Cabinet and talking over him with a patronising sneer. Her behaviour was embarrassing to witness. Lawson remembered Howe being treated like a 'cross between a doormat and a punch bag'. Betraying the continued erosion of her judgement, she failed to recognise the danger of behaving in such a contemptuous fashion.

The tipping point came a year after Lawson's resignation, at the European Community's Rome Summit in October 1990. The meeting had been convened to agree a process for European Monetary Union (EMU), moving towards the aim of a single currency. Although Howe and Thatcher were to attend together, their attitudes were poles apart. To her, a single currency was an erosion of sovereignty to be resisted at all costs. He viewed EMU as a sensible step forward, with any decision of Britain's involvement deferred until the time was right. After a long war of attrition, the Cabinet agreed that Britain would not oppose EMU in principle, but would only join a single currency if it was in Britain's interests to do so at the time. Howe stuck rigidly to that line during the meetings.

In contrast, Thatcher bludgeoned her way through the summit like a one-woman wrecking ball, declaring that Britain 'would never agree to a single currency' and dubbing the European Community 'well on the way to cloud-cuckoo land'. By the end of the summit, Britain was left isolated in sole opposition to Europe's move to closer economic unity. Thatcher saw herself as 'fighting a lone battle' against an army of French and German socialists, telling Howe that he was either 'remarkably stupid', or a traitor 'disloyal to Britain'.

Shocked at the Prime Minister's behaviour, Howe realised that his position in the Cabinet was becoming increasingly difficult to justify. Yet he resolved to make no decision about his future until he had heard Thatcher's report to the House of Commons on the Rome Summit.

He took his place on the front bench directly next to the Prime Minister. Her statement was initially encouraging, as she carefully read a speech that stuck to the moderate line previously agreed at Cabinet. But once she finished the prepared text, her tone became more aggressive. She removed her glasses and began to speak freely. In complete contradiction of her earlier platitudes, she bellowed that the European Commission was 'striving to extinguish democracy' and to 'take us through the back door to a Federal Europe', dismissing EMU on the grounds that it 'would be totally and utterly wrong' to 'abolish the pound sterling, the greatest expression of sovereignty'. Breaking the first rule of diplomacy, she began to mock the European Community president, Jacques Delors, by declaring that he wanted 'the European Parliament to be the democratic body of the Community ... the Commission to be the executive ... and the Council of Ministers to be the Senate...' To this proposition, she barked: 'No! No! No!' Her Europhobic backbenchers cheered her on, elated that she had finally broken cover and declared herself to be one of them.

Howe's disgust was obvious to all observers. Shuffling in his seat and staring resolutely at the floor, he was visibly embarrassed to be associated with the government. As soon as the statement was finished, he left the chamber to meet with his closest allies, including Lawson. They agreed that there was now no prospect of keeping the Prime Minister in check. By the end of the day he had resolved to resign, and to try to take the Prime Minister down with him.

He drafted his resignation letter the next morning before attending his final Cabinet meeting. He only had one matter to raise with Thatcher at the meeting: a minor issue of parliamentary timetabling. Several Bills to be introduced on the first day of the next parliamentary session were not ready, and he requested Cabinet approval to expedite work on them. To general astonishment, Thatcher snapped at him, barking: 'Why aren't those Bills ready? Isn't it [your] responsibility to see that this kind of thing is being done?' She might have moderated her naked contempt had she known he was preparing to plant a bomb under her premiership.

Later that day, Howe scheduled a meeting with Thatcher, telling Downing Street in advance that he would be resigning. At the meeting he handed over a deliberately anodyne resignation letter that betrayed none of his destructive intentions. Thatcher considered him incapable of causing her any significant damage, so made no effort to dissuade him, presuming that he would go quietly. Their fifteen-year partnership ended with a few stunted words and a curiously formal handshake – the first and last time they ever shook hands.

The timing of the resignation was unusually neat. Howe had quit on the day one parliamentary term ended, leaving a week-long gap before the House of Commons sat again. He resolved to keep silent for the whole week, saving the explanation of his resignation for a statement to the House to be heard as soon as it reconvened. Howe's dignified silence achieved its aim, for neither Thatcher, her advisors nor the parliamentary press were prepared for the onslaught that followed. Bernard Ingham took the opportunity he thought he had been afforded to insulate the Prime Minister, repeatedly diminishing her differences with Howe as matters of style, not policy. This obvious affront only hardened Howe's resolve. He was determined that his departure would be no damp squib.

On 13 November, MPs returned to Parliament to hear the resignation statement. It was one of the first parliamentary events to be fully televised, so Howe addressed both a packed House and a nationwide audience. He sat four rows back, directly behind Thatcher, with Nigel Lawson at his side and the threatening spectre of Michael Heseltine looming large behind them. At nineteen minutes past four, he rose to make the speech that would end eleven years of Thatcherism.

He began by curtly dismissing Ingham's briefings, declaring to widespread laughter: 'If some of my former colleagues are to be believed, I must be the first minister in history who has resigned because he was in full agreement with government policy.' After paying tribute to his long partnership with the Prime Minister, he moved to attack her counterproductive rhetoric on Europe, noting:

I believe both the Chancellor and the Governor [of the Bank of England] are cricketing enthusiasts, so I hope that there is no monopoly of cricketing metaphors. It is rather like sending your opening batsmen to the crease only for them to find, the moment the first balls are bowled, that their bats have been broken before the game by the team captain.

Speaking with a calm, polite tone that failed to mask his corrosive intentions, he observed that Thatcher seemed to look 'out upon a continent that is positively teeming with ill-intentioned people scheming, in her words, to "extinguish democracy" or to "dissolve our national identities".' Kenneth Clarke, sitting three seats down the front bench from the Prime Minister, visualised the bullets going 'thud, thud, thud' into her back.

Howe built up to a shredding conclusion, in which he directly invited his colleagues to topple the Prime Minister.

> The conflict of loyalty, of loyalty to my Right Honourable Friend the Prime Minister – and, after all, in two decades together that instinct of loyalty is still very real – and of loyalty to what I perceive to be the true interests of the nation, has become all too great. I no longer believe it possible to resolve that conflict from within this government. That is why I have resigned. In doing so, I have done what I believe to be right for my party and my country. The time has come for others to consider their own response to the tragic conflict of loyalties with which I have myself wrestled for perhaps too long.

After a final pause, he sat down. There were neither jeers from the Tory benches nor cheers from Labour. The House sat in shock, amazed to have witnessed the timid, cautious Howe attempt the daylight assassination of the Prime Minister. As Conservative MP George Walden observed: 'It was like a battered wife, finally turning on her husband.'

For Lawson, 'it was quite simply the most devastating speech I, or I suspect anyone else in the House that afternoon, had heard uttered in the House of Commons.'

Sitting through the speech was a terrible experience for the Prime Minister. She was frozen, with her back to him and face resolutely forward, remembering that 'I could turn around and see him but I didn't particularly wish to. I knew that I must keep my features very composed and calm. At the same time I had to assess what effect the speech would have.' She concluded that 'it was an experience I would not wish to go through again.' When MPs eventually got up to leave, she turned to Kenneth Baker, who was sitting beside her, and said: 'Kenneth, I never thought he'd do it.' She had expected a regretful and dignified resignation speech, not an 'act of bile and treachery', and certainly not an incitement to insurrection.

Heseltine listened to the speech with rapt attention. He 'knew instinctively' that Howe's final line 'was speaking to me, even if he did not have it in mind that he was'. Jittery with adrenaline, he paced out of the chamber, before turning to former Chief Whip Michael Jopling and asking: 'What the hell do I do now?' Jopling replied: 'Do nothing, and you'll be Leader of the Opposition in eighteen months.' Without thinking, Heseltine replied: 'I don't want to be Leader of the Opposition. I want to be Prime Minister.' He launched his long-awaited challenge the next day.

Two weeks later, Thatcher departed Downing Street in floods of tears, her eleven-year reign at an end. A muddled response to the contest, her arrogant assumption of her backbenchers' loyalty and the collapse of support from the Cabinet forced her own resignation. Thatcher was convinced that she had been ambushed by an underhand pro-European plot. In fact, she had gravely mistreated and underestimated her former friends and allies and, in doing so, spawned the most unlikely of assassins.

NIGEL LAWSON TO MARGARET THATCHER

Dear Margaret,

The successful conduct of economic policy is possible only if there is, and is seen to be, full agreement between the Prime Minister and the Chancellor of the Exchequer.

Recent events have confirmed that this essential requirement cannot be satisfied so long as Alan Walters remains your personal economic adviser.

I have therefore regretfully concluded that it is in the best interests of the Government for me to resign my office without further ado.

I am extremely grateful to you for the opportunity you have given me to serve in the Government, particularly over the past six and a half years as Chancellor; and I am proud of what we have achieved together.

I shall, of course, continue to support the Government from the back benches.

Yours ever,

Nigel

MARGARET THATCHER TO NIGEL LAWSON

Nigel,

It is with the most profound regret that I received your letter. We have spoken since and, as you know, it was my most earnest hope that you would continue your outstanding stewardship as Chancellor of the Exchequer at least for the rest of this Parliament. There is no difference in our basic economic beliefs, and Britain's economy is vastly stronger as a result of the policies which you and I and the Government have planned and pursued together.

You took a key part in preparing our party for Government before 1979. Your work at the Treasury, as Financial Secretary, on the Medium Term Financial Strategy, and at the Department of Energy in overseeing the privatisation of Britoil were landmarks in the Government's success. You have been responsible for possibly the most far-reaching reform of our tax structure this century, as well as for a period of unprecedented growth and prosperity. It is a matter of particular regret that you should decide to leave before your task is complete.

I know you will continue to support the Government vigorously from the backbenches, but all in Cabinet will miss the great ability and breadth of understanding which you have brought to our deliberations.

Please thank Therese for her splendid support.

Yours ever,

Margaret

GEOFFREY HOWE TO MARGARET THATCHER

Dear Margaret,

I am writing to explain some of the reasons for my decision to resign from the Government.

I do so with very great regret. Almost sixteen years have passed since you asked me to serve as Shadow Chancellor. Since then we have done so much together, against the odds, to rebuild the economic and political strength of our nation. Your own strong leadership has been of crucial importance in making this possible. It has been a privilege and an honour for me to have contributed to that success.

Our work has been based on common values and shared beliefs – for economic and personal freedom, for a responsible society and for greater British influence in the world. Although our principles have been sorely tested by opponents of the Government at different times over the last eleven years, I have always tried as best as I can to uphold and advance those principles in a way that united our Party and served the best interests of Britain.

It gives me all the more sadness, therefore, to acknowledge the growing difference which has emerged between us on the increasingly important issue of Britain's rôle in Europe.

As much as you, I have wanted to make the most of Britain's influence in the world, to deploy Britain's sovereignty to the best advantage of our people. Ever since our original application to join the European Community in 1962, that has clearly involved Britain's firm, practical commitment to the historic process of closer European partnership.

I was proud to have steered Britain's membership through the House of Commons in 1971, and prouder still to play my part promoting Britain's national interest in Europe, first as your chancellor of the Exchequer, and then as your Foreign Secretary, for ten hard and rewarding years.

My vision of Europe has always been practical and hard-headed. I am not a Euro-idealist or federalist. My concern is less with grand schemes than with immediate realities, as they affect our well being and prospects as a nation. Like you, I have fought too many European battles in a minority of one, to harbour any illusions on that score.

Our conduct of policy on the crucial monetary issue in Europe – first on ERM and now on EMU – has given me increasing grounds for concern. We did not find it easy, in the run-up to last year's Madrid Summit, to establish the conditions for the UK's entry into the ERM. I felt at that time that my continued membership of your Cabinet could help maintain a united approach on this issue.

Now that we are finally inside the ERM, we have a great opportunity at last to shape Europe's monetary arrangements in the years ahead. We can only do that by being and staying firmly on the inside track.

We must be at the centre of the European partnership, playing the sort of leading and constructive rôle which commands respect. We need to be able to persuade friends as well as challenge opponents, and to win arguments before positions become entrenched.

The risks of being left behind on EMU are severe. All too much of our energy during the last decade has been devoted to correcting the consequences of our late start in Europe.

It would be a tragedy, not just for our financial institutions and our industrial strength, but also for the aspirations of a younger generation, if we were to risk making the same mistake again, by trying to draw an arbitrary line under our engagement in the European process.

I am deeply anxious that the mood you have struck – most notably in Rome last weekend and in the House of Commons this Tuesday – will make it more difficult for Britain to hold and retain a position of influence in this vital debate.

Of course, there are still huge questions to be considered and resolved in this discussion. None of us wants the imposition of a single currency, but more than one form of EMU is possible. The important thing is not to rule in or out any one particular solution absolutely. We should be in the business, not of isolating ourselves unduly, but of offering positive alternatives that can enable us to be seriously engaged.

Cabinet government is all about trying to persuade one another from within. So too, within the unique partnership of nations that is making the European Community. Plain speaking certainly – but matched always by mutual respect and restraint in pursuit of a common cause.

The need to find and maintain common ground on the European issue within our own party will be crucial to our electoral success and the future of the nation. In all honesty I now find myself unable to share your view of the right approach to this question. On that basis, I do not believe that I can any longer serve with honour as a member of your Government.

I am, of course, very sad that our long years of service together should have to end in this way. The close of this Session of Parliament seems an appropriate moment for me to leave. It has been a great privilege to serve under your leadership at a time when we have been able to change Britain's future so much for the better. I shall, of course, maintain my support for your Government in following policies to that end.

Yours ever,

Geoffrey

MARGARET THATCHER
TO GEOFFREY HOWE

Dear Geoffrey,

Thank you for your letter telling me of your decision to leave the Government and the reasons for it. As I told you when you came to see me earlier this evening, I very much regret your decision, coming unexpectedly after we have worked together for so long. I shall for ever be grateful for your distinguished service and your sturdy and unflinching support in difficult times.

Your contribution to the philosophy of modern Conservatism and to the policies which we brought to Government in 1979 was great indeed. It helped to ensure that we came to office with a clear and radical programme for changing Britain and reversing the decline of the Labour years. As Chancellor of the Exchequer, you took the main burden of implementing our economic policies: and you did so with courage and fortitude in the face of many attempts to push us off course. The foundations of Britain's economic success in the 1980s were laid in those earlier years, and in particular by the budget of 1981.

As Foreign Secretary from 1983, you built on that economic success to restore Britain's standing in the world. Together we succeeded in obtaining a fair settlement for Britain's budget contribution to the European Community. Your patient negotiation with the Chinese Government secured Hong Kong's future: and you subsequently applied the same skill to the negotiations with Spain over Gibraltar. You played an important part in building up our relations with the Soviet Union and with the countries of Eastern Europe, as they emerged from the shadow of communism. In all these activities, you won the highest respect and admiration of your Foreign Minister colleagues.

Your time as Lord President enabled us to put on the statute book many of the domestic reforms which you did so much to formulate and inspire.

Your letter refers to differences between us on Europe. I do not believe these are nearly as great as you suggest. We are at one in wishing to preserve the fundamental sovereignty of Parliament. We want Britain to play a leading part in Europe and to be part of the further political, economic and monetary development of the European Community. As I made clear in my statement to the House, our aim is to find solutions which will enable the Community to go forward as Twelve. I believe the party is united behind these aims and demonstrated that very clearly in the House on Tuesday: we have always been the party of Europe, and will continue to be so.

Finally, may I say how saddened I am personally at your decision to move to the back benches. Your steadiness has been a source of great strength to the Government for more than eleven years. I am most grateful for your assurance of continued support.

May I also add a particular word of gratitude for the contribution Elspeth has made. Denis joins me in sending our best wishes to you both.

Yours ever,

Margaret

CHAPTER NINE

RON DAVIES

It was 6 a.m. when the phone went. Jack Straw, then Home Secretary, picked up to find the deputy commissioner of the Metropolitan Police on the other end of the line. Such calls would rarely bring good or expected news, but on 27 October 1998, the information imparted was particularly bizarre. Ron Davies, hitherto an unremarkable Secretary of State for Wales, and Labour's candidate to be Wales' First Minister, had been picked up by the police wandering adrift around Brixton at 4 a.m. He had had a rough night. In a corner of Clapham Common known as 'Gobbler's Gulch', he had been assaulted by a gang of strangers while apparently cruising for gay sex. The police had taken him down to the local station where he had been kept in custody for his own safety. The deputy commissioner asked Straw whether he might be able to take charge of this awkward situation. The Home Secretary, dumbfounded, called the Downing Street team to break the news. So began the first resignation from Tony Blair's Cabinet, and remained by some distance the most unusual.

Press secretary Alastair Campbell quietly ushered the Prime Minister into the dining room and shut the door. On hearing the strange tale, Blair's eyes 'got wider and wider until [he] was like someone with goitre', before he burst out laughing. He did not know Davies well, never having shared more than a fifteen-minute conversation with him. Bemused at what he had heard, Blair arranged for the police to release Davies and ferry him over to Downing Street. He arrived red-eyed and dishevelled for his first proper face-to-face meeting with the Prime Minister.

Embarrassed, Davies repeated an apparently innocent, if credulity-stretching, explanation for his late-night amble. He had been driving to London from his constituency to see his wife when he became overwhelmed by tiredness. He decided to stretch his legs at midnight on Clapham Common, where he had bumped into a Rastafarian man and the pair had got talking. They decided to go for a curry together, before meeting up with some of his mates. All went well until those friends arrived, at which point the Rastafarian pulled a knife, robbed Davies and stole his car. Davies finished his tale, asserting, hopefully, that 'it could have happened to anyone'.

As he recounted his tortuous story, Blair and Campbell looked across at each other in unblinking astonishment. Campbell remembered wondering 'what on earth he was doing there; how on earth did he get involved with a group of complete strangers; and how the hell do we explain this one?' The police claimed that Davies had offered a further detail he later declined to tell the PM – that he had had sex with the man who robbed him.

After forty-five minutes of polite questioning, tiptoeing around the more embarrassing elements of the story, Davies had failed to give a cogent account. He insisted that there was no sexual element to the evening. Blair and Campbell were unconvinced and concluded that the press and public would not be fooled either. There was nothing for it; they could not spin him out of trouble. The story was wholly implausible. Realising that this was unlikely to have been an isolated incident, Blair knew that the press would sniff out and uncover every detail of Davies's past over the next few weeks. There was no way he could remain in the Cabinet. Blair gently explained this to the beleaguered minister, who accepted his fate with equanimity.

Campbell took Davies to his office, where they drafted a resignation letter and Blair's reply to it. The pair sought to explain away the evening's events as a 'lapse in judgement', but the sexual subtext was barely disguised on the face of the letter. After all, if he had simply been robbed, there would be no need to resign. At Campbell's suggestion, Davies then called his wife to tell her the troublesome tale. Given the nature of the events that were to emerge in the public domain and their potentially profound impact on the married couple, the call was oddly perfunctory. Davies said simply that he was going to resign, that Blair had been 'very nice', and that there might be something on the news that evening.

Campbell arranged for Davies to explain his resignation in a television interview. The BBC's John Sergeant was summoned to the Welsh Office with no forewarning of what would unfold in the course of the interview. He arrived armed with a cameraman and a notebook. Before the interview commenced, Davies told Sergeant that he had 'to acknowledge that this incident is bizarre'. Relaying his story, he skirted around the question of what he was doing on Clapham Common in the first place, repeating relentlessly that he was 'guilty of an error of judgement' by 'putting himself in the position of being the victim of a crime' and was resigning to spare the government any embarrassment. He characterised the encounter as a 'moment of madness' for which he had 'subsequently paid a very, very heavy price'. In a later interview with BBC Wales correspondent Glyn Mathias, viewers noticed that Davies had the word 'sorry' written in felt tip on the back of his hand. He continued to deny that there was any sexual motive in his visit to the most notorious dogging site in the nation, insisting that he had 'a very long-term, loving, stable relationship with [his] wife, who has been marvellously supportive'.

As Campbell had predicted, the tabloids did not swallow a word of it. Their reporters fully briefed by police contacts, editors were confident enough to splash on headlines such as *The Sun*'s: 'Cabinet Minister Quits in Gay Sex Scandal' and 'Shame of Gay Sex Cabinet Minister' in the *Mirror*. The *Daily Mail*'s leader opined that he deserved his downfall for indulging in such 'reckless, corrupting and promiscuous behaviour', a position shared by two opportunistic political adversaries. Liam Fox, who fourteen years later would learn how damaging insinuations about sexual preferences could be, showed little sympathy. Then the Conservatives' constitutional affairs spokesman, he deemed Davies's actions sufficiently sordid to render the idea of him leading or continuing to lead Labour in the new Welsh Assembly 'utterly unacceptable'. Nigel Evans, the Tory spokesman on Welsh Affairs, also weighed in, declaring: 'I assume [Davies] would not wish to embarrass the people of Wales by remaining as leader of the Welsh Labour Party.' Evans came out as gay in 2010.

Although Davies had initially planned to rebuild his career piecemeal from the back benches, three weeks of moralising and speculation about what really happened on Clapham Common plunged him into a deep depression. Campbell, concerned for the downtrodden MP's wellbeing and outraged at the feeding frenzy, intervened by accusing lobby journalists of wilfully prolonging his misery, claiming that they 'probably would not care ... if he topped himself ... because it would be a good story'. His protective move backfired; its only effect was to prompt a further slew of stories about how Davies had become suicidal.

In the summer of 1999, Davies said publicly that he was having psychiatric treatment to curb his 'compulsive quest for risk' and that his wife, Christina Rees, had ended their marriage. Soon after the split, she wrote a book setting out her side of the story and gave serialisation rights to the *Mail on Sunday* and *News of the World*. In the published extracts, she alleged that throughout their marriage Davies had indulged in 'hundreds of casual sexual encounters' in secret locations across London and in south Wales. She also claimed that Davies knew the man who had attacked him on Clapham Common, as he 'was a pimp who had been supplying Ron with gay men for sex'. That evening, she said, 'Ron didn't have the money to pay for sex', so the pimp 'took his car for collateral' while awaiting final payment. Davies strongly denied his ex-wife's claims, and the book was never published. She has since apologised to him publicly and has said that the extracts were grossly misleading. In 2015, she became a Labour MP, before being made shadow Welsh Secretary in February 2017 – the job her ex-husband held twenty-one years previously.

His political career never recovered from the 'moment of madness'. Having forfeited his chance to become the leader of the new Welsh Assembly, he sat quietly on the back benches for the next three years before stepping down as an MP at the 2001 general election. Not wanting to leave public life altogether, he retreated to local politics as a member of the Welsh Assembly.

The events on Clapham Common were not Davies's last moment of madness, however. Five years later, while still an active member of the Welsh Assembly, *The Sun* followed him to a layby on Tog Hill, just north of the south-west city of Bath. They accused him of pulling up in broad daylight before heading into the bushes with a 48-year-old builder, this time only seventeen days after his new wife had given birth to their first child. Davies furiously denied the story, branding it 'completely false and without substance', and even went so far as to claim that he had been in London that day. Sticking by its story, *The*

Sun printed as proof a series of photographs of him emerging from the bushes alongside his robust denial, after which Davies altered his story. The new version had him stopping to use a public bathroom, then enjoying a lone walk in the woodlands, where he claimed he observed some badgers, before indulging in 'a brief conversation' with a stranger, with whom he walked back out to the roadside. After meeting constituency representatives and realising the full scale of the fallout, he decided this time to step down from Labour politics for good, bringing the curtain down on a career defined by two sex scandals. He has since stood for election to the European Parliament for Forward Wales, as an independent for the Welsh Assembly, and in local and Assembly elections for Plaid Cymru.

Blair was fatalistic about the implosion of Davies's Cabinet career. 'Ron's was a resignation that was inevitable,' he remarked. He was, of course, correct. Davies's testimony gave rise to several presentational problems, not least that it was riddled with holes. Yet, despite the implausibility of his tale, he never confirmed the allegations of which he was subsequently accused by the press. He maintained until the end, with intransigence, that he not been seeking sex in public.

Even if he had conceded that sex was the motivation behind his presence on the Common that night, however, he most likely would not have survived. The social mores of the time dictated that cruising for gay sex was an activity wholly incompatible with being an MP, and particularly an MP with a wife. Matthew Parris, another former Tory MP who is now a *Times* columnist, had great sympathy for Davies. Parris, who is openly gay, later admitted that he himself had cruised on Clapham Common on multiple occasions while a parliamentarian, and very nearly found himself in the same position. He was under no illusions about the fact that being caught would have ended his career.

Would the same fate befall an MP engulfed in this kind of sex scandal today, almost twenty years later? There is no doubt that the public has become more liberal on such matters. Keith Vaz, the married chair of the Home Affairs Select Committee, was in 2016 caught in a tabloid sting that revealed him to be employing the services of male prostitutes under the alias of a washing machine salesman called Jim. In addition, drugs, including cocaine, were mentioned during the episode that was secretly recorded. In the event, he did resign. Critics claimed that if he remained in post as Home Affairs Committee chair, it would present a conflict of interest, since the Select Committee presides over inquiries into prostitution and drugs. But he won support from a series of fellow MPs who paid tribute to his work on the committee, and he remained on Labour's prestigious governing body. He was treated with far more sympathy than Davies.

Perhaps, then, attitudes are changing slowly, but the unbending rule is that a swift confession of the truth is required to have any chance of redemption. Any attempt to lie or, as Davies did, fail to provide a clear explanation, was and remains fatal.

RON DAVIES TO TONY BLAIR

Prime Minister,

Thank you for seeing me this morning and for being so understanding in what are very difficult circumstances for me and my family.

As I explained, because of a serious lapse of judgment that I have made, I wish to offer my resignation as Secretary of State for Wales.

After driving back from Wales last night, I parked my car near to my home in south London. I went for a walk on Clapham Common.

Whilst walking, I was approached by a man I had never met before who engaged me in conversation. After talking for some minutes he asked me to accompany him and two of his friends to his flat for a meal.

We drove, in my car, to collect his friends, one male, one female. Shortly afterwards, the man produced a knife and together with his male companion robbed me and stole my car, leaving me standing at the roadside.

I reported this matter immediately to the police. In allowing myself to be placed in this situation, with people I had never met and about whom I knew nothing, I did something very foolish.

That is a serious lapse of judgment on my part. The whole incident will inevitably cause embarrassment not only to me and the government, but, most important, to my family.

I wish, therefore, in the interests of the government which I have been so proud to serve, to tender my resignation forthwith.

I believe it is the only sensible course. I was proud that you placed your trust in me to deliver on our pledge to establish a Welsh Assembly, and that this is so close to becoming a reality.

I will continue to give you and my successor as welsh secretary all the support and goodwill that I can as the government continues to implement the programme of modernisation on which we were elected.

RD

TONY BLAIR TO RON DAVIES

Dear Ron,

Thank you for coming to see me this morning in what are clearly such difficult times for you and for Chris [his wife].

Given the situation you described, I accept your decision to resign. I do so with a real sense of sadness.

You have done an excellent job for the people of Wales, particularly in the way you have prepared for the establishment of the Welsh Assembly.

I am grateful for your continuing offer of support, and I know that your successor will be grateful for your help and advice.

Many people will share the profound sympathy I feel, that your Cabinet career has come to an end in this way.

Yours Ever,

Tony

CHAPTER TEN

PETER MANDELSON

B ritish politics is not known for producing phoenixes; rare beasts that can sustain repeated incinerations, yet rise from the ashes each time. Whether the result of our boisterous and censorious press or a peculiar Anglo-Saxon sensibility to withhold forgiveness, redemption is hard to come by in Westminster.

Among his many talents – including for strategy, communications and withering put-downs to camera – Peter Mandelson is most distinguished for his instinct for survival. The peer and Labour Party grandee began his political life as a teenage Communist, treading an extraordinary ideological path to hold sway over every corner of the Labour Party for more than a quarter of a century. The grandson of Herbert Morrison, deputy Prime Minister in Clement Attlee's government, Mandelson's career took off in 1985, when, aged only thirty-two, he became Neil Kinnock's director of communications. He went on to serve as the party's campaign director before surreptitiously advising Tony Blair in his leadership bid under the cover of the pseudonym 'Bobby', deployed to hide his betrayal of former patron and Blair's rival, Gordon Brown.

One of the few people to make the leap across the chasm between Blair and Brown that lay at the centre of the New Labour story, his unparalleled instinct for survival allowed him to come back from two dramatic resignations.

Despite describing himself as 'tribally, habitually, congenitally Labour', the former MP for Hartlepool always divided opinion in his party, which has often appeared to love and loathe him in equal measure. His unquestionable abilities failed to mask the Machiavellian tendencies that prompted the nickname 'the Prince of Darkness'.

Mandelson was promoted to Blair's frontbench team in 1997 as a Minister without Portfolio. The elevation reflected the esteem in which the Prime Minister held him, but the lack of portfolio spoke to his relative youth and inexperience. He grandly defined his position as 'Minister for Looking Ahead', tasked with surveying all government strategy. His colleagues sneered at this assessment, branding him 'Minister Sinister', responsible only for the dark arts of political spin and the Millennium Dome. It was against this background of ridicule that, to his delight, he was promoted the following year to become Secretary of State for Trade and Industry, his first fully fledged Cabinet role.

He took to the brief with gusto and made a promising start. Blair later recalled that he was 'loved by his department', a rare accolade in Whitehall. The feeling was mutual, and even his enemies acknowledged his mastery of the portfolio. His tenure was, however, halted in its tracks after just five months. Neither incompetence nor misfortune accounted for this early stumble; he was a victim of a political assassination, and Gordon Brown's allies were behind it.

A biography of Mandelson was due to be published in early 1999, written by Paul Routledge. The author was a close friend of Brown's divisive press secretary, Charlie Whelan, so Mandelson steeled himself for a poisonous polemic. What he failed to prepare for was the revelation that he had taken a private loan of £373,000 from millionaire businessman and fellow future Labour minister Geoffrey Robinson.

Robinson had offered Mandelson the loan over dinner in 1996. They had discussed his desire to move out of his small flat into 'a home he could feel comfortable in'. Robinson, having already amassed vast wealth from success in the automotive industry, was happy to help, and suggested that he should buy something that would also be a good investment. Taking both the loan and the advice, he selected a townhouse in Notting Hill in west London, one of the capital's wealthiest enclaves.

Mandelson confessed in his memoirs that he did not think through the implications of the move that led to his first downfall. He insisted that he was entranced by the opportunity to have 'a place [he] could be proud of, with a desk on which to spread out [his] papers, shelves filled with books, and the kind of dining and living space [he] could share with friends'. His lifestyle had already caught the attention of Labour colleagues, with Blair's director of communications Alastair Campbell describing it witheringly as 'swanky'.

He proceeded to refurbish the house according to his elevated tastes. A £50,000 facelift saw the property made fit for the twenty-first century. He stripped away its original features to create a minimalist paradise. An item of clutter was permitted to disturb the clean lines: an invitation to Prince Charles's birthday party, to which he was the only Cabinet minister in attendance.

In hindsight, he acknowledged that a desire for 'high living had definitely crept into [his] soul'. He had seen 'what others enjoyed, and wanted to share it'. His material aspiration had long irritated many in the Labour Party, but by far the bigger problem was his failure to disclose the substantial loan to his Permanent Secretary at his department. Shortly after his appointment to the Cabinet, he was asked if he had any financial commitments that could create a conflict of interest. It did not occur to him to mention the loan, so the department and No. 10 remained ignorant. Unfortunately for him, among the small band of people who did know of the loan's existence were Whelan and Ed Balls – two of Gordon Brown's closest allies. As it happened, the pair had been having supper at Robinson's flat when the loan documentation was faxed through. Having caught sight of it then, they had been waiting for their moment to pounce.

Unbeknown to Mandelson, the Department of Trade and Industry (DTI) were investigating Geoffrey Robinson's dealings with the late media mogul Robert Maxwell. His department's role in investigating Robinson, while he harboured financial obligations towards the man, created a possible conflict of interest for Mandelson. Although Mandelson did not have a formal role in the investigation into his creditor, the press would leap on the appearance of impropriety.

Brown has never revealed whether he knew about the leak or if his allies simply did what they believed he would want them to do. But there can be little doubt that it was Whelan who planted the story with Routledge. Before the scandal erupted, he had boasted to a journalist that there was a 'thermonuclear device under Peter' that was 'primed to go off in January 1999'. He later claimed that he 'can't remember' whether he was the source.

A farcical mistake gave Mandelson notice of the attack; proofs of the book were mistakenly faxed to his aide, Ben Wegg-Prosser. On 16 December 1998, the loyal advisor, whose solicitor father had arranged the loan, warned his boss that it was to become public. The next morning, Mandelson told the DTI's Permanent Secretary, Sir Michael

Scholar. The unenviable task of telling Alastair Campbell about the oversight was delegated to Wegg-Prosser.

The reaction of Campbell, known for his aggressive attitude, was predictably explosive. The government had only just recovered from another row over money. A £1 million donation to the party from Formula One boss Bernie Ecclestone, made around the time that Blair exempted F1 from bans on tobacco advertising, had already sent shock waves through the nation.

In a bid to contain the fallout, Blair had declared live on television that he was a 'pretty straight kind of guy' – a strategy that can only be deployed once. A further sleaze scandal would be even more damaging. Campbell was sufficiently concerned by Wegg-Prosser's news to interrupt the Prime Minister while he was overseeing his first military action. A furious Blair joined Campbell in a three-way conference call with Mandelson's aide. Still in military mode, Blair characterised the leak as a unilateral strike by the Brownites, raging that it 'was not a story' but a 'political assassination, done to destroy Peter' and 'to damage me and damage me badly, without any regard to the impact on the government'.

Mandelson was ordered to No. 10, where Campbell told him that he was a 'stupid cunt'. The apologetic minister conceded that he had been unwise, but maintained that he had not done anything wrong. Campbell retorted that it was simply unacceptable for a Labour frontbencher to borrow vast sums of money from a multi-millionaire to live a millionaire's lifestyle. Wanting the final word, Mandelson downplayed Campbell's histrionics and told him he had 'always been a bit of a Calvinist'.

Unfortunately for Mandelson, Blair shared Campbell's view. He ordered Mandelson to pay back the loan as soon as he could, and certainly before Routledge's book came out. The repentant MP appealed to his mother and brother for help over the weekend. They agreed to pay off the loan, but could not do so immediately.

Worried that the story would emerge before Mandelson could dispose of his financial obligations to Robinson, Blair convened a meeting to discuss his fate. Despatching Mandelson to a site visit to the Millennium Dome, the Prime Minister assembled a court of his top advisors. In attendance were Campbell, Lord Irvine and Lord Falconer. Wegg-Prosser was there to represent Mandelson. Irvine and Falconer promptly dismissed the allegations of impropriety, but saw that the politics of the affair were 'very difficult'. He had too many enemies in the party and the press for matters to be smoothed over.

Conflicted, Blair took soundings from trusted Cabinet members. One after another, John Prescott, David Blunkett, John Hutton and Mo Mowlam each refused to offer their support to the master strategist. Paying the price for failing to cultivate friends in the party, Mandelson found himself wholly reliant on Blair's mercy. The Prime Minister decided to pause and see how the situation would unfold. He did not have to wait long.

The Guardian contacted Mandelson and Robinson later that afternoon. They had the story and would be running with it the next morning. The source of this second leak remains a mystery, but it is possible that Brown's team contacted *The Guardian* on discovering that Blair was trying to limit the damage.

With characteristic pugilistic fervour, Mandelson prepared to battle for his political life. After nervously rehearsing with Campbell, who played an array of hostile interviewers, he set out on a tour of television and radio stations. He intended to get his side of the story out before *The Guardian* was released. From previous hostile media coverage he had learned that 'you have to stand up to these fuckers' because 'if they scent blood, they will come for the kill'. The following day the clamour from broadcasters increased, but he maintained that his resignation was out of the question. Behind the façade, however, he felt a detached sense of inevitability akin to 'watching someone else's march to the ministerial gallows', he later said. By the end of the day, he was in floods of tears and acknowledged to friends that his career dangled by a thread.

The scandal was welcome fodder to political reporters. Abandoning their prepared Christmas 'silly season' stories and top-100 lists, they resurrected with enthusiasm the New Labour sleaze narrative. Diligent correspondents combed the register of member's interests and ministerial code for further improprieties, discovering that Mandelson had apparently neglected to tell his building society about Robinson's loan when he applied for a mortgage. Although it was later revealed that there had been no such requirement, further damage had been dealt. By the end of the day, Campbell offered only muted support, half-heartedly briefing the lobby that Blair did not necessarily see the matter as a 'hanging offence'.

As the scandal approached a third day, Blair decided that Mandelson had to resign. The media circus would continue until he departed, with follow-up stories fuelled by the barbed comments of Labour colleagues. Blair called him that evening to deliver the bad news. Again, he fought back, imploring his friend not to strip him of his job, influence and status for an innocent error of judgement. Torn, Blair agreed to 'sleep on it'.

The morning newspapers were brutal. *The Sun* asked: 'How the hell can Mandy stay?' The *Daily Mail* called him a 'master of deception' and *The Times* compared him to Becky Sharp, *Vanity Fair*'s doomed social climber. Mandelson was flicking through the papers in his office when he noticed Campbell and Jonathan Powell approaching.

Campbell ordered everyone to leave the room. He then rang the Prime Minister, who explained via speakerphone that the sooner Mandelson resigned, the sooner he could return to government. He pleaded for his job one last time, but Blair had made up his mind. By the end of the conversation, all three men were fighting back tears. The charged emotional nature of the episode did not, however, prevent Campbell taking a mental note of a Christmas card from Prince Charles in pride of place on Mandelson's desk.

Campbell swiftly drafted the resignation letter and Blair's reply to it. Mandelson signed the draft, adding only the words: 'I can scarcely believe I am writing this letter.' The rest of the afternoon was spent closing down the story. Campbell refused all interview requests, responding to a text from Sky News journalist Adam Boulton with a simple 'fuck off'.

Blair appeared anxious to avoid damaging his relationship with Mandelson, perhaps because he valued his long-standing ally's friendship or perhaps because he feared that his old confidante knew where many skeletons were buried. Either way, the Prime Minister invited him to spend the evening of his resignation with his family. Mandelson duly headed to Chequers, the sixteenth-century grace-and-favour manor house used by the incumbent Prime Minister, with his partner Reinaldo.

Over dinner, Blair's wife, Cherie, reassured him that he would 'always be part of the family' while Tony helped him plot the road back. He was to sell the house, move to a less extravagant area and repay the loan, he was told. The final piece of advice was to do the unthinkable and 'make some friends in the Labour Party'.

Despite the veneer of warmth and kindness, the Blairs were careful to distance themselves from the disgraced former minister. Journalists reported that the Prime Minister had 'moved on', and that Mandelson had 'disappeared from [his] orbit'.

Mandelson was one of three figures that had to resign over the affair. Robinson was forced out for giving the loan and Whelan was later sacked from Brown's team, reportedly under pressure from Blair, who blamed him for the leak.

The newspapers gleefully celebrated Mandelson's ruin. The front page of *The Sun* depicted his head emerging from the rear end of a Christmas turkey under the headline 'STUFFED'. A rare exception was an article in *The Times* by its former editor William Rees-Mogg, which argued that Blair was not 'loyal enough' to his allies and suggested that 'no Prime Minister can afford to butcher his friends in order to appease his enemies'. Blair gradually came to agree with Rees-Mogg, viewing his initial response as the naïve approach of a novice Prime Minister. He had lost both a trial of strength against the media and a political battle with the Brownites. He should instead have stood by his friend, he later thought, as he did in 2003 when Tessa Jowell was blamelessly entangled in a financial scandal of her own.

Mourning the loss of his seat around the Cabinet table, Mandelson felt 'adrift and alone'. The illustrious new friends he had made fell away and the royal invitations dried up. He sold the house, repaid the loan and, his short-lived stint in Notting Hill over, he embarked on a campaign to reinvent himself in the Labour Party. While sincere in intention, his progress was stymied by a series of lofty statements. At a trade union conference, he spoke of his resignation as if it were a bereavement and made the ill-judged joke: 'I have only just got out of the habit of jumping into the back of cars and wondering why they don't just move off.'

In the event, he did not have to wait long to reclaim the privilege of a ministerial car, as Blair brought him back into the Cabinet after just ten months of penance. He became the Secretary of State for North-ern Ireland, tasked with overseeing the implementation of the Good Friday Agreement that had brought peace to the troubled region. The Prime Minister hoped that this appointment would allow him to stay out of the public eye until the time was right for promotion to an even more prominent role.

Happily for Mandelson, his job came with Hillsborough Castle – a state-owned palace to rival Chequers. Content in his new role presid-ing over the estate, he released a Christmas card that pictured him at the foot of his new pile surrounded by his adoring dogs.

Disaster struck a second time, however. It was while he was engaged in a round of peace talks on 20 January 2001 that he was interrupted by his special advisor, who brought news that the next day's *Observer* featured a damaging story about him. The paper alleged that he had played an improper role in obtaining British citizenship for Indian businessman Srichand Hinduja. In his previous ministerial role, he had lobbied colleagues, the paper claimed, to ensure the application's progress in return for a promise to underwrite the cost of the govern-ment's flagship cultural initiative, the Millennium Dome.

Once again, Mandelson had prior warning that this story would emerge. The Home Secretary Jack Straw had recently responded to a parliamentary question on the topic posed by Liberal Democrat trouble-maker Norman Baker. Straw asked Mandelson for a response. He said that he had referred Hinduja to the Home Office without making any further representations. But Mike O'Brien, then Immigration minister, remembered being called up about the matter. Mandelson had no memory of making this call and insisted that he was sure the matter had been dealt with by his staff.

He told *The Observer* exactly what he had told Straw, but the head-line writers took a different view, declaring on the front page that

'Mandelson Helped Dome Backer's Bid for Passport'. Campbell called as soon as he saw the paper, wanting to know what his official response should be to journalists looking to follow up the story. Mandelson could not understand why so much had been made of the article, dismissing it as simply untrue. He was far more concerned about a piece in the *Sunday Times* about his dysfunctional relationship with Brown.

At the next morning's lobby briefing, Campbell went far beyond what he had been told. He told the assembled journalists that Mandelson 'refused' to have any involvement in the matter of Hinduja's bid for British citizenship and flatly denied allegations that Mandelson had called anybody at the Home Office. As Campbell later accepted, weeks of sleepless nights meant that he had not been 'sufficiently on top of the detail'.

He soon discovered that O'Brien remembered being telephoned by Mandelson, however, and realised that his briefing had created a dispute between ministers. He urgently arranged a series of conference calls to establish the facts. Mandelson stressed that he had no recollection of calling O'Brien about Hinduja, but said that in any case he had certainly not ever lobbied for the Indian businessman to be granted a passport. O'Brien was certain that he had been called by Mandelson to discuss Hinduja but could not remember exactly what had been said.

The story was not followed up in the next day's papers. Campbell was relieved and hoped that it had died down. He fanned the embers, however, by issuing a correction and apology to lobby journalists about the incident. He told them that Mandelson had checked his files and had discovered that he did phone Mike O'Brien. The briefing backed Mandelson into a corner, asserting as fact that he accepted he had made the phone call when, in reality, he simply could not remember. Suspicious journalists soon realised that they had been briefed questionable information for a second time about the issue and intuited that it could be worth further investigation. Campbell's errant rebuttal had led a minor story to flare up into a fully fledged scandal.

Mandelson confronted him, demanding to know why the press had been told that he had made the call to O'Brien. The response came that the Home Office had a tape of the call, so it could no longer be denied. Rattled, but taking the spin doctor at his word, Mandelson resolved to tackle the growing story head-on in a series of television interviews. He was pressed repeatedly on the tangential issue of the phone call, rather than the substantive point about any involvement in lobbying for the passport. The appearances were doing him more harm than good. It would later be revealed that there was no tape of the call after all, and Campbell strongly denies implying that there was.

By the end of the day, Blair was forced to face the reality of the deteriorating situation. Loyal Blairite John Reid was sent out to tackle breakfast radio the next morning and manfully struggled to defend the position. The story was, however, clearly building momentum. Campbell sought again to cover his tracks, complaining that he was 'fed up of having to pick up the pieces and draw so much of the blame'. Preoccupied by the impending general election set to take place a few months later, and due to face Prime Minister's Questions at noon, Blair knew he could not afford to be drawn further into the scandal engulfing his ally. If William Hague asked him about the evidence of the disputed phone call, he would be forced to repudiate his own spokesman's briefings. The laser-focused Leader of the Opposition would not miss his chance to pounce on Blair and pin him down on the matter during the gladiatorial Commons showdown, so it had to be dealt with before the Prime Minister entered the chamber.

Blair reconvened his close advisors. This time, the tribunal comprised Lord Irvine, Campbell, Jonathan Powell and the Cabinet Secretary Richard Wilson. They met in the more intimate surroundings of Blair's flat to discuss the matter. Irvine felt that Mandelson had lied to Campbell when he had initially said the story was untrue, and later sought to cover his tracks. Troublesome questions abounded over the existence and purpose of the phone call, and it was felt that Mandelson's mealy-mouthed rebuttals amounted to allegations of dishonesty against O'Brien and Straw. Against the backdrop of an imminent election battle, Mandelson would have to be sacrificed as collateral damage. Yet again, nobody came to his defence, even behind closed doors. If further impetus to sack him was needed, Straw called Blair and threatened to quit if Mandelson was not ousted.

Hardened perhaps by time and greater experience in office, Blair was more decisive this time than he had been when the loan scandal had ended Mandelson's first stint in the Cabinet. The Prime Minister was decided: there were sufficient grounds to sack his friend. He explained to his advisors: 'If I wasn't convinced he'd fibbed over the weekend then I'd have kept him, whatever the shit I'd have taken, but I was convinced he had fibbed.' Once again, Mandelson's slippery reputation had hastened his downfall.

The guillotine fell with brutal force. At 10.45 a.m., Mandelson was being chauffeured to his office to prepare for the weekly parliamentary questions on Northern Ireland that preceded Prime Minister's Questions. On the journey, he took a call ordering him straight to Downing Street, and on arrival he was hastily ushered up to Blair's flat. Blair told Mandelson outright that the situation was hopeless. Campbell spoke up from the corner of the room, demanding a line to give the 11 a.m. lobby briefing. Blair told him to say that Mandelson's fate was, for the moment, still being considered. Campbell left the journalists in little doubt that Mandelson's career was dangling by a thread.

Blair agreed to hold an inquiry into the approval of Hinduja's passport, a move that could potentially clear Mandelson's name, but insisted that he must nonetheless resign before the investigation started.

Mandelson protested. 'How can you despatch me because of a purported phone call and a bunch of inaccurate briefings and a stream of Chinese whispers? You've decided on an inquiry. Why not wait at least until the facts are established?' he asked. Blair's resolve was iron-cast; the punishment would precede the trial. With growing desperation, the courtier resorted to begging. He implored the Prime Minister not to 'end my entire ministerial career for this, without even knowing the full picture'.

'I'm sorry,' Blair said, shutting down the conversation. 'There's no other way.' As he later reflected, Blair had been 'a ruthless bastard'. For the second time, he had sacked his close friend with remarkable ease.

Campbell returned to the flat around 11.30 a.m. Blair looked wretched while Mandelson was 'pale, almost poleaxed, but trying to keep a very brave face'. The Prime Minister sat at his desk and personally wrote a public statement for Mandelson to read out.

The second resignation had been a less emotional affair than the first. Campbell later claimed that the only tears he shed that week were when his beloved Burnley football team missed a penalty. Departing Downing Street by the front door, Mandelson barked out the statement and drifted home seething with rage.

This time 'there was to be no consoling phone call from Cherie. No invitation to Chequers. No assurance I would "always be part of the family",' he later said. 'There was not the slightest sign from Tony that he saw a way back for me.' Blair left no doubt that he had disowned his friend, publicly pronouncing that 'there is no question of [Mandelson] coming back into government. I hope he will be able to get on with rebuilding his life.'

The lobby journalists were given an even starker briefing, told that 'the future for Peter Mandelson' would be to 'shut up, and then go off and have a lovely life with Reinaldo [his partner]'. Campbell's comments wounded the most. He told the press that his former friend had become 'curiously detached', implying, as Mandelson noted, that he 'was ripe not only for retirement, but residential care'.

Smug jubilation dictated the tone of the next morning's headlines, characterised by Mandelson as a 'shrieking media lynch mob'. 'Goodbye and good riddance!' howled *The Sun*, dubbing him a 'lying, manipulative, oily, two-faced, nasty piece of work who should never have been allowed back into government'. In the *Daily Express*, Peter Oborne went yet further, treading a dangerous line in claiming that 'this morning the Labour Party had the bemused and joyful air of a Transylvanian village where news has just come through that Lord Dracula will disturb them no longer.'

Mandelson was incensed and launched a savage counter-attack. He wrote a cutting riposte to Blair in the *Sunday Times*, in which he claimed that a 'relatively trivial error was turned into a huge misjudgement that led to my resignation'. Then he hired the heavyweight barrister Jonathan Caplan QC to lead his fightback at the forthcoming inquiry. Having clamoured for his resignation, the fickle press now turned on Blair for axing him without due thought.

The inquiry was conducted by the former Home Office legal advisor Sir Anthony 'Wally' Hammond. A venomous briefing war ran alongside it, in which the existence of the disputed phone call took centre stage. Mandelson's private secretary backed up his version of events and a different member of his private office said that it was she who had telephoned O'Brien.

Hammond's report was released just five weeks after Mandelson's resignation. Dead-batting the thorny issue, he concluded that everyone involved had acted with total propriety. On the question of the troublesome phone call, he 'could not reach a view with any certainty', and found that all parties had been 'frank and honest'. Nonetheless, he concluded that the call probably had occurred, for the junior O'Brien was more likely to remember it than Mandelson.

This exoneration of Mandelson was, for Blair, a pathetic finale to a miserable episode. The sacking, designing as an act of self-protection, had been ineffective and – it turned out – unnecessary. It confirmed his reputation for being led by press opinion and demonstrated an oversensitivity to allegations of corruption that gave the impression he had something to hide.

Jonathan Powell cited the Hinduja affair as an example of the Blair government's 'speed addiction', arguing that 'we were so mesmerised by the press that we believed we had to respond to journalists' questions by the time of the 11 a.m. press lobby or we would bleed to death'. He concluded that, 'as a result, we rushed into dismissing Peter precipitately'. Mandelson took a similar view, blaming the press operation at Downing Street, which turned a misunderstanding into a dispute between ministers where one had to be lying. Campbell had, he argued, deliberately misrepresented the position to protect himself.

Following his second resignation, he knew that there could be no return to frontline politics under a Blair government. Many colleagues assumed he would stand down as an MP in the upcoming general election. Confounding his critics yet again, however, he reinvented himself as a diligent constituency representative and embarked upon a battle to retain his Hartlepool seat. Telling friends that his 'credibility and future in public life were on the line', he declared the election a 'personal referendum' on him. He faced formidable leftist opposition from Arthur Scargill, former National Union of Mineworkers leader and one-time nemesis of Margaret Thatcher, who ran as a candidate for his own party, Socialist Labour.

On 6 June 2001, the evening of the election, a gaggle of Fleet Street sketch writers travelled up to his County Durham seat, in quivering anticipation of Mandelson's final humiliation. In the end, he emerged victorious, retaining nearly 60 per cent of the vote – a surprise to all, including the returned MP.

It is a political orthodoxy that successful candidates in safe seats rarely give notable victory speeches. They usually offer a platitude to their opponent and thanks to the hapless local policemen nodding off in the corner. Mandelson's broke this mould, however, and he landed the defining sound bite of the 2001 election. Commanding the attention of the news bulletins, he delivered a defiant speech in which he declared that 'my career was in tatters … well, they underestimated the people of Hartlepool, and they underestimated me'. Voice cracking with emotion, he slammed the palm of his hand on the desk before him and bellowed: 'I am a fighter and not a quitter!'

The phrase has lived with him since. Three years later, however, bored of constituency surgeries and with no prospect of a Cabinet return, he decided that he might be a quitter after all. He resigned as an MP and waved goodbye not just to Parliament but to Britain itself, taking a job as Trade Commissioner for the European Union. Few were sad to see him go.

Even fewer anticipated what was later to follow: the great survivor was to enjoy a third act in UK politics. It came about some four years after his departure from the House of Commons. By that time, October 2008, Gordon Brown had finally realised his dream of trading up from No. 11 to No. 10. But he faced many problems, including his profound unpopularity. In the face of chilling and well-orchestrated attempts to oust him, he turned in desperation to his former foe, now four years into his job in Brussels. The pair had been enemies for fourteen years, circling around each other in rival factions, but now they needed each other. Brown required Mandelson's mastery of strategy;

Mandelson craved a return to Westminster, which was contingent on Brown's favour. The offer was extended and Mandelson seized it with both hands, coming back to Britain as the Baron Mandelson of Hartlepool and Foy, the Prime Minister's unofficial gatekeeper and the Business Secretary. He strode with a swagger up Downing Street on his first public visit to see his new master, sporting a vermillion jumper and a wide grin, before quipping to the waiting press pack that it would be 'third time lucky'.

Soon he was collecting new titles at will, becoming First Secretary of State, Lord President of the Council and President of the Board of Trade. Within the year his reach had extended into every vein of government. Over thirty junior ministers reported to him and he sat on thirty-five of the forty-three Cabinet committees. Each threat to Brown's leadership was met by a television appearance from the omnipotent Baron, whose eyes betrayed the danger hidden by his emollient tone. He had emerged from the shadows to become one of the most powerful men in British politics.

Mandelson used his party conference speech in 2009 to rouse his colleagues, wearied by thirteen years in government and teetering on the brink. He told them to follow his own example of survival, saying: 'I came into politics to help remake Labour as a party of government … it made us not just modernisers but fighters – and certainly not quitters. Electorally, we are in a fight for our lives … but if I can come back, we can come back!'

PETER MANDELSON TO TONY BLAIR

Dear Tony,

I can scarcely believe I am writing this letter to you. As well as being one of my closest friends you are a close colleague whose leadership and political qualities I value beyond all others.

As you have, I have reflected overnight on the situation concerning the loan I took from Geoffrey Robinson and I have decided to resign from the Government.

As I said publicly yesterday, I do not believe that I have done anything wrong or improper. But I should not, with all candour, have entered into the arrangement. I should, having done so, told you and other colleagues whose advice I value. And I should have told my permanent secretary on learning of the inquiry into Geoffrey Robinson, although I had entirely stood aside from this.

I am sorry about this situation. But we came to power promising to uphold the highest possible standards in public life. We have not just to do so, but we must be seen to do so.

Therefore with huge regret I wish to resign. I am very proud of the role I played in helping you and previous leaders of the Labour Party to make our party electable and to win our historic victory last May.

I am proud of the trust you placed in me both at the Cabinet Office and at the DTI. In just 18 months you have helped to transform this country and the government has made huge progress delivering on our manifesto and its programme of modernisation.

I will always be a loyal Labour man and I am not prepared to see the party and the government suffer the kind of attack this issue has provoked.

You can be assured, of course, of my continuing friendship and total loyalty.

Yours ever,

Peter

TONY BLAIR TO PETER MANDELSON

Dear Peter,

You will know better than anyone the feelings with which I write to you. You and I have been personal friends and the closest of political colleagues.

It is no exaggeration to say that without your support and advice we would never have built New Labour.

It was typical of you, when we spoke last night, that your thought was for the reputation of the Labour party and the government and that you believed that since there had been a misjudgment on your part, then, as you said to me 'we can't be like the last lot' and that what we are trying to achieve for the country is more important than any individual.

But I also want you to know that you have my profound thanks for all you have done and my belief that, in the future, you will achieve much, much more with us.

Yours ever,

Tony

GEOFFREY ROBINSON TO TONY BLAIR

Dear Tony,

I am writing to ask you to accept my resignation from the Government.

I have enjoyed the work of the last 18 months and have welcomed in particular the opportunity to work on the economic strategy that is designed to secure the renewal of our country. But, as you know, I have been subjected to a persistent – and I believe unfair – set of allegations about my business affairs.

I have already accepted responsibility and have apologised to the House of Commons for oversights in the past concerning registration of interests.

But although my affairs have been under full political and media scrutiny for more than a year, it is clear that I have not misused my position either as an MP or minister.

I have done nothing wrong in any of these areas and I will vigorously defend myself against any allegations.

In the case of the loan to Peter Mandelson, I merely considered myself in 1996 as someone in a position to help a long-standing friend, with no request for anything in return.

There comes a time when, after more than 12 months of a highly charged political campaign, the point has been reached when I feel that it is no longer right that you or your Government should be affected by or have to contend with these attacks.

I will always remain totally loyal to the Government and will continue to support it in whatever way I can in the future.

Yours,

Geoffrey

TONY BLAIR TO GEOFFREY ROBINSON

Dear Geoffrey,

Thank you for your letter. I accept your decision with regret. I know that you have felt these past months hounded by the campaign against you.

I want you to know, however, that what I remember and thank you for, is your immense contribution to the Government.

The windfall tax which helped fund the New Deal for the unemployed; the reform of the corporate tax system; the saving of the coal industry; the agreement with the private sector to give the biggest boost to science we have ever given to Britain; the reinvigoration of the Private Finance Initiative; for all your business sense and helpful advice, we thank you.

You have performed the task of public servant with great dedication in circumstances of extraordinary difficulty. I look forward to working with you in the future.

Yours ever,

Tony

MANDELSON'S RESIGNATION SPEECH

I am today resigning from the government and wish to set out the background to my decision.

I do not accept in any way that I have acted improperly in respect of any application for naturalisation as a British subject.

I do, however, accept that when my office spoke to a Sunday newspaper at the weekend, I should have been clear that it was me personally, not my official, who spoke to the Home Office minister.

As a result of that reply, incorrect information was given to the House by the Culture Secretary, and to the press by the Prime Minister's spokesman. I accept responsibility for that.

I have said to the Prime Minister that I wish to leave the government and he has accepted that.

I would only ask people to understand that my sole desire and motivation throughout was to emphasise that I had not thought to influence the decision on naturalisation in any way at all, merely to pass on a request for information, and the Prime Minister is entirely satisfied with this.

I confess in reaching my decision that there is another factor. As a reading of today's newspapers shows all too graphically, there must be more to politics than the constant media pressure and exposure that has dogged me over the last five or so years.

I want to remove myself from the countless stories of controversy, feuds and divisions, and all the rest, all the other stories that have surrounded me. I want, in other words, to lead a more normal life, both in politics and, in the future, outside. That is my decision and I hope that everyone will respect that.

Finally, it has been the greatest privilege of my political life to play a part in the peace process in Northern Ireland, something far bigger and more important than any one individual or his career.

We are so close now to a final settlement, to a complete implementation of this government's, as well as others', achievement – the Good Friday Agreement. I only hope and pray that everything that we have worked for, and the parties in Northern Ireland have worked for, now comes to pass and I wish the people in Northern Ireland every success and peace in the future and I thank them for their kindness to me.

The Prime Minister has asked me to do Northern Ireland Questions in the House this afternoon. I shall then listen to Prime Minister's Questions and then formally I will resign from the government.

CHAPTER ELEVEN

STEPHEN BYERS

Stephen Byers was an outrider for Tony Blair's modernising project. Atoning for his youthful Trotskyite sympathies to become New Labour's chief missionary, he was charged with road-testing ideas that made the rest of his party squirm. His suggestion in 1996 that Labour should break their foundational link with the trade unions cemented his status as a pariah among party members. His comrades never forgot this original sin and delighted in the cascading series of disasters that befell him. The luckless Byers's eventual resignation from the Cabinet stands apart from the others in this book as it was not caused by personal error, indiscretion or political infighting. Instead he was crushed by his own civil servants, who disliked him even more than his party did.

Byers entered the Cabinet in July 1998 as part of Blair's first re-shuffle. In the aftermath of the 2001 election victory, he boasted to journalists that he was to be granted the role of Education Secretary, tasked with driving through reforms that would be the centrepiece of the second term agenda. But reshuffles rarely go to plan, and he was shunted down the Cabinet hierarchy to the Department for Transport, Local Government and the Regions (DTLR). This proved an unhappy inheritance, for the railway system lay in crisis and local government creaked from years of Tory neglect.

Byers soon began to make substantive progress and was highly rated by many of the people and institutions he dealt with. Admirers ranged from railway executives and shareholders to the General Secretary of the Trade Union Congress, who surprisingly reported that his 'stock was high in the trade union movement'.

The problems that led to his departure were caused not by his mastery of the brief, but by the attitude of his own staff. An atmosphere of discord was caused by the creeping influence of special advisors, Byers's political appointees whose dictatorial style was despised by his civil servant staff.

His most controversial special advisor was Jo Moore. She was a battle-scarred veteran of the Labour right who taunted stray Trotskyites by wearing a brooch in the shape of an ice pick. Her stint as Labour's head of press in the early 1990s had made her an experienced media handler, and she was highly rated by the party leadership. Bringing to DTLR a professionalism gleaned from prior experience in the private sector, she was determined to craft a communications operation fit for the twenty-first century. However, she was not a born diplomat, and the more experienced civil servants, despising the entitled attitude of the new arrival, stood implacably opposed to her modern methods. Their antipathy was partly a cover for their underlying dislike of Byers, who was openly nicknamed 'fuckwit'.

The minister's long ordeal began on 11 September 2001, when Moore made a naïve and foolish blunder. As the terrorist attack unfolded in New York, the DTLR staff gathered around a small television in the open-plan office. While others saw only the horror and devastation, Moore spied an opportunity for political gain. Shortly before the first World Trade Center tower collapsed she sent a now-infamous email to the departmental press secretaries, instructing them that 'it is now a very good day to get out anything we want to bury. Councillors' expenses?'

Burying bad news is a long-established political tactic. Fleet Street hacks, politicians and special advisors are all capable of cynicism and ruthlessness equal to or worse than Moore's. As columnist and former Tory MP Matthew Parris has admitted, the email was 'just the kind of idiotic thing I might have written'. Her real sin was presentational; she should have realised that the email could be used against her by its recipients.

Armed with the offending missive, a small cabal of embittered civil servants launched a savage attack upon Moore and Byers. Having left sufficient time for the wall-to-wall coverage of 9/11 to die down, they leaked the email to the newspapers on 9 October. They didn't, after all, want their story to be buried.

The story led the news bulletins, and the press leapt at the chance to resuscitate their perennial complaint about New Labour's culture of spin and deceit. Moore immediately apologised and offered her resignation to Byers. Refusing to let her fall on her sword, he instead rang the Prime Minister's director of communications and strategy, Alastair Campbell, for advice. Although incensed at what he saw as a 'classic civil service move', Campbell sensed that Moore would eventually be 'hanged, drawn and quartered' and recommended that she should depart quickly. Blair, however, was more benevolent, recognising that 'if they get her, every special advisor will be vulnerable to leaking by the civil service … it will be open season'. He ruled that the value of her 'great service over the years' was not to be erased by this momentary lapse of reason, and that she should be retained if she was sufficiently penitent. Her only punishment was an official reprimand from the DTLR's Permanent Secretary and a public admonishment from Blair.

Moore's enemies were not finished. Astonished at their foe's capacity for survival, the group began to intensify the leaks. Moore and Byers were soon accused of orchestrating an underhand plot to discredit London's transport commissioner and only days later further leaks revealed that Railtrack, the company that operated all train infrastructure, had used a financial bailout orchestrated by Byers to pay £137 million to its shareholders. It was a leak that could have come only from his own department.

The minister's run of extremely bad luck then began with Railtrack slipping into financial ruin. Byers was forced to chair crisis talks to keep the trains running while still fending off outrage at Moore's email. Placing Railtrack into special measures, he effectively renationalised rail infrastructure and, in doing so, made himself a fresh set of enemies: the company's disenfranchised shareholders. They threatened to sue him and his department if they lost out from the nationalisation and began a vicious briefing war in which Byers was assigned an unfair proportion of blame. It was the worst possible moment for a minister to be at loggerheads with his own press office.

After headlines about Moore and the bullying culture of the DTLR spilled into a second week, Campbell ordered her to make a public apology. She duly delivered a statement live on television, standing awkwardly in the open-plan office in front of the staff that were still trying to oust her. Meekly gazing into the camera, she acknowledged people's disgust at what she had written and added that she found it difficult to believe that she had written it. The event had been a success until the last moment, when she smirked in response to a reporter's heckle. The newspapers all carried the picture of the smirk and refused to accept the contrition. As Campbell noted in his diary, the 'general feeling was that Jo's public statement has backfired and made things worse'.

Railtrack's woes persisted through November and December. As soon as Byers had convinced shareholder groups not to take the DTLR to the courts, the outraged company executives threatened to sue him personally for abuse of office. His travails were soon seized upon by the Conservative transport spokesperson, the up-and-coming Theresa May. She accused Byers of recklessly risking the 'life savings' of the 10,000 railway workers and pensioners who had invested in Railtrack. Beginning the inevitable calls for his head, she argued that 'it is perfectly clear Mr Byers cannot run his own office, let alone a transport network. He should go.'

Furious at the behaviour of the DTLR's press team, Campbell scheduled an urgent meeting with Sir Richard Wilson, the head of the civil service. The pair agreed that the DTLR would recruit a new departmental head of communications to bridge the gulf between Byers's political staff and his press team. They chose Martin Sixsmith, a former BBC journalist who had previously worked for other New Labour ministers. Arriving for his first day at work, Sixsmith was immediately squared by the most senior official at the DTLR, Permanent Secretary Sir Richard Mottram, who briefed him on the department's caustic culture and asked him to keep a close eye on Moore's activities.

There was to be no respite for Byers over the Christmas and New Year period. After being hammered in the press for holidaying in India, on his first day back at work he faced anonymous briefings claiming that the Prime Minister planned to sack him at an 'appropriate time'. He also came under sustained fire from Gordon Brown's Treasury team, who forced him to drop a £3 billion commitment to improve rail safety after it was deemed too expensive.

Fighting back against his civil servants, Byers proposed a top-down reorganisation of departmental staff, taking control of recruitment from the officials. Senior staff saw this as nothing short of a declaration of war, and the proposals were immediately leaked. Anonymous sources denounced his plans as 'an abuse of power' and, for good measure, accused Moore of 'having a detrimental impact on the operation of the department'.

On 14 February, the civil servants struck a decisive blow by leaking a second email to the *Daily Mirror*. This was allegedly sent by Sixsmith to Moore, and apparently reprimanded her for trying to repeat the tactic of suppressing bad news. The email supposedly read: 'There is no way that I will allow this department to make any substantive announcements next Friday. Princess Margaret is being buried on that day. I will absolutely not allow anything else to be.' Junior members of the Downing Street team quickly rang Sixsmith, who gave them the impression that the story was correct.

Moore was gobsmacked. She furiously denied the allegations, and immediately involved Campbell and Jonathan Powell, Blair's chief of staff. Campbell remembers that he immediately 'smelled a large rat', having recognised that 'Jo was being done in'. He was right. Moore had not proposed to make any announcement that clashed with Princess Margaret's funeral, and Sixsmith had not in fact sent the quoted email to her. The story had been wholly concocted and was designed to cause maximum damage.

The next morning Campbell confronted Sixsmith, who accepted that the story was nonsense and retracted the confirmation that he had given the day before. Taking personal control of the situation, Campbell made the brutal decision that, despite her innocence, Moore had to be sacked. The department's civil servants had proved that they would stop at nothing to destroy her, including scuppering their own policies. Their actions could not be allowed to damage the government further. Byers reluctantly accepted the decision but demanded Sixsmith's resignation in return.

At Campbell's request, Sir Richard Mottram took Sixsmith for lunch that day and told him that he should resign. To Mottram's dismay, Sixsmith initially refused to go quietly and laid out his terms. He would only agree to leave if he was paid a large severance payment, received a public exoneration and Jo Moore also quit. After a long lunch, Mottram returned to the department believing that they had reached an agreement.

He spoke to Byers at 5 p.m. and assured him that Sixsmith would resign. Wanting to set the matter to rest before a third day of bad press, the minister made a live television statement admitting that there had been a 'breakdown of trust within the department', announcing Moore's and Sixsmith's departures, and adding they had both 'done the right thing by offering their resignations'.

Sixsmith heard Byers's statement on the radio while driving back to the DTLR from a dental appointment. He was surprised to hear that he had offered his resignation, and promptly rang Mottram to say that he had not resigned and, now Moore had been sacked, had no intention of doing so. Mottram had been played for a fool by the wily Sixsmith, who in an instant doubled the severance payment he could demand. As soon as the call ended, a mortified Mottram was overheard shouting at a bewildered colleague: 'We're all fucked. I'm fucked. You're fucked. The whole department's fucked. It's been the biggest cock-up ever and we're all completely fucked.'

In Campbell's opinion, this was something of an understatement. That night he noted in his diary that he was 'fed up with the whole thing'. Now well beyond the end of his tether with the crisis, he had begun to think: 'fuck the lot of them'.

Sensing that he had lost Campbell's support, Byers decided to take matters into his own hands. He arranged a long interview on television with ITV's Jonathan Dimbleby, in which he repeated that he was pleased that Sixsmith had been dismissed but claimed to have had no role in his departure, insisting: 'I do not get involved in personnel matters.' This turn of phrase jarred with Campbell, who noted at the time that it 'wasn't a hundred per cent true, and would cause us real problems'.

The war of words escalated as Sixsmith released a statement responding to the interview. He claimed to have evidence that Byers had demanded his sacking and was now brazenly lying. As Sixsmith had cannily anticipated, this intervention made the story about Byers's integrity, finally permitting *The Sun* to lead with a headline it had been holding in reserve for months: 'Liar Byers ... Pants on Fire!'

Campbell despatched Byers's Cabinet colleagues to defend him against the allegations of dishonesty. They faced what is known in golfing circles as a 'difficult lie'. Education Secretary Estelle Morris won the prize for the most tortured attempt to justify the minister's comments. She claimed that 'it wasn't an attempt to deceive – he couldn't possibly have thought that people wouldn't have known that they would have had that conversation. What I call a lie is when you say something to somebody and hope to get away with it because they won't find you out...'

Buoyed by his victory, Sixsmith decided to press the nuclear button. Ten days after his resignation had been prematurely announced, he gave the *Sunday Times* an interview, revealing that he had never resigned, that Byers was still trying to force him out and that No. 10 had now unleashed a smear campaign against him. He concluded that, as far as he was concerned, he was entitled to turn up for work the next day and would be doing so. Theresa May leapt at the chance to pin Byers down, deeming the affair 'the most clear example in human history of a man being caught out lying' and demanding an explanation to the House of Commons. Byers had been cornered.

Blair had decided that, whatever happened, Byers's ministerial days were numbered. He had failed to control his department, had no answer to the charge of misleading the public, and the tabloids had moved into kill mode. The only decision was whether to sack him now or quietly despatch him in a later reshuffle. Adopting his usual approach when ministers were in crisis, Blair asked Lord Falconer and Lord Irvine to examine the evidence and report back to him. The two lawyers felt that Byers's dishonest statement meant that Blair could not risk a session of Prime Minister's Questions. Campbell and Jonathan Powell stood up for Byers, arguing that he had done nothing egregiously wrong and should be protected if feasible. The Prime Minister acquiesced to his political advisors, and decided that his minister would be thrown into the gladiator's ring to see if he could survive.

Byers entered the House of Commons that afternoon to give a statement on the Sixsmith affair. Apologising for his performance on the Dimbleby programme, he said: 'If my answers … gave the impression that I did not put forward a view [on Sixsmith's employment] or make clear my views to others inside and outside the Department, that is obviously something I regret and I welcome the opportunity in this House to clarify matters.' Most assembled MPs felt that Byers had given a convincing account of himself, but the outcome would ultimately depend on the performance of his opposite number. Sharp, forensic questioning would expose his lie and leave him without any escape.

Under pressure, Theresa May floundered. The Leader of the House Robin Cook, who sat next to Byers during the session, deemed May's response to be 'one of those rare defining occasions where the mood of the House perceptibly shifts'. The parliamentary sketch writers agreed, comparing her failure to Neil Kinnock's inability to land a blow on Margaret Thatcher at the height of the Westland Affair.

Realising that his days as a minister were numbered, the luckless Byers thought that matters could get no worse. He was wrong. At lunchtime on 10 May 2002, a train derailed at Potters Bar station, killing seven people and injuring a further seventy-six. Poor maintenance of the line had contributed to the accident, so Byers's department bore its share of responsibility. Although he dealt competently with the crisis and its fallout, the disaster provided further ammunition to a press corps determined to get their man.

He managed to limp on for two more weeks, before the Transport Select Committee delivered the decisive blow. They published a report that deemed his recently released ten-year rail plan 'incomprehensible'. After reading yet more poisonous briefings from factional rivals in Gordon Brown's team in the newspapers the next day, he decided that he could not put up with any more.

He slipped over to Downing Street to see Blair, interrupting discussions about an imminent reshuffle in which he would undoubtedly have been sacked. He told the Prime Minister that he was going to 'pack it in', as he had become 'a liability to the government and a liability to [you]'. Blair remembers that he seemed mentally 'shot through' and agreed that a dignified resignation would be in everyone's best interests.

He returned to 10 Downing Street the next morning, and was granted the unprecedented honour of delivering his resignation statement in the grand pillared room of Downing Street. This was, according to Blair, so 'he would still be seen as a friend'.

Campbell and Byers took pleasure in confusing journalists and commentators by announcing that there would be an important Downing Street press conference, but not revealing the subject matter. The pair cackled as they watched Sky News's Adam Boulton receiving the news of the press conference live on air. With no inkling what the announcement might be and not wanting to seem out of the loop, he was forced to improvise. He speculated that there might be a declaration of war, that Blair might be resigning on health grounds or that he was finally handing over to Brown. The rapidly assembled press corps were shocked to see Byers emerge into the pillared room instead of his boss. He solemnly read out a long statement, concluding: 'I am leaving because I am sure it is the right thing to do for the government and the Labour Party' and stressing that 'the people that know me best know that I am not a liar.'

Jonathan Powell, watching from the back of the room, was particularly impressed by the statement, considering it by far Byers's best performance in office. The pestilent Sixsmith, however, remained intent on making mischief. He appeared at the gates of Downing Street asking to be let in and claimed to the awaiting cameras that he was still Byers's press secretary. This proved, as Campbell noted in his diary, 'just how big a twat [he] was'.

The fallout from Byers's downfall was extensive. Blair, incandescent with the behaviour of the DTLR's civil servants, asserted his authority by abolishing the entire department. The other four ministers were sacked or moved and the offending press team split up or fired.

Sixsmith was incensed to find that his payoff deal prevented him from writing a tell-all memoir, but managed to channel many of his experiences of DTLR life into the magisterial BBC satire *The Thick of It*, for which he acted as a 'reality consultant'. As for Jo Moore, she retrained as a teacher and by 2003 was working at a north London primary school.

There was little that Byers could have done to avoid his downfall. Faced with a hostile department whose problems pre-dated his arrival, he suffered from a series of crises that embedded his hapless status. The tabloids thrived on the surfeit of willing sources for negative stories, and once the narrative moved against him, there was little he could have done to recover. Blair recognised this problem, but was reluctant to bow down to the inevitable and allow his loyal ally to be removed by supposedly apolitical civil servants.

An earlier resignation might have left open the possibility of a return to frontline politics. Instead, Byers remained a backbench MP until 2010, when he retired at the general election in disgrace after offering his lobbying services to undercover journalists for £5,000 a day. His final demise coincided with the death of the New Labour project for which he had once been a passionate herald.

JO MOORE TO STEPHEN BYERS

Dear Steve,

I have today decided to offer my resignation as your Special Adviser.

Last September I made a terrible error of judgement by sending an e-mail for which I have been rightly condemned.

I had hoped that my apology would be accepted for the genuine, heart-felt apology it was and that I would be able to continue my work for you and our Labour government.

But it has become increasingly obvious to me that this is not possible.

Clearly there are some individuals in the department who are not prepared to work with me and are even prepared to invent stories about me as they have done this week.

I have devoted most of my adult life to working for the Labour Party because I am committed to achieving a fair and just society.

I do not want to be an obstacle to achieving this goal.

Yet stories like the one this week, despite the fact they are totally untrue, are allowing opponents to denigrate the real achievements of the government and are a distraction from our priority of investing in and reforming key public services like railways and the London Underground.

It therefore seems to me that the right thing to do is resign.

Yours sincerely,

Jo

BYERS'S RESIGNATION STATEMENT

Thank you very much for coming this afternoon. I am going to make a personal statement but I will be taking no questions.

Yesterday morning I asked to see the Prime Minister and told him I have decided to leave the government.

I am leaving because I am sure it is the right thing to do for the government and the Labour Party.

It has been my privilege to serve in the government since 1997 and it was not an easy decision to resign. I know the political obituaries will be full of talk of spin doctors, emails and who said what to whom.

In today's political world that is inevitable. But I hope people will also remember the part I played in raising school standards when I was at the Department of Education, the role I played as Chief Secretary to the Treasury in helping to lay the strong economic foundations we now enjoy.

I hope they will remember the national minimum wage and the Fairness at Work legislation that I introduced as Trade Secretary and I hope they will see that the long-term decisions I have taken to restructure the rail industry will stand the test of time.

I stand by the major policy decisions I have taken and the programmes that I have implemented but I also recognise that in other areas there are things I should have done differently.

Government ministers take many decisions, and I know that I have made mistakes, but I have tried at all times to behave honourably and with the interests of the British people at heart.

And the people that know me best know that I am not a liar.

What is clear to me, however, is that I have become a distraction from what the government is achieving, but the debate we need to have about key policy issues is being distorted by my involvement.

But by remaining in office I damage the government. Having worked for the Labour Party all my adult life, it is not easy to admit to that reality but I cannot and will not allow this to continue.

The support I have received from parliamentary colleagues, Labour Party members and members of the public has been very important to me.

Now I return to the back benches to represent the interests of my constituents in North Tyneside and to put the case for further modernisation and reform in order to deliver economic stability, rising living standards and social justice, the things I have always believed in and always will.

This has been a government I wanted to serve in but now I know I must leave. I do so with many regrets and with much sadness but I know with absolute certainty that it's the right thing to do for the Labour Party and, above all, for the government.

Thank you very much.

CHAPTER TWELVE

ROBIN COOK AND
CLARE SHORT

The decision to go to war in Iraq is now seen as the defining mistake of the New Labour years. Although the war was to split the party top to bottom for years to come, it only prompted two top-level resignations. The departure of Labour Cabinet ministers Robin Cook and Clare Short are often cited as master classes in, respectively, how to resign and how not to resign. On the basis of his departure, the former has been hailed as a principled, decisive and respectable politician, while the latter has been dismissed as a hesitant, silly and vain figure.

The story behind their resignations begins in 2001, with the events that eventually prompted the invasion of Iraq. In the wake of 9/11, George W. Bush made a threat that set the course of the twenty-first century. As the Western world reeled in horror and shock at the attacks, the US President declared: 'Every nation, and every region, now has a decision to make. Either you are with us, or you are with the terrorists.'

Within days the Bush administration despatched a confidential message to Iraq's intelligence agency, demanding that Saddam Hussein's regime fall in line on the right side on the newly declared War on Terror. Saddam replied personally and, with characteristic recklessness, mocked the American reaction to the attack on the Twin Towers, the most lethal terror attack on domestic soil in US history. He contended that UN sanctions had killed far more in his lands than the 9/11 attacks had killed Americans in New York. The Butcher of Baghdad was picking a fight.

That ill-conceived riposte prompted the latest crisis in the fraught and tortuous relationship between the two nations. George Bush Sr had failed to destroy Hussein in the First Gulf War of 1990–91. The Iraqi dictator's tight control over his inner circle rendered an assassination attempt or coup impossible; toppling him now meant war. While Iraq's government had no direct links to Al-Qaeda or the Taliban (the organisations linked to the atrocity), the nation was brought to its knees by a vengeful US in the aftermath.

While Saddam jeered at Bush and baulked at the US's demand for Iraq's co-operation, Tony Blair shredded his schedule and dashed across the Atlantic to pledge his support to the US President in person. As the Americans' intentions became clear, Blair's own views on terror hardened. He instinctively agreed that Saddam must be toppled, and that Britain should stand shoulder to shoulder with its ally come what may. That position was revealed in his now infamous note to Bush on 28 July 2002, in which he pressed the President to seek the backing of the United Nations (UN) before launching military action against Iraq, but added: 'I will be with you, whatever.' Despite his apparent indication that the UK would agree to partner the US in armed action against Iraq without UN support, Blair was motivated by his Foreign Secretary Jack Straw to try and convince Bush to seek a mandate from the global organisation.

The diplomatic line of attack pursued by the US against Saddam rested on the Iraqi dictator's failure to comply with restrictions on his weapons programme. After much wrangling at the UN headquarters in New York, the organisation passed Resolution 1441, which ordered the Iraqi government to provide evidence that it no longer possessed the weapons of mass destruction it had previously deployed against the Iranians and Kurds. Saddam failed to comply within the deadline.

Bush and his hawkish advisors believed this breach of the resolution comprised sufficient justification to depose Hussein with the backing of the UN. Convinced that the Iraqi strongman had immediate access to biological and chemical weapons, the US argued that further delay would prolong the forthcoming war by granting Saddam time to prepare for it. Thousands of American troops began to build up on Iraq's borders, poised to strike.

In Britain, opposition to military action was growing. In February 2003, over a million protestors took to London's streets in the biggest demonstration the country had ever seen. The burgeoning anti-war movement emboldened Labour's left flank, which had lain dormant as New Labour's centrists soared. The left-wing faction, united by a common hatred of what they saw as the right-wing economics and antiquated imperialism of the American administration, presented an acute political problem for Blair. He believed there was a bona fide case for just war against Iraq, but knew that to survive within his party he must convince the Labour movement and the public at large of the necessity of taking action.

His first concern was that he would not be able to persuade his party and country that military action was justified without a further UN resolution authorising it. Public debate fast became dominated by technical arguments about international law. Some believed Resolution 1441 already permitted invasion by stating that Iraq would face 'serious consequences' if it did not 'comply with its disarmament obligations', which it had not. But Blair was aware that this argument was disputed by many of Britain's leading jurists and international allies.

He returned to the US to press Bush to push for a second UN resolution. Again he was successful, despite vehement opposition from Bush's neoconservative advisors, many of whom considered the UN a waste of time. Bush had 'decided that if Tony Blair needed [this] for political purposes, it was important for us to go the extra mile for our ally'. But consensus to pass that second resolution proved elusive. President Vladimir Putin of Russia could not tolerate an American bridgehead in his sphere of influence. France's President Jacques Chirac moved to protect his country's economic interest in the region by privately agreeing with Putin to veto any further UN resolution. Chirac then astonished the world's commentators by announcing in a television interview on 17 February 2003 that 'regardless of circumstances, France will vote no. France sees nothing at the moment to justify war to disarm Iraq.'

In the absence of a second resolution, many Labour MPs, members and party supporters considered a war unnecessary and illegal. Among Labour's staunchly anti-war cohort were two prominent members of the Cabinet: International Development Secretary Clare Short and Commons leader Robin Cook.

After twenty years as a frontbencher, Cook's command of the House was unrivalled. His fearsome intellect was envied across the chamber, and he swatted aside opponents with scorn and ease. While his powers of analysis and his skill wielding sardonic put-downs commanded respect, he did not attract a close following among his colleagues. Bordering on curt and dismissive, Cook was not widely liked.

Nonetheless, Cook's talent and experience could not be ignored, and despite being no natural ideological bedfellow of Blair's, he was made Foreign Secretary after the 1997 election. He sought to reposition Britain on the global stage, embracing internationalism, abandoning the traditional West–East prism, and adopting what he dubbed an 'ethical foreign policy'. But, despite this successful exercise in rebranding, after the 2001 election Cook was shunted down the Cabinet pecking order to become the Leader of the House of Commons. The demotion was not viewed as a verdict on his performance; instead it belied Blair's fears over an upcoming battle over the euro. Cook, a zealous pro-European, had to be moved from his influential berth at the Foreign Office.

In 2002, amid the first steps in the march towards war in Iraq, Cook indicated to friends that the issue could prompt his resignation from government. For him, 9/11 had not provided any justifiable reason to deviate from the strategy of sanctions and inspections that had successfully contained Saddam up to that point. Although no pacifist, he could see no proper case for war on the facts before him, a view most now consider vindicated.

Short's approach to politics was the opposite of Cook's. A pugnacious idealist and flagbearer for the Labour left, she styled herself as the government's 'conscience'. Her strict Catholic upbringing had, she has said, inculcated in her a moral absolutism and desire to do the right thing. Belief in her own ethical intuition was twinned with a reckless streak. She developed a taste for resignations over foreign policy early in her career, first quitting as a shadow minister in 1988 over Northern Ireland and then again in 1991 over the First Gulf War.

Her idealism sat uneasily with the Prime Minister's pragmatism. Furthermore, she always disliked Blair on a personal level, later saying he 'set her teeth on edge'. The feeling was mutual, but he tolerated her presence in government for two reasons: she protected him from accusations of excluding the Labour left and was a good fit to lead the newly established Department for International Development.

Short had always had a knack for provoking colleagues. She

sanctimoniously denounced the sinister forces behind New Labour as 'people who live in the dark' in 1996, and then publicly condemned Blair's 'vile and dishonest' spin doctors when in government. As soon as the prospect of war arose, her instinctive anti-Americanism, distaste for Bush and loyalty to the Labour left presented her with a quandary: should she resign on principle, giving up the department she loved and the chance to make a difference, or remain and fight to change Blair's mind?

Cook and Short were allied in sentiment over the Iraq War, but were prevented from forming a united front of opposition in Cabinet by their intense antipathy for each other. The pair were barely on speaking terms. Cook's chief advisor joked that if he were offered a choice he would have opted for a 5,500-mile trip to Ulan Bator in the hold of a cargo plane over a ten-minute amble across St James's Park in Westminster to see Short in her department.

For months, both ministers kept private their respective misgivings about the looming conflict, paying heed to the doctrine of collective ministerial responsibility. Short was the first to break cover. Her intervention was made in a manner that critics derided as characteristically slapdash. Without any warning to No. 10, on 9 March 2003 she let rip her thoughts on BBC Radio 4's *Westminster Hour*, a late-night Sunday radio programme. After some gentle prodding from presenter Andrew Rawnsley, she accused the Prime Minister live on air of encouraging actions that were 'deeply reckless. Reckless for the world, reckless for the undermining of the UN in this disorderly world, reckless with our government, reckless with his own future, position and place in history.' It would be 'indefensible' to act without a UN mandate, she said, and made clear that if war were declared 'there was no question' that she would resign.

Her comments took Blair, his team and the rest of her colleagues by surprise. One Cabinet minister, who had been listening to the programme while in bed, was so enraged by her pious pronouncements that he seized his radio and hurled it at the wall. Blair called Short later that evening to deliver a simple message: she would find out the next morning if she still had a job.

Against the advice of his advisors, Blair decided that Short should receive a reprieve. He would not permit her becoming a martyr for the cause, calculating that he would gain a far greater victory if he could persuade her to change her mind. Alastair Campbell, his director of communications, scoffed at the improbability of a minister effecting such a volte-face. With consummate confidence, Blair winked and told him: 'I have my ways.'

Blair asked her outright what the price for her loyalty would be. She responded that she required a 'clear legal opinion about the circumstances under which military action without a further resolution could meet the UK government's commitment to respect international law' and an early agreement on a UN Security Council mandate for the civil administration of post-war Iraq. Before any military action took place, she insisted on the publication of a Middle East peace process road map, supported by the US. In all, this represented a major climbdown by Short. Her key demand for a legal opinion had already been accepted by the government. It was the first of a series of agonising retreats, which justified Blair's tactical decision to keep her inside the Cabinet for as long as possible.

Blair used Prime Minister's Questions to distance himself from Short's comments, saying: 'I cannot answer for the comments of every member of every administration around the world – including occasionally my own.' In the same session, he confirmed that any colleague who did not support the government's position on Iraq would have to resign under the doctrine of collective responsibility.

A few days later Cook visited Blair's chief of staff, Jonathan Powell. He told Powell that, regardless of the verdict of the coming legal opinion, he would not support war without a second UN resolution, for which Britain was pushing. He repeated his message the next day, telling John Prescott that he would resign in the absence of the second resolution. He made no public comments and did not brief the press.

Blair saw Cook before the Cabinet met on 13 March, four days after Short's broadcast intervention. Cook began by joking with Blair about the level of pressure the Prime Minister's allies were heaping on him to avoid resigning. He quipped he was 'getting so many regular checks from colleagues that I'm beginning to think I'm on suicide watch. I wouldn't be entirely surprised if someone came along and took away my belt and shoelaces to keep me out of harm's way.' He then told Blair that his mind was made up, however, and that he would not be persuaded otherwise. Blair did not seek to, only asking him not to make any public statements while the second resolution remained a possibility.

The forthcoming war was the main agenda item at the Cabinet meeting that followed. Blair was greeted at the Cabinet room door by his deputy John Prescott, who stood to attention and saluted his commander-in-chief, sending the room into fits of giggles before the meeting began. Blair updated his ministers that work continued in the UN to obtain a second resolution, despite French President Chirac's threat to veto it. Straw noted that although the government was aiming to secure the resolution, it was not 'an absolute necessity'. Cook then intervened, astutely laying the groundwork for the fight that was to come by observing: 'The intensity of our efforts to get agreement in the Security Council means we cannot now pretend that it does not really matter if we fail to get agreement.'

Short also contributed to the meeting, setting out her views on the strategy that should be taken with the UN. Her colleagues ganged up on her, greeting her lengthy speech with dismissive eye-rolling. In particular, Charles Clarke and John Reid reportedly made no attempt to disguise their contempt, theatrically whispering: 'How very helpful' and 'I'm sure Tony couldn't have thought of that on his own' while she spoke. Eventually, David Blunkett interrupted her and issued a call for all colleagues to stand by the Prime Minister. In a pointed reference to Short's *Westminster Hour* appearance, Blunkett denounced Chirac as 'reckless'. Blair did not call out his lieutenants for their rudeness, either in Cabinet or afterwards, and Short left the meeting shaken at how she had been treated. She noted in her diary that she was 'getting near [the] end of the line' and 'feeling sad and tearful'.

When hope for a second resolution at the UN finally dissipated over the next few days, Blair set about ensuring that Parliament would vote for war without one. He redoubled his efforts to keep Short in the Cabinet, calling her each day for advice on how to present his position on the international stage and asking her to prepare to take a key role in Iraq's reconstruction. He even enlisted her political mentor Gordon Brown to persuade her to stay. She could not decide whether to resign or not, and spent each evening alone pacing around her living room.

Blair met Bush in the Azores, a set of islands in the Atlantic Ocean, on 16 March to set in place the final preparations for war. They agreed that there would be no military action before 18 March, when the vote in Britain's Parliament was scheduled. The Azores summit was, according to Blair, a 'slightly surreal event'. He said:

> On the face of it we were still pushing for a political solution. There were some last-minute hopes of an Arab initiative to get Saddam out; or of a Saddam capitulation. George was content to adopt the line that we were going to hold out every last hope for peace.

But Blair conceded that he himself, alongside the other world leaders and all informed commentators, 'knew the die was cast'.

Blair returned to England on 17 March, when it was at last formally announced that the quest for a second resolution had been abandoned. A special session of Cabinet was convened for 4 p.m. that day, where, as promised, the legal basis for war could be scrutinised. Straw was scheduled to make a statement to the Commons immediately afterwards.

Blair met Short in his office before the meeting. He reminded her of his promise of a leading role for her in Iraq's post-war reconstruction, even arranging a phone call from Kofi Annan, the Secretary General of the UN, to discuss the plans. Short agreed to come to the Cabinet meeting, but would not give a cast-iron guarantee that she would remain on board.

The Prime Minister saw Cook soon after Short. Cook cordially told Blair that as the second resolution had been abandoned, he would be resigning in accordance with the terms he had previously set out. The meeting was, according to Cook, 'a very civilised affair'. Blair 'had given up on trying to talk me out of resignation. Anyway, I had come armed with the final edition of my resignation letter signed and sealed. I, in turn, had given up on trying to talk him out of going to war.'

Cook decided against 'doing a Heseltine' and walking out of Cabinet to announce his resignation straight to the media on the steps of Downing Street. Instead, he booked a slot in the Commons that evening to announce his departure.

Having shaken hands and parted amicably with the Prime Minister, Cook headed downstairs to co-ordinate the presentation of his resignation with Alastair Campbell. The pair sat together in Campbell's office and drafted Blair's reply to the resignation letter. Despite the fraught nature of such a task, the pair spent time mocking Short's vacillations. Campbell then took Cook to the side door out of No. 10, where a car had been arranged to whisk him away unseen by reporters. They also shook hands, and Cook told his friend: 'I really hope it doesn't all end horribly for you all.' With that parting remark, he strolled over to the car, humming to himself. It had been an unusually courteous resignation.

Blair proceeded downstairs and swept into the Cabinet room. Having been given no warning that he was to resign, Short was shocked to see that Cook was not present. Blair began the meeting by announcing that there would be a road map for the Middle East peace process which would 'open the way to a full and final settlement within three years', and that Bush would 'seek a UN mandate for the post-conflict reconstruction of Iraq'. Aware that many in the party would raise the issue of oil, he reassured his colleagues that 'oil revenues would be administered under the UN's authority'. He then moved on to consider the legality of the proposed invasion. The Attorney General, Lord Goldsmith, was sitting in Cook's vacated seat and presented a brief advice to the ministers in which he argued that there was a firm legal basis for war in the absence of a second resolution. He did not disclose an earlier advice which had set out the various counter arguments before reaching an equivocal conclusion. Blair then summed up the government's position: they would support the US in their upcoming military action.

Ministers who had previously expressed doubt rallied round their leader. Prescott made a strong intervention, telling his colleagues that 'we should do the brave thing, and not be cowards.' One by one, the other Cabinet members expressed their support, each accepting their share of the responsibility for the war. Peter Hain remembered thinking: 'History is probably like this – you make decisions which have momentous consequences, without either being casual or sitting on the edge of your seats. Instead, we had adopted a course which seemed the logical conclusion of the preceding week's events.'

Short was the only one present to offer resistance. She made a tor-turous attempt to scrutinise the Attorney General's advice, eventually simply asking him if he had any doubts. He replied that legal opinions were never certain, but he was confident in his position. She then made a short speech that prompted further derision from her colleagues. She announced she had still not decided whether to resign, and was 'going to have a little agonise tonight. I owe it to all of you.' The other ministers jeered at her to keep quiet.

Despite Short's intervention, which Blair later branded 'ridiculous', the Prime Minister was happy with the way Cabinet had gone. He continued his attempt to secure Short's vote for the war and prevent her resignation, arranging for Brown to call her after the meeting and appeal to her personal loyalty. Blair then spoke with her again, selling hard his previous offering of a legacy-building role in Iraq's recon-struction. No Cabinet minister can ever have been indulged so heavily by a Prime Minister in the modern age, but Blair had calculated that the effort was worth the political reward.

Later that day, Straw told a packed Commons that Parliament would vote the next day on whether the country should go to war. Robin Cook then rose gracefully from the back benches to set out his reasons for his resignation. He was heard in silence, the audience hanging on every word. Standing several rows behind the government, and just in front of leading anti-war campaigners Tony Benn and Bob Marshall-Andrews, he delivered a devastating analysis of Blair's case for war, regarded as the most significant backbench speech of his generation.

He opened by praising Blair's domestic achievements, noting that he was resigning for one reason alone: he 'could not support a war without international agreement or domestic support'. Drawing on his experience as Foreign Secretary, he declared presciently that

Iraq probably has no weapons of mass destruction in the commonly understood sense of the term – namely a credible device capable of being delivered against a strategic city target. It probably ... has biological toxins and battlefield chemical munitions, but it has had them since the 1980s when US companies sold Saddam anthrax agents and the then British government approved chemical and munitions factories.

He proceeded to ask the two key questions to which Blair had never provided a credible answer: 'Why is it now so urgent that we should take military action to disarm a military capacity that has been there for twenty years and which we helped to create?' he demanded, and 'Why is it necessary to resort to war this week, while Saddam's ambition to complete his weapons programme is blocked by the presence of UN inspectors?'

Identifying this key contradiction in the government's position, he said: 'We cannot base our military strategy on the assumption that Saddam is weak and at the same time justify pre-emptive action on the claim that he is a threat.'

Turning to the foreign policy implications of the war, he warned of a strong sense of injustice throughout the Muslim world that would be caused by invading Iraq while tolerating Israel's indiscretions. There seemed to be 'one rule for the allies of the US and another rule for the rest'. Equally importantly, he argued that Britain's relations with their European allies had become one of the casualties of a 'war in which a shot has yet to be fired'.

Seeking to capture the mood of the nation, he claimed that Britons

do not doubt that Saddam is a brutal dictator, but they are not persuaded that he is a clear and present danger to Britain. They want inspections to be given a chance, and they suspect that they are being pushed too quickly into conflict by a US administration with an agenda of its own. Above all they are uneasy at Britain going out on a limb on a military adventure without a broader international coalition and against the hostility of many of our traditional allies.

He concluded by telling the House that he intended 'to join those tomorrow night who will vote against military action now. It is for that reason, and for that reason alone, and with a heavy heart, that I resign from the government.'

As Cook retook his seat, his colleagues eschewed the parliamentary convention against clapping to endorse his speech with a round of applause and a standing ovation. He gave no interviews after his resignation, becoming the first politician in the 24-hour news age to resign without uttering a word to the media. The speech prompted yet more anguish for Short. She booked her own slot for a resignation statement the next morning, but changed her mind again overnight, eventually resolving not to abandon the government and deciding, 'with a heavy heart', to authorise the invasion with her vote.

When the Downing Street staff heard that Short had scheduled a press conference the next morning, they presumed it would be a resignation statement after all. They were delighted to discover that the press had been assembled to be told that she would vote with the government. Blair's plan had worked perfectly, and Campbell noted gleefully in his diary: 'Clare was making a complete fool of herself.'

Blair was never worried that he would lose the Commons vote, as the Conservatives had pledged their support. He knew, however, that his authority would be fatally damaged unless he carried most Labour MPs with him. If he had failed, his own resignation would have been demanded and the Cabinet would likely have had to resign with him.

Before the parliamentary debate commenced, every cog in the well-oiled New Labour machine worked furiously to bring the parliamentary party into line. This was a fight to secure a project that had been a generation in the making. Blair worked side by side with Brown for the first time since he had become Prime Minister. Blairites Pat McFadden, John Reid and Alan Milburn sat planning strategy with their sworn enemies from the Brownite camp Nick Brown and Douglas Alexander. Co-ordinating with the Chief Whip Hilary Armstrong, all ministers were given a list of MPs to lobby. The whips deployed all their political capital, and Blair made use of his powers of patronage, promising ambassadorial roles, directorships and future honours. His wife Cherie led the battle to convince wavering female MPs.

With cruel ruthlessness, Blair deployed Short as a human shield. Campbell pressured the press to make her U-turn the prevailing story of the morning. When she arrived in the House for the debate, she was ordered to sit next to the Prime Minister, displayed as a trophy to commemorate his victory over the left of his party.

Blair then delivered to the House the greatest speech of his career. Every rhetorical trick in his arsenal was deployed: the slight pause, the small sigh, the vocal crack, the thrusting hands and the biblical references. In a rousing conclusion, he declared of Saddam:

> The only persuasive power to which he responds is 250,000 Allied troops on his doorstep. To retreat now would be to put at hazard all that we hold dearest. If we do act, we should do so with a clear conscience and a strong heart … We will confront the tyrannies and dictatorships and terrorists who put our way of life at risk … to show at the moment of decision that we have the courage to do the right thing.

The speech received rapturous reviews from the press gallery and, in a rare demonstration of the power of persuasion, swung public opinion firmly in favour of the war. The next day, opinion polls recorded a fifteen-point boost in favourable sentiment towards war from the week before. The *Daily Mail* set aside its long-held loathing of Blair to deem it 'the speech of a lifetime … one of those rare Parliamentary performances that can change hearts, minds and votes'. Even the anti-war *Independent* was forced to praise Blair's delivery as the 'most persuasive case yet by the man who has emerged as the most formidable persuader for war on either side of the Atlantic. The case against President Saddam's twelve-year history of obstructing the United Nations has never been better made.' *The Sun* went furthest: 'Tony Blair has won his place in history alongside Winston Churchill and Margaret Thatcher.'

After Blair's speech, the whipping operation resumed apace. McFadden co-ordinated the government's operation from Downing Street, while Cabinet strongmen Prescott and Reid were sent to collar any would-be rebels. According to Straw, the last-minute efforts to persuade the fifty or so 'wobblers' became desperate: 'By the end we were just pouring alcohol into them.'

The revolt was successfully contained. The Commons voted to authorise war by 412 to 149 votes. Eighty-nine Labour MPs voted against, and a further forty supported an amendment condemning the government's strategy, representing a record rebellion, but nowhere near the majority of the party. Campbell presented the vote as a triumph for Blair. The exhausted Prime Minister returned to No. 10 that evening, picked up the phone and called Bush. He confirmed that British troops would be supporting the upcoming invasion.

The war began the next day, with US forces moving into Iraq without the UK's knowledge. Joint airstrikes began shortly after. Saddam's resistance crumbled swiftly and Baghdad fell by 9 April.

Short remained in the Cabinet for two months after the war began, but had become a figure of ridicule. Dubbed 'depleted Claranium', she was subjected to an avalanche of vitriol from all sides of the party. Scorn was poured upon her by the Labour left, the wider anti-war movement and even her own mother. Fellow Birmingham MP and former friend Lynne Jones publicly denounced her, claiming that she had 'pretty well burnt her boats' with everyone. Another former leftist ally claimed that 'we didn't want her anyway … she had alienated so many people by making her threat to resign rather than just doing it that she was of no use to us any more'. In turn, Blair's supporters dubbed her a busted flush. Her old enemy Campbell delighted in briefing the press that she was 'pretty much finished as a political figure' and that she was destined for the scrapheap at the next reshuffle.

For the meantime, she was marginalised in government. Her involvement in the post-war administration was limited as other departments took their decisions without consulting her. Straw took overall control of the reconstruction effort and, finding Short reluctant to engage and unwilling to commit Department for International Development resources, proceeded to ignore her. He noted with thinly disguised disdain that Short was a 'handicap but not an overwhelming impediment' to progress.

Deeply hurt by the collapse of her reputation, Short recalled that 'people who were sort of buddies and friends, who previously would come and crawl all over [me] and ask [me] to speak at their constituency dinners, now sort of look the other way.' By May 2003, two months after the vote, she could carry on no longer, and resolved finally to go through with her much-mooted resignation. Her pretext was that the new UN resolution on the reconstruction of Iraq, which she played a large role in drafting and promoting, failed to meet her requirements. Having skipped a key Commons vote and Cabinet meeting, she delivered the news of her resignation to Campbell on 12 May.

With Cook's example in mind, she requested a slot for a resignation statement to the House. Unlike the former Commons leader, she used her departure to try and deal as much damage to the government as possible. She began the statement by excusing her failure to resign over Iraq and restating that the build-up to war had been very poorly managed. Her attack then broadened to draw a link between the failures over Iraq and 'the style and organisation of our government'. Firing volley after volley at Blair, she claimed: 'There is no real collective responsibility because there is no collective – just diktats in favour of increasingly badly thought-through policy initiatives that come from on high.' She ended her speech seeking to rouse Labour activists under her banner, calling on them to 'work together to prevent our government from departing from the best values of our party'.

She was not finished. In interviews with *The Guardian* and the *Financial Times*, she directly called for Blair's resignation and for an immediate hand-over to Brown. Every element of her resignation was calculated to damage the government, but in effect managed only to destroy what was left of her reputation. Just one of Labour's 410 MPs expressed public support for her position, and the press mocked her mercilessly. *The Times*'s leader writer summed up the prevailing mood by warning readers 'never to underestimate Clare Short's ability to make a total prat of herself'.

On the back benches, Short's bitterness towards Blair mutated into outright hatred. Imagining that she would become a Joan of Arc figure for the Labour left, she attempted to lead a fight for the party's principles. Instead, she found herself alone, bereft of allies and influence. She eventually decided to leave the party altogether, resigning the Labour whip in 2006 before leaving Parliament for good in 2010. Tragically, if she had resigned before the war, she could, after Cook's death in 2005, have become the public face of the anti-war movement and even a credible contender for Labour's leadership.

The popular consensus is that Cook and Short's departures are examples of how to resign well and badly. Cook is remembered as a man of principle who left government with honour and decency. Short has been portrayed as an embittered hypocrite who could not make up her mind. That assessment is unfair. For all its superficial dignity, Cook's resignation was in many ways pointless: he missed his chance to change policy over Iraq, and did not attempt to persuade Blair of his views. If he had resigned at an earlier stage, when he first received the intelligence dossiers he later dismissed as 'alphabet soup', he could have convinced colleagues to follow suit and rendered British involvement in the war inconceivable. Instead, unwilling to attempt to build an alliance around the Cabinet table, his departure now looks self-serving. Despite her myriad failings, Short at least tried to convince her colleagues and the public of her position. Her indecision was prompted by a genuine desire to lead a humanitarian recovery project, and naïve reliance upon the promises of a manipulative Prime Minister. She has been judged harshly.

ROBIN COOK TO TONY BLAIR

Dear Tony,

At Cabinet for some weeks I have been frank about my concern over embarking on military action in the absence of multilateral support. I applaud the heroic efforts that you and Jack [Straw] have put into the attempt to secure a second resolution at the UN.

It is not your fault that those attempts have failed. However, the evident importance that we attached to a second resolution makes it all the more difficult now to proceed without one, and without agreement in any other international forum.

As I cannot give my support to military action in these circumstances, I write with regret to resign.

You and I have both made the case over the years for an international order based on multilateral decisions through the UN and other forums. In principle I believe it is wrong to embark on military action without broad international support. In practice I believe it is against Britain's interests to create a precedent for unilateral military action.

As our Foreign Secretary I was impressed by the energy and skill with which you ended Britain's isolation in Europe and achieved for our country equal status and influence to Germany or France. I am dismayed that once again Britain is divided from our major European neighbours. As president of the Party of European Socialists, of which the Labour Party is a member, it troubles me that I know of no sister party within the European Union that shares our position.

I regret leaving my post as Leader of the House of Commons, in which I have had two fulfilling years modernising the procedures of a Parliament for which I have a deep affection. I also am proud of the real achievement of your government. Among those many achievements, I take particular satisfaction from our record on delivering devolution, investing in hospitals and tackling poverty among children.

All of these have only been made possible by your successful leadership and two record election victories which were your personal achievement. You will continue to have my personal support as leader of our party. I am only too sorry that our differences on the present crisis mean that I can no longer continue to serve you in Cabinet.

Yours sincerely,

Robin

TONY BLAIR TO ROBIN COOK

Dear Robin,

Thank you for your letter confirming your wish to resign from the Cabinet. You were good enough to tell me some days ago that you would resign in the event of our failure to secure a new UNSCR [United Nations Security Council resolution] that authorised military action.

You have been a good friend and colleague over many years, and I regret that you will not be part of the team that leads the country through this difficult and dangerous crisis.

Particularly when you were Foreign Secretary, we have worked together closely on a number of grave issues – Operation Desert Fox, Kosovo, Sierra Leone and many others – and I always valued your counsel and support.

You also secured notable diplomatic achievements such as agreement to an International criminal court and surrender of the Lockerbie suspects.

I want to thank you for the contribution you made in your two Cabinet posts, and no doubt will continue to make, to forging better relations between Britain and the rest of the EU. When the current crisis is over, this will be particularly important.

I also want to thank you for the modernising energy you have brought to your position as Leader of the House.

On your resignation, I have always tried to resolve this crisis through the UN, as you recognise in your letter. But I was always clear that the UN must be the way of dealing with the issue, not avoiding dealing with it.

The government is staying true to Resolution 1441. Others, in the face of continuing Iraqi non-compliance, are walking away from it.

As I have said to you, the threatened French veto set back hugely the considerable progress we were making in building consensus among UNSC members.

I passionately believe that if the international community had stayed rock solid in its determination and unity around Resolution 1441, Saddam could finally have been disarmed without a shot being fired.

But, just as he has done for the past 12 years, he has divided the international community and used his dictatorship to exploit our democracies and weaken our will. My will is as strong as ever, that he must be disarmed.

Saddam has had 12 years to disarm, and many last chances and final opportunities. The surprise now is not that action may take place but that the process has been strung out over so long, despite repeated resolutions, and repeated judgments that Iraq is in material breach of them.

I want to thank you for the kind comments in your letter, and know that we will remain friends if no longer Cabinet colleagues.

Yours ever,

Tony

CLARE SHORT TO TONY BLAIR

Dear Tony,

I have decided that I must leave the government.

As you know, I thought the run-up to the conflict in Iraq was mishandled, but I agreed to stay in the government to help support the reconstruction effort for the people of Iraq.

I am afraid that the assurances you gave me about the need for a UN mandate to establish a legitimate Iraqi government have been breached. The security council resolution that you and Jack have so secretly negotiated contradicts the assurances I have given in the House of Commons and elsewhere about the legal authority of the occupying powers, and the need for a UN-led process to establish a legitimate Iraqi government. This makes my position impossible.

It has been a great honour for me to have led the establishment and development of the Department for International Development over the past six years. I am proud of what we have achieved and much else that the government has done.

I am sad and sorry that it has ended like this.

Yours,

Clare

TONY BLAIR TO CLARE SHORT

Dear Clare,

Thank you for your letter of resignation from the government.

As you know, I believe you have done an excellent job in the department, which has the deserved reputation as one of the best such departments anywhere in the world.

That is in no small measure down to you.

Our record on aid and development is one of the government's proudest achievements and I would like to thank you for your role in bringing that about.

I know you have had doubts about the government's position on Iraq, but I was pleased you stayed to support the government during this military conflict.

Had you stayed on, there was clearly an important job to be done in the continuing efforts to bring about the reconstruction of Iraq.

My commitment to that effort remains as strong as ever.

I am afraid I do not understand your point about the UN. We are in the process of negotiating the UN resolution at the moment.

And the agreement on this resolution with our American and Spanish partners has scarcely been a secret.

As for who should lead the process of reconstruction, I have always been clear that this is not a matter of the UN leading or the coalition leading.

The two should work together. That is exactly what the resolution stipulates.

Yours ever,

Tony

CHAPTER THIRTEEN

LIAM FOX

Most government ministers do not take their friends along to top-secret meetings. Still fewer choose to bunk up with a gaggle of students after a long night on the town, or sneak into nightclubs under a nom de plume – but nobody has ever accused Dr Liam Fox of being a consensus man. Throughout his career, his ability to combine hard work with hard partying has raised eyebrows, once prompting a colleague to dub him a 'reckless bastard with no judgement'.

An eloquent Brexiteer and neoconservative, Fox became the darling of right-wing Conservative members during his rapid ascent from humble beginnings to the top levels of his party. Having entered Parliament in 1992, Fox kept above the fray while the Tories sank into their first destructive bout of infighting over Europe and emerged from the Major years with his reputation burnished. As the party settled into a long stint in opposition, Fox soared up the hierarchy. His big break came in 1999 when he secured the coveted position of shadow Health Secretary. Having condemned the 'wasteful' NHS and called for 'huge restrictions' on abortion, he has cemented his status as a pariah of the left and flagbearer for traditional Tories.

The reckless streak that his colleagues had noticed many years before was publicly revealed when he joked in 2000 about the Spice Girls being 'four dogs and a blackbird', a comment that would now result in immediate dismissal. He managed to survive the ensuing furore, however, and retained his role after the Tories' 2001 election defeat. Having played a pivotal role in securing the party leadership for his friend Michael Howard, he was rewarded by an appointment as party chairman, which has become a key post for any Tory harbouring leadership ambitions.

On Howard's departure in 2005, the 44-year-old Fox sensed that it was his moment. Presciently anticipating that the leadership race would be won by a fresh-faced young candidate, he decided to stand against the bookies' favourite, the battle-hardened David Davis. Tory leadership contest rules dictate that members choose from two candidates shortlisted by MPs. Fox failed to make the final two, having been edged out at the last moment by the eventual victor, David Cameron, who was even younger, sparkier and from the party's liberal wing.

Although he was alive to the dangers of alienating an obvious future rival, Cameron could not let Fox continue in the influential role of party chairman. Fox's rumoured disdain for the new flagship policy of additional funding for the NHS precluded a return to the post of shadow Health Secretary. Eventually, Fox agreed to shadow the role of Defence Secretary, a move he considered to be a demotion.

His eighteen-year wait for a Cabinet role came to an end after the 2010 general election. He survived the cull of shadow ministers that was required to accommodate Liberal Democrat coalition ministers, becoming Defence Secretary. His first year was a successful one, in which he defied budget cuts to execute a strategic defence review and a series of technology upgrades achieving, he claimed, the goal of getting more for less. At the same time, he competently presided over the armed forces, which were engaged in complex conflicts in Afghanistan and Libya.

Like many unmarried politicians, Fox faced recurrent whispers about his sexuality. He found this repeated innuendo 'irritating beyond belief' and addressed the matter directly in his 2005 leadership campaign by saying:

I know that some people use smears and I have heard them for years. They'd say: 'Why are you not married? You must be a playboy, or a wild man, or gay, or whatever?' To which I'd reply: 'Well, I'm getting married in December and I'm perfectly happy with my private life.'

His engagement was met with scepticism by many in the press, who implied that it had been deliberately timed to coincide with his leadership bid. Patrick Hennessy, then editor of the *Sunday Telegraph*, relayed the news in prose laden with sarcasm, quipping: 'As is the case with many politicians who reach their early forties as a bachelor, Dr Fox has been dogged by persistent rumours about his sexuality … However, he has put that all to rest by announcing his engagement last week to Jesme Baird.' An infuriated Fox insisted he had fallen in love and dismissed the press speculation as baseless smears.

It was these persistent rumours that ultimately destroyed Fox's ministerial career, although the tabloids could not fully unleash them without a pretence. Their trigger was the press attention that fell upon his relationship with his best man and best friend Adam Werritty, who was seventeen years his junior.

The pair first met in 1998, when Werritty was vice-president of the Edinburgh University Conservative Association and Fox was Tory spokesman for constitutional affairs. Fox attended the Association's Burns Night supper as their star guest. Despite their age gap, they swiftly became close friends, bonding over their mutual reverence for the Iron Lady. He had made such an impression that Fox returned to Edinburgh later that year to celebrate his thirty-seventh birthday with Werritty and his friends. From then on, the pair saw each other frequently, enjoying karaoke nights with other Edinburgh students, during which the shadow minister would belt out hits under the name 'Barry from Bournemouth'.

On his graduation from Edinburgh, Werritty, like many of his peers, was attracted by the bright lights of London. Unlike them, he lived rent-free in Liam Fox's riverside flat.

His subsequent career choices neatly shadowed his friend's successive promotions. When Fox was made shadow Health Secretary, Werritty set up a research and lobbying firm named 'UK Health Group'. After Fox's appointment as shadow Defence Secretary, the focus shifted into defence procurement. The pair then began to attend professional events together, travelling twice to Sri Lanka and attending the Herzliya Conference in Israel – a summit for politicians, military leaders and intelligence officials.

They continued to travel abroad together after Fox entered the Cabinet in 2010. In the first months of his tenure as Defence Secretary, Werritty was present for Fox's official visits to Bahrain and Singapore, brokered a meeting with the Sri Lankan Foreign Minister and dined in Florida with an American general. He also frequently travelled to and from Fox's ministerial engagements, often on private flights paid for by Tory donors. In early 2011, they enjoyed three holidays together: a jaunt to Dubai, a skiing holiday in Europe and a trip to Abu Dhabi, where Werritty played third wheel to Fox and Jesme, who by then had been married for six years. It was unprecedented for a professional lobbyist to be granted that kind of access to a government minister, let alone one with such a sensitive portfolio.

The close working and personal relationship continued until the spring of 2011, when Fox's special advisors raised the alarm. They had discovered that, despite having no official role, Werritty had printed business cards emblazoned with the green parliamentary portcullis that read: 'Advisor to the Rt Hon. Liam Fox MP'. Appreciating the danger, Fox ordered Werritty to stop handing out the cards, and no longer invited him on government business.

The relationship was brought into the public domain by military technology kingpin Harvey Boulter. Without telling Fox, Werritty had set up a meeting to allow Boulter to lobby the Defence Secretary. The meeting was staged by Werritty in the lobby of a Dubai hotel so that Fox would think it had been a chance encounter. The three men then sat in the hotel bar to discuss a range of procurement issues. At the time, Boulter was facing a multi-million-pound lawsuit brought by a US conglomerate, and after the meeting he emailed his opponents, apparently intimating that Fox would strip their CEO of his knighthood unless the claim was settled. This absurd threat led, unsurprisingly, to Boulter being accused of blackmail.

On 8 August 2011, the height of journalism's 'silly season' in which the press grasp around for any available story, *The Guardian* ran a short piece about Fox's meeting with Boulter and the subsequent blackmail allegations. By 19 August, they had revealed that the meeting had not been a chance encounter but that it had been set up by Werritty, who had described himself as an advisor despite not being employed by the MOD. The *Guardian* article was spotted by John Mann, a perceptive, opportunistic Labour backbencher always on hand to wade into a partisan battle. Mann began to fire parliamentary questions at Fox, asking him who Werritty was, which meetings he had attended and whether he had been exposed to classified information. In his replies, Fox skirted around the truth, stating that 'Mr Werritty is not an employee of the Ministry of Defence and has, therefore, not travelled with me on any official overseas visits.' Far from shutting the story down, this slippery turn of phrase piqued the attention of Labour MPs and journalists well versed in the underlying rumours about his sexuality.

By October, leaked records revealed that Werritty had visited Fox on fourteen occasions since 2010 without any official explanation. Although Fox insisted that the visits were 'not in any official capacity', he was forced to refer the matter to his Permanent Secretary Ursula Brennan for an internal inquiry. Announcing the investigation, Fox said that 'a number of baseless accusations have been made in recent days. For the sake of clarity, I have asked my Permanent Secretary to establish whether there has been any breach of national security or the ministerial code. She will report back in due course.'

He remained confident that the inquiry would draw a line under the matter and, returning to business, departed the next day on a trip to war-torn Libya. As the minister responsible for the armed forces, he was there to co-ordinate an operation preventing Colonel Gaddafi's embattled regime from slaughtering its own citizens in the town of Benghazi. Hampered by the Royal Air Force's targeted strikes, Gaddafi's forces were fighting street by street, and the dictator clung to power by a thread.

On landing in Libya, Fox was taken to the city of Misrata. He met with survivors of the civil war who were rebuilding their ruined city. Faced with the desolation before him, he could not bring himself to engage with the media storm that was brewing back at home. Also, from his second day in Libya, he could not keep in touch with London even if he had been inclined to, as NATO bombing missions had destroyed much of the country's communications infrastructure. Out of phone contact and devoid of internet access, he had no idea of the scale of the developing scandal.

Neither Fox nor Gaddafi would survive October. In the minister's absence, the newspapers had begun to run day after day of embarrassing stories about him, subtly shifting the focus away from the security angle and onto the more fertile ground of his relationship with Werritty. With Fox's sex life now deemed a matter of public interest, ten years of hushed whispers were poured across the pages of the tabloids.

The Prime Minister became directly involved for the first time, demanding an interim report from Ursula Brennan to shut down the scandal. He hoped that the report would clear Fox of any security breaches, and thereby stem the flow of damaging stories. On Fox's return, Cameron told him that he must issue a statement setting out his side of the story. Fox followed his leader's advice to the letter. He publicly accepted that it had been wrong to meet Boulter in Dubai without any officials present and acknowledged that he should not have permitted others to receive the 'misleading impression' that Werritty was his advisor.

Despite Fox's statement, the Sunday newspapers led with the story for a second week. Sniffing around and hinting at a hidden scandal, the tabloid editors made implications that might usually have been considered libellous. The *Mail on Sunday* dialled up the rhetoric, unearthing pictures showing Fox and Werritty dressing in identical clothes, and, pushing the limits of credibility, found a 'behavioural expert' to supply the following insightful comment: 'When people are very close and friendly there is often a tendency to start looking alike, even down to the posture they adopt and the way they dress.'

Those pictures formed the basis of a merciless skit on the BBC's *Have I Got News For You*, bringing the story to an audience far beyond the bounds of the Westminster village. Other emerging allegations included a bizarre story about a burglary at Fox's flat in April 2010, when the police had apparently noted that a different young male friend was staying over.

The Defence Secretary's personal life had become a serious

distraction for the government. Fox was forced to cancel his press conferences, and Ed Miliband used Prime Minister's Questions to keep the story alive, basing his questions on the Werritty matter. On 10 October, Fox was forced to give a further statement to the House of Commons denying any wrongdoing, but accepting that he had blurred the lines between his ministerial responsibilities and loyalty to his friend. That statement was well received both by colleagues and newspaper editorials, who emphasised that mere innuendo was not sufficient to force a resignation – that required proved wrongdoing. The feeling was that Fox would finally be allowed to move on.

That evening, however, Cameron received Ursula Brennan's interim report. It revealed that Werritty had been present in the MOD on twenty-two occasions – far more than previously revealed. When the report swiftly became public, Werritty's various contacts and the meetings he attended were splashed across the papers. Particularly damaging were the findings that he had met with the Israeli ambassador apparently under government auspices, and had been granted direct access to Fox's diary without the most rudimentary security clearance. Downing Street promptly issued a statement accepting that 'serious mistakes' had been made and announcing that the full inquiry into Fox had been transferred over to the Cabinet Secretary Sir Gus O'Donnell.

The shadow Defence Secretary Jim Murphy, a fellow Scot and pugnacious streetfighter, seized the opportunity to move in for the kill. Entering all-out attack mode, he declared:

This gets murkier and murkier. People will be shocked Liam Fox is unable to provide straight answers to straight questions. We have previously raised serious concerns about his insistence on visiting a Sri Lankan government failing to produce an independent and transparent investigation into allegations of war crime. We need a full explanation for his visit as well as clarification of the role of Adam Werritty. Mr Werritty's role is unclear and is now becoming a real concern.

Fuelled by the details released in Brennan's interim report, the broadsheets honed in on the corruption angle. As the disclosures revealed a lifestyle that could not have been sustained by the small profits generated by Werritty's companies, reporters began to investigate where the funding had come from. *The Times* soon identified a diverse range of backers, from a corporate intelligence company with a close interest in Sri Lanka to a pro-Israel lobbying group.

As further details emerged, Fox's enemies across the political spectrum saw their chance to pile in. Some became convinced that there were more sinister explanations for Werritty's actions, and he soon found himself simultaneously accused of seeking to identify further army budget cuts and trying to obtain arms supplies for the Sri Lankan regime.

The wildest allegation came from the hard left. Outspoken anti-Israel campaigner and former diplomat Craig Murray sought to prove that the young lobbyist stood at the apex of an Israeli plot to topple the Iranian government, orchestrated by their secret service Mossad and Britain's first Jewish ambassador to Israel. Murray alleged that:

Evidence continues to mount that, rather than simply pursuing commercial interests with then Defence Secretary Liam Fox, Adam Werritty was involved centrally in working with the British and Israeli intelligence services to try to engineer war against Iran … Werritty's role as a go-between with MI6, Mossad and Iranian pro-Shah groups came briefly into view as a result of what the press thought was a ministerial gay scandal, but government and a complicit media and opposition have sought to bury it as quickly as possible, before the real truth is revealed.

He added: 'I am not going to let that happen.'

Usually such far-fetched speculation would receive limited attention, but Murray managed to co-opt several MPs to assist him. According to Murray's website, among them was Jeremy Corbyn, then a rebellious and disaffected backbencher. As a committed pro-Palestinian activist that had long been suspicious of Fox's atlanticism, Corbyn submitted a series of parliamentary questions about Werritty's meetings with Britain's ambassadors to Israel.

The feeding frenzy soon began to affect Fox's ministerial work. He struggled to balance defending himself against the slurs and rumours with deciding which Libyan targets would be hit on the ground while receiving distressing reports of civilian casualties. By 14 October, he realised that he could not carry on any longer, having spent his final day as a minister being hounded by a BBC reporter at St Pancras station who repeatedly barked: 'Dr Fox, do you think this is a witch hunt?' Resisting all attempts to persuade him to stay, he chose to exit the fray before he suffered further damage. It was a tactical retreat.

Sir Gus O'Donnell's report into Fox's conduct was released four days later, and he would not have survived it. O'Donnell concluded that Fox had been guilty of a 'failure of judgement', and had not lived up to the standard expected of ministers. The involvement of Werritty had 'posed a degree of security risk not only to Dr Fox, but also to the accompanying official party'. O'Donnell also noted that the problem was exacerbated by the 'frequency, range and extent' of Fox's contact with Werritty and by his failure to tell any officials in the department about it. Finally, Werritty's use of business cards describing himself as an advisor 'risked creating the impression that Mr Werritty spoke on behalf of the UK government'. The report did, however, confirm that neither Fox or Werritty made any inappropriate financial gains.

Fox might have been able to survive had he addressed the matter earlier and more comprehensively. He later told his colleague Rob Wilson:

> I think that your instinct is to get on with your work and I think probably we should have stopped and said: 'We have to deal with this and then move on rather than just try to continue.' But it was slightly more difficult when you're in the middle of a war and in the circumstances, I might probably do the same again. Then, of course, as with all these things, you are slightly at the mercy of events. Would things have been different if we'd have caught Gaddafi a week earlier?

The story was whipped up, however, by insinuations surrounding his relationship with Werritty. Fox maintains that he was the 'victim of a hate campaign' and of 'whispering in the weeds' about his sexuality. There is clearly an element of truth in this, for the tabloid coverage of his relationship with Werritty seems, in hindsight, outdated and offensive. However, Fox's breaches of the ministerial code alone were probably resigning issues, and, as proved by his later appointments, he was wise to jump before he was pushed.

In his only comment on the affair, Werritty denied any allegation of corruption, noting that

> one man's 'clandestine' meeting is another man's informed and fascinating discussion. I guess it really just boils down to a difference of perspective. But when the saga about my role and who funded it

snowballed, the hunt was firmly on – especially after the extent of my foreign travel was revealed, and how much of it coincided with Liam's travel programme.

What remains unknown is exactly what he was doing in the meetings and trips he made abroad. This was the question that most troubled Cameron, who as early as 2010 had identified the role of lobbyists as the next great scandal waiting to befall the political class.

Fox returned to the back benches to become a trenchant critic of government policy and a go-to man for lobby journalists seeking a lacerating quote about the Prime Minister. He also took an increasingly prominent role with the group of Conservative MPs agitating to secure a referendum on membership of the European Union. As soon as Cameron made the fateful promise of an in–out referendum on Europe in 2013, Fox made his position clear – he would be backing Brexit. Having played a muted role in Vote Leave's triumphant victory in the subsequent referendum and Cameron's subsequent downfall, he once again sensed that his moment had come.

After another profile-raising tilt at the Tory leadership, he entered Theresa May's first Cabinet in the newly created position of Secretary of State for International Trade. His role was to travel across the globe laying the ground for the free trade arrangements made possible by the UK's exit from the EU, a post that he had waited his whole career to fill. On the night that he was appointed to his dream job, he celebrated in customary fashion, knocking back eight bottles of House of Commons champagne on the terrace of the Palace of Westminster. Adam Werritty was chief among the revellers.

LIAM FOX TO DAVID CAMERON

Dear David,

As you know, I have always placed a great deal of importance on accountability and responsibility. As I said in the House of Commons on Monday, I mistakenly allowed the distinction between my personal interest and my government activities to become blurred. The consequences of this have become clearer in recent days. I am very sorry for this.

I have also repeatedly said that the national interest must always come before personal interest. I now have to hold myself to my own standard. I have therefore decided, with great sadness, to resign from my post as Secretary of State for Defence – a position which I have been immensely proud and honoured to have held.

I am particularly proud to have overseen the long overdue reforms to the Ministry of Defence and to our armed forces, which will shape them to meet the challenges of the future and keep this country safe.

I am proud also to have played a part in helping to liberate the people of Libya, and I regret that I will not see through to its conclusion Britain's role in Afghanistan, where so much progress has been made.

Above all, I am honoured and humbled to have worked with the superb men and women in our armed forces. Their bravery, dedication and professionalism are second to none.

I appreciate all the support you have given me – and will continue to support the vital work of this government, above all in controlling the enormous budget deficit we inherited, which is a threat not just to this country's economic prosperity but also to its national security.

I look forward to continuing to represent my constituents in North Somerset.
Yours ever,

Liam

DAVID CAMERON TO LIAM FOX

Dear Liam,

Thank you for your letter.

I understand your reasons for deciding to resign as Defence Secretary, although I am very sorry to see you go.

We have worked closely for these last six years and you have been a key member of my team throughout that time.

You have done a superb job in the 17 months since the election, and as shadow Defence Secretary before that.

You have overseen fundamental changes in the Ministry of Defence and in our armed forces, which will ensure that they are fully equipped to meet the challenges of the modern era.

On Libya, you played a key role in the campaign to stop people being massacred by the Gaddafi regime and instead win their freedom.

You can be proud of the difference you have made in your time in office, and in helping our party to return to government.

I appreciate your commitment to the work of this government, particularly highlighting the need to tackle the deficit, and the relationship between Britain's economic strength and our national security.

You and Jesme have always been good friends, and I have truly valued your support over the years. I will continue to do so in the future.

Yours ever,

David

CHAPTER FOURTEEN

CHRIS HUHNE

It was his routine weekly commute, but this time the journey he had travelled scores of times had profound and far-reaching consequences. Chris Huhne, a Liberal Democrat MEP, had caught a flight from Brussels to London as usual. Arriving at Stansted airport shortly after 10 p.m., he collected his baggage and made his way to the long-stay car park. He climbed into his sleek black BMW, replete with personalised H11HNE number plates, and set off on the short drive south to his Clapham home. Halfway through the journey, he realised he had been flashed by a speed camera. Glancing at the dashboard, he saw that he was driving almost 70 miles per hour in a 50 miles-per-hour zone. Panic set in, for he already had nine points on his licence, and a further speeding ticket would mean a six-month ban. That was unthinkable, for he was seeking selection as a parliamentary candidate, and badly needed his car. When the speeding ticket arrived in the post weeks later, his wife agreed that she would take the blame for him by filling in the police form to say that she had been driving the car.

Seven years later, this mundane episode condemned three senior public figures to jail: Huhne himself – the only Cabinet minister to trade his red box for an orange jumpsuit; his wife, leading economist

Vicky Pryce; and Pryce's friend Constance Briscoe, the first black British woman to become a judge. The saga was marked by the depths Pryce plumbed to avenge her husband's infidelities, and the extent Huhne was willing to lie in public to save his own skin.

Having retained his driving licence and secured the candidacy for the parliamentary seat in Eastleigh, Huhne won the seat in the 2005 general election. Charles Kennedy stepped down as Liberal Democrat leader shortly afterwards, and young favourite Mark Oaten's leadership bid collapsed amid revelations of his proclivity for male prostitutes. Demonstrating the chutzpah that had riled his MEP colleagues, Huhne nominated himself as an alternative leader despite having been an MP for only a few months. He ran eventual winner Menzies Campbell close, earning himself further promotion to become party spokesman for the environment.

When Campbell retired two years later, Huhne ran again. This time he was expected to win, but was pipped to the post to another young former MEP, Nick Clegg. During that fractious campaign, he began the tryst that would break up his marriage and ruin his career. Carina Trimingham was a PR consultant and fourteen years Huhne's junior. Outrageously described by *Daily Mail* columnist Richard Littlejohn as a 'comedy lesbian from central casting', she was notorious in media circles for spoon-feeding political scandal to gossip columnists. Her affair with Huhne intensified during the 2010 general election campaign when he decided to walk out on his marriage, resolving, however, to wait for his youngest son to complete his A Levels before breaking the news. During the election campaign, Huhne had the gumption to portray himself as a family man, splattering his literature with references to his wife and children and proclaiming that 'family matters to me so much. Where would we be without them?'

Shortly before the 2010 election, news of Huhne's misdemeanours reached Neville Thurlbeck, the infamous chief reporter at the *News of the World*. He did not follow up the lead as he deemed Huhne insufficiently significant to be of interest. That changed when Clegg took his party into coalition with David Cameron's Conservatives, and Huhne was awarded the prized role of Secretary of State for Energy and Climate Change. As a Cabinet minister and strong supporter of further investigation into tabloid phone-hacking, his scalp had become infinitely more valuable. The *News of the World* despatched a private detective to tail Trimingham, and soon obtained pictures of the pair kissing. The newspaper decided to run with the story on 20 June 2010.

Huhne was tipped off the day before when he spotted a photographer following him around Waterloo station. Resolved to limit the damage, he headed straight to the family home. When he arrived, Pryce was upstairs watching a football match. At half time, she came down to the kitchen where he sat her down and confessed all. Explaining that they had only 'thirty minutes to kill the story', he said that he would be issuing a statement announcing the end of their marriage. The news came as a complete shock to Pryce, who had not picked up any sign that he was having an affair. Huhne, acting with disconcerting banality, drafted a succinct press release and headed off to the gym.

His statement achieved the aim of extracting the sting from the story. Although a media frenzy had been avoided, Pryce was left utterly humiliated. As Huhne left the home for good, he turned to her and said sharply: 'Don't talk to the newspapers.' She should have taken this advice.

She was instead overcome by an uncontrollable desire for revenge. When he later popped back to the family home, she is said to have left him with two black eyes and no further plans to return. Choosing to disregard his earlier exhortation, she formed a close relationship with *Sunday Times* reporter Isabel Oakeshott.

Oakeshott has been unfairly portrayed as an Iago figure in the tragedy. But Pryce was not so naïve. The pair met at her instigation, and she openly admitted her purpose was to damage her ex-husband in any way she could. Handing over copies of his confidential financial documents disclosed in the divorce proceedings, she claimed that he had exaggerated his past financial success. Oakeshott told her politely that there was no news story in the technical details of the divorce, and the pair parted. Pryce said that she would soon be back in touch with something else that could, this time, be weaponised.

Dropping Oakeshott for the time being, she instead sought out the *Mail on Sunday*. She told them that Huhne forced one of his constituency aides to take driving points on his behalf. This tall tale was easily rebutted as the aide had no driving licence at the time. Spurned by the *Mail on Sunday*, Pryce reverted to Oakeshott. Over lunch, she again insisted that her husband must be brought down. When Oakeshott asked how, this time Pryce was ready with an answer. Leaning across the table, she dramatically whispered: 'I took his points!'

Oakeshott's immediate reaction was that this was a minor transgression. However, misleading the police amounts to perverting the course of justice, which is punishable with an unlimited prison sentence. No Cabinet minister could survive being convicted of such a serious offence.

The pair exchanged emails over the next few days. Initially, Oakeshott sought to persuade her not to give the story to the *Mail on Sunday*, which she dubbed 'fairly downmarket' and 'a bit tawdry'. Such 'tabloid muckraking' would jeopardise her long-term aim of being given a seat in the House of Lords. On the other hand, if the *Sunday Times* ran the story, Pryce could achieve the 'dual objective of bringing Chris down … without seriously damaging your own reputation in the process'.

Oakeshott added: 'You know we could have quite a lot of fun doing it …We could perhaps go away somewhere nice for a few days, work on it in complete privacy and in relaxed surroundings. It wouldn't have to be anywhere fancy (though it could be!) and I'm sure the *Sunday Times* would help foot the bill.'

Pryce's reply noted that she 'would need some reassurance that it would indeed bring CH down', prompting the response that there are no guarantees about politicians resigning – 'some get away with the most extraordinary behaviour; while others have to stand down over more minor things'. Despite this warning, Pryce gave Oakeshott the go-ahead, writing: 'I have no doubt as I definitely want to nail him. More than ever actually and would love to do it soon.'

She soon became aware that she was also placing herself in danger of criminal prosecution, and began to lose her nerve. Seeking to persuade Oakeshott to run alternative stories, she again referred to financial misdemeanours and wild smears about alleged homosexual encounters. But Oakeshott held firm: if Pryce wanted to 'nail' Huhne, she would have to go on record about the speeding points. Oakeshott added that 'there is a minor risk of you being prosecuted, but we think it is highly unlikely, especially if we handle it right … the bottom line is that the story WILL bring Chris down, if you are prepared to go on the record about what happened – with the minor risk that this carries.'

After several days of further prevarication, a frustrated Oakeshott wanted to know that her time was not being wasted. Pryce told her to proceed, and with the help of the newspaper made repeated attempts to record Huhne confessing, once trying to wire herself up for a face-to-face meeting. But he was too canny an operator to fall for such tricks, and all attempts to record a confession failed. He was skilfully quelling the brewing storm.

Oakeshott's editor decided that the story could be run without a taped confession, but required Pryce to make a written statement. But at the last minute Pryce retreated again, and would not permit the paper to reveal that she took the points. She did not want to go into any details that might implicate her, instead seeking to destroy his career without the risk of friendly fire.

The *Sunday Times* published the interview on 8 May 2011. Most of the copy was anodyne, with the driving points allegation innocently slipped in at the end. Oakeshott wrote that 'a rumour has been circulating among senior Lib Dems, [that] Huhne managed to avoid being banned from driving by persuading somebody to accept penalty points for speeding on his behalf.' Pryce commented:

> Oh gosh. Yes, he did. I am surprised you are raising this. I would rather not get into it ... but, look, there is such huge pressure on politicians to be everywhere at once, especially early in their career, so that they are visible – huge pressure – and he does drive a bit like a maniac.

The leading news story accompanying the interview, however, solely focused on the speeding allegations.

Huhne's reaction was to dismiss the story as 'simply incorrect', adding that the claims had 'been made before and they've been shown to be untrue'. By the end of the week, Oakeshott found herself under pressure to provide a follow-up, and tried in vain to contact Pryce. She discovered that she had been double-crossed, as Pryce had granted an exclusive interview to the *Mail on Sunday*. Smarting at the failure of the previous week's article, Pryce revealed for the first time on the record that it was she who had taken the penalty points.

This confession unshackled Huhne's political enemies. Simon Danczuk, Labour MP for Rochdale and an old adversary of the

Liberal Democrats, immediately complained to the police. He also issued a press release accusing Huhne of 'serious criminal behaviour', calling on him to 'stand aside from his position in the Cabinet while the investigation is conducted'.

The police interviewed Huhne and Pryce before passing their files to the Crown Prosecution Service. The CPS's role is to decide whether suspects face charges, and cannot proceed unless there is a realistic prospect of conviction and it would be in the public interest to go to trial. That decision ultimately lay with the Director of Public Prosecutions, Keir Starmer, later a Labour frontbencher.

Huhne maintained his denial, accusing his wife of inventing the story in a fit of pique. His decision to lie was calculated carefully. Realising that the case might well not be pursued and that accepting the truth would end his career, he knew that he had nothing to lose.

The Liberal Democrat hierarchy nervously awaited Starmer's decision. Huhne had reluctantly promised Clegg that he would resign as a Cabinet minister if charged, realising that it would be impossible to 'go on being Secretary of State … Obviously you could argue that you're innocent until you're proven guilty; but in practice, the relationship with your colleagues is such that I think it would be very, very difficult.'

Starmer was set to announce his decision on 3 February 2012. All senior Liberal Democrats, excepting Huhne himself, had gathered at a budget hotel in Eastbourne for a strategic away day, and, by mid-morning, were enduring a presentation on campaign techniques. Attentions were obviously wandering, for David Laws remembered 'everyone from Nick Clegg downwards was looking at their watches and BlackBerrys for the news from London and the CPS'. Steve Webb was the first to pick up Starmer's statement, spinning around to give his colleagues the thumbs down. The CPS had decided that both Huhne and Pryce would be charged with perverting the course of justice, prompting sharp intakes of breath and scandalised whispering through the hall.

Clegg took to the stage, realising that focus on the strategy presentation was in terminal decline. He explained that Huhne was to resign as a minister and would fight to clear his name. Suddenly, Stephen Lloyd, ignorant of recent developments, broke the gloomy atmosphere with a pre-planned surprise. As soon as Clegg had finished, the hapless local MP burst through the back doors, accompanied by a tall man dressed as a fluffy bee. Affecting his best game-show host voice, Lloyd hollered: 'Can I introduce you all to the Eastbourne Buzz! Here to promote the greatest town on the south coast!' The bee proceeded to dance around the room while Clegg and his team attempted to escape.

Huhne was the first Cabinet minister to be forced from office by criminal prosecution. He continued to deny the allegations, lying to interviewers, reporters and news anchors alike. Why did he continue to lie? The main reason is that he thought he would get away with it. He had seen no firm evidence against him and there was no CCTV – it was his ex-wife's word against his. He later explained:

> I justified my denial to myself by saying that it was a relatively minor offence committed by 300,000 other people ... it was not a murder charge, not carousel fraud with £29 million squirrelled away, not even keeping a secret Swiss bank account – and 1,100 people have just been given immunity from prosecution and anonymity by the Treasury for lying about what they actually owe in taxes and having repeatedly lied on their tax returns. I think most people would regard sending back a form about a speeding offence as being of a lesser order of magnitude than any of those things, and for such disproportionate consequences for your family, for your career, not just for me but for my ex-wife as well.

His conclusion was that 'most people would do what I did'.

Starmer's decision to prosecute had not been an easy one. The key evidence, of which Huhne remained ignorant, was the corroborating testimony of Pryce's friend and neighbour, Constance Briscoe. Briscoe, a part-time judge, had given a statement to the CPS confirming that she had been told about the points swap in 2003. In Starmer's view, the 'unimpeachable' evidence of the judge solidified the prosecution case by corroborating Pryce's account. The problem was that Briscoe's statement was false. It had been invented to help her friend Pryce induce the prosecution.

Briscoe twinned her legal ability with a rare talent for self-promotion. Despite her relatively junior status, she had built up a media profile by offering comments on a wide array of legal issues. Her appearances on the BBC's *Any Questions?* and *Question Time* had enraged many fellow barristers, for whom she was an attention-seeking fantasist. Even her supporters, including Baroness Helena Kennedy QC, acknowledged that 'Constance doesn't make friends easily.' One friend she did manage to retain was Vicky Pryce.

Around the time Huhne deserted Pryce, Briscoe's husband left her for a law student fifty years his junior. The two women bonded over their shared heartbreak, and Briscoe offered to advise Pryce in her negotiations with the *Sunday Times* and *Mail on Sunday*. Her first transgression was to lie to the *Mail on Sunday*, telling them that she knew about the points swap in 2003. That was enough to ensure that the newspaper printed the story. When Essex Police began their investigation, they asked her to repeat her comments on oath, and she signed a sworn statement – the document that induced the CPS to prosecute Huhne and Pryce.

The CPS's lawyers swiftly became suspicious about their star witness. In her first statement, Briscoe concealed her role as an intermediary with the *Mail on Sunday*. She then tried to cover her tracks, giving further inconsistent statements to the police and tampering with documents on the police file. Deciding to drop her from the case, the prosecution dramatically declared that she could not be 'relied upon as a witness of truth'. Later convicted of perverting the course of justice, Briscoe spent sixteen months in jail. Her part in the conspiracy to destroy Huhne ultimately destroyed her career and left her penniless, rendering her the truly tragic figure in the scandal.

Huhne was convinced that Briscoe's disgrace would prove to be his ticket out of trouble. At a court hearing the day before the full trial was due to commence, his barrister pressed the judge to throw out the case. John Kelsey-Fry QC summarised the case against him as 'at best gossamer thin'. There was no CCTV evidence against Huhne, the principal witness had been abandoned, and the only other testimony was from Pryce – a co-defendant with an obvious motive to attack him. Arguing that Huhne's trial could never be fair, Kelsey-Fry pointed to a YouGov poll that showed 60 per cent of the population already thought he was guilty. The conclusion was that 'this isn't only trial by media' but that 'they have also published a verdict.' There seemed to be fruitful grounds to have the case dismissed without a trial. When Kelsey-Fry sat down, he was confident that his brazen gamble had paid off.

Throughout the course of the afternoon, Andrew Edis QC, the prosecution barrister, persuaded the judge that there was a case to answer. Edis's argument was that Huhne's explanation of events made no sense. His story was that Pryce was the one who had speeded, having picked him up from the airport to drive him home. But there was no good reason for her to have done that – she had been on a panel at the London School of Economics that evening, and if Huhne's story was correct, would have travelled to Stansted after 8 p.m. by public transport before driving forty miles to ferry her husband back. This behaviour must have been very unusual, yet Huhne maintained that he had no memory of it. Edis also referred to a series of texts between Huhne and his son Peter. Peter said: 'We all know that you were driving' and 'Are you going to accept your responsibility or do I have to contact the police and tell them what you told me?' Huhne failed to respond. Edis asked why, if he was not the driver, he did not reply to say so. He concluded that such difficult questions must be answered by a jury.

The judge was convinced, and denied Huhne's application to dismiss the case. He ordered the trial to commence the next day. Unknown to all but Huhne himself, Huhne had played his final hand. To proceed to trial and maintain his lies on oath, he said,

> would have been truly horrendous, and I did not want to be in that position ... I had very much the examples of Jonathan Aitken and Jeffrey Archer to mind: both of them had perjured themselves in court, which is a far more serious offence than the one of which I was accused. I personally preferred – both for the reasons of not dragging my family through any further proceedings, and because I did not want to perjure myself – to step back.

Huhne rang Nick Clegg late that night. Calm and in control, he explained that the lawyers' assessment was not promising, and that he wanted to spare his family the attention that would accompany a full trial. As a result, he planned to plead guilty the next morning. Clegg was stunned, as the guarded Huhne had protested his innocence in public and private. He insisted that Huhne must stand down as an MP immediately, for even the Liberal Democrats' famous munificence did not extend to tolerating the incarceration of a sitting MP.

On the morning of 4 February 2013, the media gathered outside Southwark Crown Court to report on the first day of the trial. Huhne arrived hand in hand with Trimingham. He asked to be read the charges again as soon as proceedings began, and his admission that he was guilty of all charges prompted gasps of shock from the public benches. Leaving the court with a warning from the judge to expect a jail sentence, Huhne emerged into a paparazzi scrum. On the steps of the court, he told the assembled press that, 'having taken responsibility for something I did ten years ago, the only proper course of action for me is now to resign my Eastleigh seat in Parliament, which I shall do very shortly.'

Huhne had offered the CPS a deal by which his ex-wife would be let off if he pleaded guilty, but they had refused. So Pryce remained on trial, having pleaded not guilty on the basis of an archaic defence called marital coercion – essentially claiming that her criminal behaviour was induced by her husband's manipulative demands.

Her trial began the day after Huhne's confession, and provided a very public example of the flaws of the jury system. Many jurors failed to understand the case, their role or the most basic concepts of justice. A note was sent up to the presiding judge asking several questions, including: 'Can a juror come to a verdict based on a reason that was not presented to the court and had no facts or evidence to support it?', 'Can we speculate about the events at the time that Vicky Pryce signed the form, or what was in her mind at that time?' and '...please advise on which facts in the bundle the jury shall consider to determine a not guilty or guilty verdict'. The judge met these queries with disbelief, and dismissed the jury before they could reach a verdict. It took until 7 March for a second jury to reject Pryce's defence, and she was also convicted of perverting the course of justice.

The pair of convicts returned to court on 11 March to hear their sentences. Sitting uncomfortably next to each other in the dock, they looked resolutely straight ahead and failed to exchange a single glance. Huhne called several character witnesses, including Labour MP Bob Marshall-Andrews, known as the 'underdog's overdog' for his unerring support for those in trouble, and an ex-girlfriend from university who told the judge that Huhne was less arrogant than he appeared. Despite these pleas, Mr Justice Sweeney decided that both parties would be sentenced to eight months in prison – a particularly harsh sentence for the offence.

His accompanying remarks were scathing. To Huhne, he said:

No doubt you thought that you would get away with it. After all, only you had been in the car at the time of the offence, it had taken place at night, the camera was forward-facing, and you could choose who, if anyone, to share the secret with.

And you did get away with it for some eight years ... you have fallen from a great height (albeit that that is only modest mitigation given that it is a height that you would never have achieved if you had not hidden your commission of such a serious offence in the first place) ... this was as your counsel accepts a serious offence, indeed as it seems to me a flagrant offence of its type...

He reserved equal disdain for Pryce, finding her to have been 'motivated ... by an implacable desire for revenge, and with little consideration of the position of your wider family'. She 'decided to set about the dual objective of ruining [Huhne] whilst protecting [her] own position and reputation in the process. [Her] weapon of choice was the revelation of his part in the offence in 2003. But it was a dangerous weapon because it had, in truth, been a joint offence.' She had then falsified a defence of marital coercion, and 'in doing so, just as you did in your dealings with the media ... demonstrated that there is a controlling, manipulative and devious side to your nature'. His comments on Pryce leave a sour taste in the mouth, for her motives in reporting the offence did not alter its gravity. She seems to have been punished for self-reporting a serious crime – an action that usually merits a discount in sentence rather than a withering insult from the judge.

Pryce served her time in Holloway Prison writing a book on the economics of the jail system. Huhne was sent to Wandsworth Prison, dubbed Britain's worst jail. Two days later, *The Sun* reported that a prison officer had ridiculed Huhne on his first morning, calling him down to breakfast with a loud 'Order! Order!' and adding over the PA system: 'The Right Honourable Member for Wandsworth North – down to the office.' Huhne later insisted the story was 'complete and utter nonsense'. He and Pryce were both released after serving two months of their sentences.

Huhne describes prison as 'a humbling and sobering experience', but it was 'quite a long way down the list of what was least pleasant' about his downfall. He ranks losing his job as a Secretary of State as 'the worst part of the penalty'. That was, apparently, even more painful to him than the breakdown of his relationship with his children.

CHRIS HUHNE TO NICK CLEGG

Dear Nick,

I am writing to resign, with great regret, as Energy and Climate Change Secretary. I will defend myself robustly in the courts against the charges that the Crown Prosecution Service has decided to press. I have concluded that it would be distracting both to my trial defence and to my official duties if I were to continue in office as a minister.

It has been a privilege to serve with you in the first group of Liberal ministers in a British government since 1945. As Liberal Democrats in government, we have put the national interest first. When we negotiated the coalition agreement, Greece had been hit by financial crisis. Since then, Portugal, Ireland, Spain and Italy have all been hit, vindicating our decision to tackle our own bigger budget deficit. We have had an essential role in ensuring that those decisions are fair. Our decisions are putting in place the foundations for a long-lasting recovery, a rebalancing of the economy, and durable jobs.

Our role in the coalition has ensured that growth in the green economy – already accounting for more than a million jobs – will be a large part of the solution. We have legislated in the first Energy Act 2011 for the pioneering pay-as-you-save Green Deal which will revolutionise our energy saving efforts, provide jobs across the country, and save householders money. The white paper on Electricity Market Reform has mapped out a new policy to encourage the billions of investment that we need in all three families of low carbon electricity generation – renewables, nuclear and clean coal and gas. The Green Investment Bank will support this goal, and this will also create new industries in which the UK will have a head start.

We have put consumers' interests – today and in the long term – at the heart of our policy, encouraging more competitors in the electricity and gas markets, working with Ofgem to simplify the confusion of tariffs, and getting tough on abuses.

I am proud that the UK has played a leading role in the revival of international climate change talks through the United Nations at Cancun and Durban. Climate change is an area where working with our European partners can help us to achieve national goals which would be out of reach if we were isolated and alone.

The Liberal Democrats under your leadership are playing an essential role in ensuring that the coalition government reflects liberal values at home and abroad. I have been proud to help put our commitments to freedom, fairness and the environment into practice, and to demonstrate once again that liberalism is alive and well in the country of its birth.

Best Wishes,

   Chris Huhne

NICK CLEGG TO CHRIS HUHNE

Dear Chris,

Thank you for your letter.

I am immensely grateful for the huge contribution you have made to the government over the past 18 months; both in the trailblazing work you have undertaken as Energy and Climate Change Secretary and in your wider role in government as a key architect of the coalition.

You have shown real leadership in your time at DECC [the Department of Energy and Climate Change], driving forward a key part of the government's agenda tackling the challenges of climate change and driving green growth and jobs. The Green Deal and other major initiatives that you pioneered will deliver major dividends to the public while marking a major step change in the UK's approach to the environment.

I fully understand your decision to stand down from government in order to clear your name but I hope you will be able to do so rapidly so that you can return to play a key role in government as soon as possible.

Best wishes,

Nick Clegg

CHRIS HUHNE TO DAVID CAMERON

Dear David,

This letter is to submit with much regret my resignation as Energy and Climate Change Secretary. I intend to mount a robust defence against the charges brought against me, and I have concluded that it would be distracting both to that effort and to my official duties if I were to continue in office.

It has been an honour to negotiate and then serve in the first coalition government of modern times which has substantial achievements both in reducing the economic dangers faced by our country, and in making progress with policies to tackle climate change and provide energy security. Internationally, we have helped to build a coalition of ambitious countries in Europe and beyond to put the United Nations process back on track.

It has been a privilege to be a minister in the coalition government, and I wish the administration every success with the environmental and economic challenges that lie ahead.

Best wishes,

Chris Huhne

DAVID CAMERON TO CHRIS HUHNE

Dear Chris,

Thank you for your letter informing me of your decision to resign from the Government. I believe you have made the right decision under the circumstances.

You have made a very significant contribution to the Government, of which you can be justly proud.

You were a member of the team which negotiated the formation of the Coalition Government between the Conservative Party and the Liberal Democrats in those crucial days after the General Election, with our shared commitment to come together as two distinct political parties and govern in the national interest.

As Secretary of State for Energy and Climate Change, you have led the Government's efforts to live up to its responsibility to tackle climate change with great passion and distinction. You played a key role in securing the progress made at the Cancun and Durban summits, and I pay tribute to the leadership you showed at both. You have been determined to deliver on our pledge that this should be the greenest Government ever, recognising that cutting carbon emissions is not a luxury but a necessity. And you have relentlessly championed green growth.

Thank you too for the important contribution you have made as a member of the National Security Council since its inception, not only on security of our energy supply, but also in our discussions on Afghanistan, and during the Libya campaign.

Like the Deputy Prime Minister, I am sorry to see you leave the Government under these circumstances and wish you well.

David

CHAPTER FIFTEEN

ANDREW MITCHELL

Government ministers are best advised to restrain themselves from insulting members of the public. Taking on the police can be fatal. In 2012, David Cameron's Chief Whip Andrew Mitchell destroyed his career by having an ostensibly minor tiff with the policemen stationed at the Downing Street gates. Powerless to respond when later accused of calling the constables 'plebs', he soon learned that the key to a successful political career is not to make the wrong enemies.

The Prime Minister's residence has been under 24/7 police guard since the IRA bombing campaign of the late 1980s. Most ministers enjoy a good relationship with the ever-present bobbies that lend them a friendly smile on their way in and out of Downing Street. But tensions developed with Mitchell as soon as he entered the Cabinet in May 2010. The police guard refused to accede to his requests to cycle in through the back gates, instead ordering him to go around to the front entrance each time to be formally identified. After a series of further confrontations, in which the police obstinately refused to let him pass without proving who he was, he ordered a leading civil servant to his office. A stern authoritarian, nicknamed 'Thrasher' since his schooldays, Mitchell railed against the constables' attitude, dismissing them as officious jobsworths and reportedly barking that they 'should have fucking known who I am'. Seeking to placate their new minister, the Cabinet Office submitted a formal complaint in which it was noted: 'There have been a handful of incidents where Cabinet ministers (including Andrew Mitchell, Secretary of State for International Development) have either not been allowed access … or have not been recognised/identified within a reasonable time period.'

The officers reluctantly accepted that they had to let Mitchell through once or twice a week without forcing him to produce identification. But when he became David Cameron's Chief Whip in September 2012, he was granted an office in Downing Street and began to cycle in and out of the front gates every day. In revenge for his earlier complaint, a group of guards began refusing to let him pass through the main gates on his bike, instead forcing him to dismount and wheel it through the pedestrian side entrance.

The incidents that led to Mitchell's demise began on the evening of 18 September 2012. Heading home at the end of a long day, he began to cycle down from his office in Downing Street and towards the main gates. One of the attendant constables asked him to dismount and use the side exit, prompting the retort: 'I am the government Chief Whip [and] I will be leaving via these gates.' The officer on duty angrily opened them for him, but that evening sent a memo to his superior, recording that Mitchell 'keeps requesting to leave Downing Street via the main vehicle gates', and was 'adamant he WAS GOING THROUGH THOSE GATES'. The protection squad vowed never to let him do so again, setting the stage for a major confrontation.

The next evening, Mitchell left his office for a meeting at the Carlton Club. As they had agreed, the policemen on duty refused to open the main gates for him. The events that followed remain hotly disputed. Everyone agrees that Mitchell demanded that the gates be opened

but was flatly refused each time. When he realised that further protest was futile, he got off his bike and stormed over to the pedestrian
gate, scowling and muttering under his breath. He was escorted by a
42-year-old constable named Toby Rowland. In his later note of the
incident in his log book, Rowland recorded that Mitchell had shouted
at him: 'Best you learn your fucking place ... you don't run this fucking
government ... you're fucking plebs...' It was also noted that there were
'several members of the public present', who were 'visibly shocked' by
the outburst. Mitchell remembered the altercation differently. He has
always vehemently denied calling the police 'plebs', but does admit
that he lost his temper and said with sarcasm: 'I thought you guys were
supposed to fucking help us.' According to Mitchell, he then got back
on his bike, told Rowland that he would be pursuing the matter with
his superiors, and cycled away.

News of the altercation reached the Prime Minister's private secretary the next morning. After a brief *mea culpa*, Mitchell promised
to apologise to Rowland for snapping at him. But, before he had the
chance to contact the policeman, he received a call from Ed Llewellyn,
Cameron's chief of staff. Llewellyn opened the call by saying: 'Hou-
ston, we have a problem.' The political editor of *The Sun* had been
in touch to say that they had the story and would be putting it on
the next day's front page. Mitchell was gobsmacked to hear for the
first time that he stood accused of calling the policemen 'plebs' and
'morons'.

He was soon summoned to a meeting with Cameron, Llewellyn,
Chancellor George Osborne and director of communications Craig
Oliver. The seniority of the attendees immediately worried the Chief
Whip – clearly the story was going to be a big problem. Protesting his
innocence, he emphatically repeated that he had not called anybody
a 'moron', let alone a 'pleb'. Cameron's priority was to minimise the

political fallout, because the allegations played neatly into the narrative portraying the Tories as a snobby elite dominated by sneering Old Etonians. Cameron knew that the opposition would not hesitate to play the 'class war' card. Desperate to prevent a public dispute between a well-heeled politician and a police officer, the Prime Minister ordered Mitchell to keep out of sight.

The press descended upon his various homes. Twenty photographers were stationed outside his constituency house in Sutton Coldfield, a further five went to his London flat, and eight more camped at the end of his drive in Nottinghamshire. His father and mother-in-law were chased for comment, his neighbours canvassed and his children followed. As he hid away, the newspapers published stories recounting his brusque manner and short temper, with examples drawn from his schooldays to his time as a minister. Hiding behind the blackout curtains he had erected, his mental health rapidly deteriorated. Having lost over a stone of weight in three weeks, he took to chain-smoking cigarillos while repeatedly checking his BlackBerry for any further updates. Unable to sleep and compulsively turning over the events in his mind, he desperately tried to remember any detail that might vindicate him. He later recounted: 'As I faced the wall at three in the morning, I wondered if I could really go on facing much more of this.'

After two weeks of constant headlines, the story showed no sign of calming down. Craig Oliver decided that the strategy must change, and ordered Mitchell to come out of hiding for an interview with Sky News. He was to apologise profusely on camera in the hope that his contrition would dampen the growing calls for his departure. George Osborne strongly disagreed with Oliver's suggested approach, and rang Mitchell in a forlorn attempt to advise him against it.

As Osborne had predicted, the interview was a disaster. Mitchell, who seemed flustered and uncertain, could give no satisfactory answer to the key question of whether he had used the word 'pleb' or not, merely stating that he had not used all the words attributed to him. As soon as it had been broadcast, he took a call from his friend, the political publisher and blogger Iain Dale, who asked him: 'Who the fuck told you to do that?' Far from bringing the curtain down on the story, Mitchell's faltering response ensured that it would continue into another week.

Later that day, the deputy Chief Whip, John Randall, arrived at Downing Street with some disturbing news. He had received an email from a constituent named Keith Wallis, who claimed to be a tourist that had witnessed the incident. According to Wallis's email, he had been sightseeing with his nephew and remembered Mitchell's 'yobbish' and 'totally unacceptable' behaviour. Crucially, Wallis said that he heard Mitchell shout 'you fucking plebs' as he marched towards the pedestrian gate. After telling Cameron's team, Randall called Mitchell to relay the contents of the email. The beleaguered Chief Whip was 'absolutely horrified' by what he heard, immediately shouted that he was being stitched up and hung up the phone. He later described this as the worst moment of his life.

The apparently independent corroboration of the police's account unsurprisingly undermined Cameron's faith in his Chief Whip. Mitchell later recalled: 'It was truly Kafka-esque. I was being systematically destroyed, and I knew it was not true but it had the apparent acquiescence of a senior whip, people in Downing Street and the media. I was on my knees with everything exploding around me.' The Prime Minister called him the morning after to say that he looked 'bang to rights' and should resign. If he refused, Cameron intended to sack him there and then. Having prepared carefully for the call, Mitchell was decisive in response. He insisted that he was being set up, and appealed strongly to Cameron's personal loyalty, asking him how he would feel 'when it is shown that this is a lie'. Faced with Mitchell's insistent denials and the implied threat that he would not go quietly, the Prime Minister acquiesced. He postponed his decision, and instead asked the Cabinet Secretary Jeremy Heywood to conduct a full inquiry into the affair.

Heywood came to a swift conclusion. On assessing the available CCTV and Wallis's emails, he found 'some inaccuracies and inconsistencies' between the various police accounts. He was also troubled by the apparently independent witness's blanket refusal to co-operate with his investigation. He advised the Prime Minister that there was not sufficient evidence to sack Mitchell, and suggested that there were unanswered questions about the reliability of the testimony. Conscious of the toxicity of the affair, however, Cameron decided to let matters rest as they were.

The press were not satisfied either with Heywood's verdict or Cameron's lack of action, and the story entered its third week. It even managed to eclipse revelations of the sex offences of the DJ Jimmy Savile as the BBC website's top news item. To avoid becoming an unwelcome distraction, Mitchell was forced to skip the Conservative Party conference in Birmingham, despite his constituency being in the city.

The ongoing campaign against the Chief Whip was loudly supported by the Police Federation, the body that functions as a trade union for police officers. Only the bravest politicians take on the Federation, a highly organised outfit that counts over nine out of ten officers as members and nurtures a visceral hatred of Tory governments. Within a week, policemen had been photographed across the country wearing shirts emblazoned with 'PC pleb and proud' and cufflinks with 'pleb' written on them. The organisation's London chairman joined the attacks by posting Mitchell's email address on Twitter and inviting his followers to get in touch. Within a week, Mitchell had received over a thousand abusive emails, with one calling him an 'upper class superior dick' and another simply reading: 'Resign, you despicable man!'

He received only lukewarm support from his colleagues. Home Secretary Theresa May, herself no friend of the Police Federation, maintained a studied silence. She and her fellow Cabinet ministers had decided not to wade into an unwinnable fight. Work and Pensions Secretary Iain Duncan Smith openly joked about his colleague's imminent demise, delighting in the plight of a man who had, ten years previously, helped to oust him as Tory leader. It was left to the unlikely figure of Chris Mullin, the former Labour minister and veteran exposer of police misconduct, to stand up for him. Mullin wrote in *The Times*: 'No sensible Prime Minister should surrender to the mob and the "mob" in this case is being orchestrated by the Police Federation, as big a bunch of head-bangers as one is ever likely to come across within the realms of sanity.'

After the Tory conference, Mitchell's local West Midlands Police Federation branch took matters further still by demanding a face-to-face meeting, ostensibly to let the Chief Whip explain himself. He accepted the invitation on the condition that the location, date and time of the meeting were kept private. In breach of that agreement, the details were leaked to the press, who were told that it would be a showdown during which Mitchell would finally be confronted.

The nation's media accordingly descended on Sutton Coldfield, with representatives from the Police Federation's PR agency arriving early to brief assembled journalists. After making his way through the crowds of reporters, Mitchell met the police representatives for forty-five minutes. They abruptly ended the meeting to ensure their subsequent public statement would make the six o'clock news. The

Federation representative announced to waiting cameras that Mitchell had failed to give a proper account of what he had said to PC Rowland: that is to say, he had, again, refused to accept that he had said 'pleb'. The Federation concluded that 'his position is untenable … he has to resign'.

The scandal was almost a month old when Parliament returned from its conference season break. Mitchell was relieved to get back to work, and sought sanctuary in the day-to-day life of the Whips' Office. His optimism was ill-founded, however, as it became clear that he had lost the support of his parliamentary colleagues. Cutting an increasingly gaunt and nervous figure, it was obvious that he was mentally shot through. A brutal Prime Minister's Questions followed, in which his reputation was savaged. Cameron struggled to defend him. At a crunch meeting of the backbench 1922 Committee that evening, four speakers denounced him, prompting a senior MP to describe him as a 'dead man walking'.

The killer blow was dealt by the Labour front bench, who contrived a clever ploy to force Mitchell's hand. They threatened to deploy an arcane parliamentary procedure that would censure him for uncourteous behaviour by docking his salary. As they had arranged for the motion to be put to a full debate in the House of Commons, Mitchell would have to whip his disgruntled colleagues into voting to save his own salary. This was a bridge too far for the proud Chief Whip, and he finally decided that it was time to go.

He sent the Prime Minister his letter of resignation on 20 October 2012. Explaining that he could no longer continue to bring the party into disrepute or put his family through the ordeal, he still refused to accept that he had called Rowland a pleb.

Mitchell was then immediately faced with a further dilemma. Cameron's advisors pleaded with him to drop his battle with the Police

Federation and withdraw from the limelight, but his friends took a different view, urging him to preserve his chances of a political comeback by exposing the police stitch-up. This time, Mitchell chose to fight.

Knowing that he could not enter the fray on his own, he asked his closest political ally David Davis to take charge of the response. Mitchell identifies Davis as a 'very, very rare thing in politics: a man who, if I were caught between enemy lines lying in a fox hole with a bullet in my leg with the tracer rounds flying over the top, would come and get me'. The affair had piqued the interest of Michael Crick, one of British politics' longest standing investigative broadcasters. The persistently obtrusive Channel 4 reporter determined to get to the bottom of the matter. He was the perfect man for the job. With a penchant for supposedly lost causes, he has cultivated a formidable reputation in Westminster for relentlessly exposing untruths and half-truths. Few wriggle off the hook on his watch.

Crick and his team at Channel 4 soon discovered that Keith Wallis, the 'tourist' whose corroborating testimony had proved fatal to Mitchell, was in fact a serving police officer. When interviewed by Crick, Wallis admitted that he had not even been in Whitehall that night. Further, CCTV footage obtained by Crick revealed that, contrary to the logbook entries, the street appeared to be almost deserted at the time.

Crick's findings were broadcast on 18 December 2012 in a special episode of Channel 4's *Dispatches*. The Prime Minister happened to be at home on the evening the programme screened, and was outraged at what he saw. He immediately ordered the Metropolitan Police Commissioner Bernard Hogan-Howe to get to the bottom of the conspiracy. Promising a 'ruthless search for the truth', Hogan-Howe launched an internal investigation codenamed 'Operation Alice', assigning thirty officers to co-ordinate the effort. They took over a thousand depositions and analysed hundreds of hours of phone records in the biggest internal review of its kind. In what some quipped was an ironic role reversal, Hogan-Howe utilised one of his more controversial powers and accessed *Sun* journalists' phone records without their permission.

This intrusion achieved its aim. It emerged that on the night of the incident, one of PC Rowland's colleagues, PC Glanville, Googled 'the Sun' before calling in and leaving a message for the political team. *The Sun*'s political editor returned the call and asked for paper records to corroborate the story. Glanville then texted another officer, PC Weatherley, who had witnessed the outburst, before forwarding her police logbooks to the press. Soon after, Weatherley sent a text to another officer boasting that she 'could topple the Tory government'.

Glanville and Weatherley were both sacked for leaking information and then lying to Operation Alice investigators about it. Glanville, who now works as a used car salesman in Essex, remains unrepentant, saying: 'I have no regrets about coming forward. I thought the public deserved to know how someone that senior in the government behaved … nobody was going to do anything about it. The Met's hierarchy are always more afraid of upsetting politicians than looking after their own.'

When questioned by Hogan-Howe, Wallis openly admitted that he had lied, but would not reveal how he had heard about the incident or which other officers were involved. He was dismissed from his job as a policeman and later sentenced to a year in jail.

The phone records revealed that Wallis was not the only person to offer fraudulent corroboration of Rowland's story. On the evening of the altercation, a woman called *The Sun*'s newsroom claiming to be a tourist that had witnessed the events. She was the source for the allegation that Mitchell had used the word 'moron'. It later emerged that the call had been made from Hitchingbrooke Hospital in Cambridgeshire, apparently by an on-duty nurse who was the partner of another of the policemen on the gates.

After Hogan-Howe's inquiry, Wallis had been jailed, three other police officers sacked and a further two placed on final written warnings. Newspaper columnists lined up to write apologetic pieces praising Mitchell's bravery. He should have let the matter rest there and quietly awaited a return to the Cabinet as a rehabilitated, indeed enhanced, figure. However, emboldened by the revelations and furious at how he had been treated, he could not resist wallowing in his victory. In an extensive interview with the *Sunday Times,* he accused the police of destroying his career in a smear campaign designed to promote their own political agenda. He later began a libel action against *The Sun* for printing the 'pleb' story. Despite the evidence of the subsequent stitch-up, PC Rowland continued to insist that he had been telling the truth, and in turn sued Mitchell for defamation. The final verdict on the whole affair lay with the courts.

It took nearly two years for the cases to be heard, ironically because the Court of Appeal decided to use a preliminary hearing to crack down on inefficient practice in the British legal system. The trial finally began in November 2014, over two years after the initial incident. The judge, Sir John Mitting, was required to answer a simple question: was it more likely than not that Mitchell used the word 'pleb'?

Rowland gave an inconsistent account at the trial. He offered several different descriptions of the location of Mitchell's outburst and claimed to have made his logbook entry as soon as the incident occurred, despite the CCTV footage showing that he did not. That footage also revealed that he had made a phone call after the altercation from the police phone box at the end of Downing Street. He claimed to have forgotten making this call, and insisted that he had no recollection of who had been on the other end of the line.

In contrast, Mitchell performed robustly in the dock under heavy fire from *The Sun*'s barrister, who accused him of being a 'Jekyll and Hyde character' with a 'capacity for menace'. He called upon a wide array of character witnesses to vouch for him. Tory grandee Ken Clarke said Mitchell was 'never dishonest or untruthful to my knowledge' and was 'a considerable public servant', while Sir Bob Geldof said that although he was prone to use all manner of swear words, Mitchell had never used the word 'pleb' in his earshot. Mitchell's former commanding officer General Sir Antony Walker declared that it was 'highly unlikely' that Mitchell would 'talk down to anyone'.

Set against the former minister, however, was the corroborated testimony of the police officers and several contemporaneous police logs supporting their allegations. He also stood accused of being involved in a similar incident in 2005 outside the Palace of Westminster, in which he apparently told a security officer that he was 'too important to stop for you', before telling him to 'stop being so aggressive, you little shit'.

It took the judge two weeks to reach his verdict, which he read out to a crowded courtroom on 27 November 2014. The air was thick with tension as the assembled onlookers waited for the result. The former minister sat in silence at the back of the court. Mitting kept everybody in suspense until the very end of his long judgment, when he finally revealed that, in his view, Mitchell probably did use the word 'pleb'.

The judge reached this conclusion for three main reasons. First, the timing of the CCTV fitted Rowland's account of the amount of words that were exchanged better than Mitchell's. Second, Mitchell could not be sure of what he had said, while Rowland specifically remembered hearing the word 'pleb'. Third, and critically, Mitting found Rowland to be an entirely trustworthy character. For Mitchell to win the case, the policeman would have had to have invented the use of the word 'pleb' and then chosen to maintain his lie. Having considered their respective characters, the judge concluded that Rowland was 'not the sort of man who would have had the wit, imagination or inclination to invent on the spur of the moment an account of what a senior politician had said to him in a temper' and 'still less to perform the pantomime which their invention would require'. He finished the judgment by saying: 'For the reasons given, I am satisfied at least on balance of probabilities that Mr Mitchell did speak the words alleged or something so close to them as to amount to the same, including the politically toxic word "pleb".'

Rowland left the court in triumph, marching onto the steps of Fleet Street to tell the awaiting journalists and photographers that it was 'a huge regret that what happened at the gates of Downing Street more than two years ago has ended up here' and adding that he was delighted that 'my innocence, my integrity and my reputation as a police officer has been recognised'. Rowland called the pain he and his family had been through 'indescribable' and said it was 'particularly saddening because I was merely following procedures'.

It was then Mitchell's turn to face the press, flanked by the ever-loyal David Davis. After calmly thanking his legal team, family and friends for their support, Mitchell admitted that he was 'bitterly disappointed', but said that it was now 'time to bring the matter to a close and get on with our lives'. The affair had taken a major toll both on his mental health and his wallet. He was forced to pay PC Rowland £50,000, contributed around £500,000 to News Group's legal bill and had to pay hefty fees to his own solicitors. This necessitated a long departure from the public eye, as he took on several additional jobs, including acting as a consultant for an investment bank and offering a strategic intelligence firm his expert advice on controlling reputational damage. Mitchell decided against quitting as an MP, and still nurses hopes of a comeback. His best chance is if his friend David Davis, now Brexit Secretary, manouevres his way into No. 10.

What really happened at the gates of Downing Street? There are only three possibilities. First, that Mitchell did use the word 'pleb'. Second, that Rowland misheard what Mitchell said to him. Finally, it is possible that Rowland invented the 'pleb' insult to damage Mitchell. Whatever the truth, merely being accused of saying 'pleb' placed Mitchell in a political Catch-22 situation from which he could never recover. If the allegation was that he simply swore at the policeman, he would have apologised profusely and survived, whether he did so or not. But the injection of a class element to the dispute was always going to prove fatal. Once the allegation had been made, the truth became irrelevant. Mitchell's most impressive achievement was managing to survive for so long.

ANDREW MITCHELL TO DAVID CAMERON

Dear David,

It is with enormous regret – not least because of the tremendous support and loyalty you have shown me during recent weeks – that I am writing to resign as your Chief Whip.

Over the last two days it has become clear to me that whatever the rights and wrongs of the matter I will not be able to fulfil my duties as we both would wish. Nor is it fair to continue to put my family and colleagues through this upsetting and damaging publicity.

I have made clear to you – and I give you my categorical assurance again – that I did not, never have, and never would call a police officer a 'pleb' or a 'moron' or used any of the other pejorative descriptions attributed to me. The offending comment and the reason for my apology to the police was my parting remark 'I thought you guys were supposed to f***ing help us'. It was obviously wrong of me to use such bad language and I am very sorry about it and grateful to the police officer for accepting my apology.

I am immensely grateful to you for giving me the opportunity to serve as your Development Secretary for seven and a half years, both in Opposition and in Government. I believe Britain, under your leadership, has made real progress in transforming the lives and the opportunities of some of the world's poorest people and that we will continue to do so as we deploy an expertise and commitment which show Britain at its best.

I now intend to concentrate on serving my constituents in the Royal town of Sutton Coldfield to the best of my ability and giving you the strong support you rightly deserve from all members of the Conservative Party.

With every good wish,

Yours ever,

Andrew Mitchell

DAVID CAMERON TO ANDREW MITCHELL

Dear Andrew,

Thank you for your letter. I was sorry to receive it, but I understand why you have reached the conclusion that you have, and why you have decided to resign from the Government.

I regret that this has become necessary, and am very grateful for all you have done, both in Government and in Opposition – as well as for the kind words in your letter.

I am in no doubt that your work in the field of international development has made a really important contribution – not only to the Conservative Party, but more importantly to Britain's standing in the world, and above all to international efforts to tackle deep and sustained poverty.

You brought real passion to the job in Opposition, which you turned into more than two years of very successful work in Government.

You brought immense energy and dedication to the role, a focus on the world's poorest, and decisive progress on the key issues of vaccination against preventable diseases, maternal health and family planning that make the greatest difference to the greatest number of people.

You have also brought a proper accountability and transparency to the Department for International Development's work.

Under your leadership of the Department, Britain achieved a leading global role, which will be continued as Britain chairs the United Nations High Level Panel.

As we discussed in advance of the reshuffle, I wanted you to bring your organisational skill and energy to the important job of Chief Whip. It was clear to me that you had already made a strong start.

As you have acknowledged, the incident in Downing Street was not acceptable and you were right to apologise for it.

You have much to be proud of from your service on the Frontbench both in Opposition and in Government, and in your continued service to your constituents in Sutton Coldfield. I hope that, in time, you will be able to make a further contribution to public life.

Yours,

David

CHAPTER SIXTEEN

DOUGLAS CARSWELL
AND MARK RECKLESS

In March 2012, the rebellious Tory backbencher Douglas Carswell got to his feet in the House of Commons. As had happened so often before, he strayed from the whips' suggested list of questions, instead grilling the government on the Child Benefit Bill. Fellow Conservative Claire Perry, sitting in the next row, leaned across the front of her seat, face contorted with disgust, and reportedly shouted: 'Why don't you just fuck off and join UKIP?' She probably came to regret the suggestion two years later when he did cross the floor, taking his colleague Mark Reckless with him. By giving UKIP's populist insurgency a parliamentary presence, the pair played a key role in hastening the UK's departure from the European Union, the bloc they had despised for their whole lives in politics.

In a country where small parties usually fail to make an impression, UKIP managed to shake the political system to its foundations. Launched as the Anti-Federalist League in 1991 by an assortment of disaffected Thatcherites, the party initially provided a repository for politically homeless right-wingers. Over the next twenty years, however, its repertoire was expanded by tapping into growing rage against political correctness and multiculturalism. They began to attract a uniquely diverse base of supporters under the leadership of chain-smoking, beer-swilling demagogue Nigel Farage. In the south of England, former shire Tories were drawn in by the leader's irreverent disdain for Brussels' grey bureaucracy. But they also attracted scores of working-class ex-Labour supporters seeking to punish an establishment that had long ignored them, and who found a ready scapegoat for their problems in UKIP's anti-immigration message.

David Cameron inadvertently became UKIP's chief recruiting sergeant by breaking a promise to hold a referendum on the EU's Lisbon Treaty and then forming a coalition government with the pro-European Liberal Democrats. Yet more 'kippers' flocked to their self-declared 'people's army' when the Prime Minister scornfully labelled its supporters 'loonies, fruitcakes and closet racists'. They still lacked MPs, however, as Britain's 'winner-takes-all' electoral system makes small parties work disproportionately hard for limited rewards.

As the coalition parliament progressed, UKIP began to hoover up votes across the country. They were particularly successful along England's deprived eastern seaboard, stealing support from the main parties to win a series of local council seats. Most Tories feared that a crucial part of Thatcher's electoral empire had permanently broken free.

Teetotal, socially liberal and pro-migration, Douglas Carswell and Mark Reckless were unlikely 'kippers'. Apart from advocating as swift a divorce from Europe as possible, they shared almost no ideological purpose with the party to which they defected. Carswell, a radical libertarian, was the self-appointed brains of the pair. Although popular with his constituents, relentlessly enthusiastic and a sophisticated campaigner, he lacked his Prime Minister's easy charm. Colleagues described him as prickly and overly cerebral, and he felt 'shut out from the word go' when Cameron began to modernise the party in 2005. He soon settled into the role of a prematurely embittered backbencher.

Mark Reckless was the MP for Rochester and Strood, another poor coastal constituency. He cut a very different figure to the supremely confident Carswell. Timid, restrained and uncomfortable in his own skin, Reckless's instinct was to back away from confrontation. Despite this, his opposition to the European Union was as fervent as his colleague's and he was keen to do anything to advance their joint cause.

During the coalition parliament, the pair of dissidents exploited the government's small majority to heap pressure upon the Prime Minister. Aware that the previous two Tory governments were destroyed by the European question, Cameron, a pragmatic Eurosceptic, succumbed to widespread demand and, in 2013, promised that a future Tory government would hold an in–out referendum on EU membership. He did not, however, intend for Britain to leave the bloc or even to hold the referendum. With an overall majority at the next general election beyond his best expectations, there seemed little prospect that the referendum would happen. Cameron hoped that the meaningless promise would placate his Europhobic backbenchers and halt UKIP's advance.

It did neither. In January 2014, ninety-five Tory MPs signed a letter demanding a parliamentary veto on all past and future actions of the EU. As they all knew, this was incompatible with continued membership. Carswell didn't bother to maintain the pretence, admitting when he signed that 'my agenda in all of this is to get this country out of the EU'.

UKIP continued to surge on the back of Farage's jingoistic populism. Escaping sanction for comments that would have destroyed any conventional politician, the leader announced publicly that he was upset by foreigners speaking different languages on trains and would be uncomfortable with Romanian neighbours. With each outrageous statement, UKIP's support soared further, propelling them to an electoral high point in May 2014. They gained 127 council seats in the local elections in areas as diverse as Essex, Hull and Rotherham. More importantly, they beat the Conservatives, Labour and Liberal Democrats to win the European parliamentary elections. For the first time, the British people had elected over 25 per cent of their MEPs with express instructions to undermine the UK's membership of the EU and UKIP had won a national election.

Despite that, Carswell and Reckless identified a growing problem with UKIP's success. Voters undecided on the EU issue were, they realised, put off by UKIP's 'pound-shop populism' and Farage's divisive rhetoric. They knew that it would suit those campaigning to remain in the EU to make the Leave movement synonymous with Farage, for he repelled as many people as he attracted. As Carswell observed: 'If it became a choice between being rude about Romanian immigrants versus the economy, we would lose [any referendum] 60–40.' This 'Farage paradox' was confirmed by polling data: the more attention UKIP received, the fewer voters wanted to leave the EU.

For this reason, a clandestine group of Tories hatched a bold plan to take back control of Euroscepticism. They would infiltrate UKIP and neuter it from within. The idea was first conceived by Carswell and Reckless's close friend, the MEP and libertarian polemicist Daniel Hannan. The trio began to meet regularly in the Tate Britain, a location they deemed beyond the limited horizons of parliamentary journalists and safe from eavesdroppers. During those sessions, they laid the ground for the two MPs to defect, arranging top-secret meetings between Carswell and former UKIP leader Lord Pearson of Rannoch. Carswell later had lunch with Farage to make the offer in person.

The UKIP leader failed to spot the trap that had been laid for him and willingly snatched the bait. To him, the defections seemed the perfect way to crown his triumphant year. The plans were kept a closely guarded secret and, apart from the Tate Britain plotters, only Farage knew what was to come when a small crowd gathered for a late-summer press conference at the Institute of Civil Engineers in Westminster. The few journalists present were astonished to see Carswell stride into the room, take to the lectern and say: 'Good morning. I'm today leaving the Conservative Party and joining UKIP.' A visibly elated Farage bounced around the room afterwards, declaring the move 'just about the bravest and noblest thing I have seen in British politics in my lifetime'.

Carswell knew that his defection would dominate political coverage for days to come and initiated his detoxification campaign immediately. He used his short speech to tell his new party that they must drastically change, calling upon them to embrace feminism, disability rights and equality, before adding: 'UKIP must adapt to survive ... and let me make it absolutely clear: I'm not against immigration.' Refusing to follow the precedent of previous MPs who had crossed the floor of the House of Commons without seeking their constituents' permission, he announced that he would be resigning as an MP and stand in the consequent by-election under the UKIP banner. At the time, he said this was 'the only honourable thing to do'. He also realised that a by-election campaign would bring with it further publicity and a chance to project a new image of a respectable UKIP.

On the morning of Carswell's defection, the Prime Minister was relaxing at Chequers with his closest friends and advisors at what they called the 'start of term gathering'. When the announcement began, the whole team was discussing how they would move the agenda on from UKIP's recent gains. On cue, messages began to pepper their mobile phones from outraged colleagues. The team rushed into a little room by the front entrance and gathered around the small television to watch their colleague's treachery.

Cameron was surprisingly sanguine. Having worked with Carswell for many years, he respected him as an independent thinker who had always been upfront about his beliefs. Although he had defected, his voting pattern was unlikely to change, so he posed no immediate threat to Cameron's majority. Nonetheless, the team agreed that they must fight the upcoming by-election hard to deter any other defectors and arrest UKIP's momentum. The party's election guru Lynton Crosby, who was with Cameron at Chequers, texted his friend Boris Johnson, then London Mayor, angling for him to be the Conservative candidate. Johnson replied in seconds with a curt: 'No thanks!' Certain defeat to Carswell was not a tempting offer for the ambitious blond.

Chief Whip Michael Gove was despatched to root out any other would-be defectors. He was soon assured by one MP after another that there was no threat. Over a long lunch, Reckless promised that he would be staying put come what may. In fact, now reassured that Carswell's gamble had been successful, he was also ready to jump ship.

Only days after the lunch with Gove, Reckless ambushed his former allies on the eve of their party conference. Emerging on stage at UKIP's own conference, he was met with rapturous applause by an audience that had immediately guessed what was coming. After breathlessly blurting out that he was leaving the Conservatives to join UKIP, his voice was drowned out by the army of activists chanting: 'UKIP, UKIP, UKIP'. This was yet another blow dealt by the 'people's army', and seemed to be a further step towards electoral success.

Cameron was squashed up next to his advisors on a packed train when the news of Reckless's treachery was whispered into his ear. Although usually calm in a crisis, he could barely suppress his rage for the remainder of the journey. As soon as he made it to the safety of his car, he railed against Reckless, denouncing his erstwhile colleague as a malevolent liar and pathetic sidekick hanging onto Carswell's coattails. Touring around the conference drinks receptions that evening, he continued to abandon his usual discretion, complaining that party activists had 'knocked on doors, stuffed envelopes, licked stamps to get [Reckless's] fat arse on the Commons benches, and this is how he repays them'. He promised to 'throw the kitchen sink' at the upcoming by-election.

Coverage of the Tory conference was dominated by the twin defections. Farage then trailed news of a major announcement on the morning of Cameron's keynote speech, timed to take place just before the Prime Minister took to the conference stage. Panic spread among the Downing Street team. Glued to the television, they let out sighs of relief when Farage announced that the new convert was not another MP, but a former Tory donor called Arron Banks, who had previously pledged to give £100,000 to UKIP. After Foreign Secretary William Hague ridiculed that prior donation, adding that he'd never heard of Banks, the bombastic, attention-seeking insurance magnate upped his donation to £1 million. This generosity secured his dominance over UKIP politics for the next three years; as he put it, he 'had Farage by the short and curlies'.

As expected, Carswell trounced his former party in the Clacton by-election. He chose to spend the political capital he had earned at once, using his victory speech to set out a manifesto for a new UKIP, no longer obsessed with migrants or fearful of change, but focused upon disrupting the received wisdom of the past thirty years. He said:

> To my new party I offer these thoughts: humility when we win, modesty when we are proved right. If we speak with passion, let it always be tempered by compassion. We must be a party for all Britain and all Britons: first and second generation as much as every other. Our strength must lie in our breadth. If we stay true to that there is nothing we cannot achieve.

The rest of his speech channeled early English theologian John Wycliffe and Abraham Lincoln, imploring UKIP to campaign for government of the people, by the people, for the people' and calling for them to break down borders, not curb migration. This cerebral and overtly libertarian manifesto was lost on many members of his new party, who took little interest in the niche philosophy of their recent recruit. Farage thought it was a bizarre speech, perhaps fit for a nine-teenth-century coffee house, but not the front line of modern politics.

But at that stage the UKIP leader's more pressing concern was the Rochester and Strood by-election, in which Reckless was facing a tougher battle than Carswell had. The Tories co-ordinated a massive effort to defend the seat and halt UKIP's advance. Party chairman Lord Feldman diverted all available resources to the fight and David Cameron visited the constituency five times during the campaign. Farage responded in kind, spending a good deal of Banks's million-pound donation, despatching every activist he could to Rochester and fighting tirelessly door-to-door throughout the final days.

Reckless won the seat by 3,000 votes, in a victory described by Farage as a 'massive, massive' moment in his party's 'David v. Goliath battle' against the establishment. Over a series of celebratory pints, he triumphantly declared that UKIP was targeting 100 seats in the upcoming general election, adding that 'the balls are up in the air [in British politics]', and 'it is completely impossible now to say what will happen next'. Yet Reckless's victory was to mark the highest point of UKIP's fortunes, as their heightened profile brought with it greater scrutiny.

Political journalists feasted on the undisciplined movement and all manner of oddballs emerged from within their ranks. Long-standing 'kipper' Godfrey Bloom jovially described countries receiving gov-ernment aid as 'Bongo Bongo Land', characterised feminism as the pastime of 'shrill, bored middle-class women of a certain physical genre' and claimed that wives who failed to clean behind the fridge were 'sluts'. He was one of the saner characters to emerge. Another elected official blamed recent storms and heavy flooding across Britain on the government's decision to legalise gay marriage, saying that the Prime Minister had acted 'arrogantly against the gospel', prompting God to visit 'storms, disease, pestilence and war' upon the population. Perhaps the most damaging comments came from former leader Lord Pearson of Rannoch, who had declared in the past that Britain was under threat because 'the Muslims are breeding ten times faster than us' and the government would soon 'no longer [be] able to resist their demands'.

With only months to go before the general election, a pronounced split emerged between Farage and his two MPs. Carswell delivered a further speech urging members to stop making racist remarks, adding that the party should no longer tolerate 'pejorative comments about people's heritage and background'. Going further than ever before, he dismissed his members' desire for a bygone era by pointing out that 'far from being Merrie Olde England, life in pre-industrial Britain was grim'. Adding that 'a dislike of foreigners is not merely offensive, but absurd', he again implored his party to promote an inclusive internationalist agenda with an optimistic outlook for the sunlit uplands that lay ahead. He supplemented the speech with an act of pure idolatry by writing an article in *The Times* in which he argued that Enoch Powell, author of the infamously reactionary Rivers of Blood speech and a hero to most kippers, had been 'wrong about immigration'.

Farage considered the article tantamount to a palace coup, and vowed to meet fire with fire. Dismissing the former Tory's electoral tactics as 'PPE bollocks', he removed him from all strategic roles in the general election campaign and reset UKIP's core message to be 'immigration, immigration, immigration and Nigel'.

Farage hired a new set of advisors on the recommendation of friends in the American alt-right movement, which would later propel

Donald Trump to the White House. Prominent among them was a Twitter shock-jock named Raheem Kassam, who had previously headed up the British outpost of the alt-right Breitbart website. Their strategy was to inflame UKIP's natural supporters by saying the unsayable, breeding publicity and shifting the debate onto Farage's ground. Kassam was reportedly responsible for the new tactics, which became known as 'shock and awful'. Long-term UKIP staffers soon spotted the change in Farage, with one of his MEPs describing him as 'snarling, thin-skinned and aggressive', while long-serving press officer Gawain Towler admitted that Kassam helped unleash a side of his personality 'that had not been given the same amount of licence in the past'. According to Towler, he had previously 'floated above the nastier side of UKIP', and 'everybody had liked him', but 'in the campaign, suddenly he became as toxic as the party, and that was a big change'.

Farage leapt at every chance to make a controversial intervention in the general election campaign. He scandalised many by responding to a brutal terrorist attack in Paris by claiming that there was 'a fifth column' of Islamists living in the UK fuelled by mosques 'pushing a deeply unpleasant and anti-Christian heritage culture'. Barely out of the headlines as polling day approached, he also complained about women breastfeeding in public, and then used a televised debate to accuse sick foreigners of flocking to the UK for free HIV treatment.

Carswell and Reckless realised that their plan to detoxify the party was doomed, and decided instead to focus solely on winning their seats. Running a wholly independent campaign, Carswell excised Farage from his election literature and even rang the central office to ensure that UKIP advertising vans bearing Farage's face did not stray into his constituency.

On 7 May 2015, David Cameron's Conservatives won an astonishing and unexpected general election victory, while UKIP had a terrible night. Reckless lost his seat to his former party by 7,000 votes, his gamble a miserable failure. Farage fell over 2,800 votes short of victory in South Thanet, failing to enter Parliament at the seventh time of asking. Although UKIP soared into a strong second place in seats across the country, their lack of electoral nous meant that they ended up with fewer MPs than they started with. Carswell was the only winner.

There was one upside to UKIP's dismal performance – the Tories' surprise majority meant that an in–out referendum on membership of the EU was unexpectedly within touching distance. Carswell was also delighted when Farage confirmed his resignation as UKIP leader. He took to the airwaves on the Sunday after the general election to call for a fresh start for UKIP, adding, in a thinly veiled criticism of his former leader, that 'optimism works in politics and I think perhaps we needed a little bit more of it'.

This intervention prompted Farage to reconsider his position. As rumours swelled that he might backtrack and return to the leadership to lead the fight to leave the EU, he received a call from Carswell. It was the first time the pair had spoken in months. Farage's aide Chris Bruni-Lowe, who heard the call, remembered a panicked Carswell saying: 'You can't do that, you're toxic. You'll damage the cause,' prompting Farage to think, 'well, fuck this', and decide to make a return to the leadership. Untroubled by the procedural niceties, UKIP's governing body swiftly offered to forget his previous resignation. With Farage officially back, the party descended into open warfare as Carswell joined with fellow cast-offs to lead an open insurrection against the restored leader.

Soon after the general election, the Prime Minister embarked upon a frenzied effort to renegotiate Britain's relationship with the EU. While he toured European capitals, his internal opponents stepped up their preparations for the forthcoming 'Leave' campaign by setting up a group called Business for Britain. This was ostensibly a think tank led by Carswell's friend, political strategist Matthew Elliott. Working with Tory backbenchers, the group intended to apply to the Electoral Commission to be chosen as the official 'Out' campaign for the referendum, granting them a free mailshot, a suite of TV broadcasts, £600,000 of public funds to spend and the right to raise a further £7 million. Elliott, like Carswell, was determined to sideline Farage from the campaign. This incensed UKIP donor Arron Banks, who decided to found a rival group called Leave.EU and compete for the designation. Dismissing Elliott as a tedious careerist, interested only in becoming 'Lord Elliott of Loserville', Banks started to collect data from UKIP supporters.

Farage used his speech to UKIP's conference in September 2015 to announce that the party would be fully supporting Leave.EU in their attempt to be designated the official 'Leave' campaign. Chris Bruni-Lowe confirmed that Farage did this chiefly because 'it would piss off Carswell'. He achieved his aim. Assembled delegates saw the party's only MP, who had been watching from the back of the room, storm off seething with anger. His worst fears had been realised, for he was convinced that a Farage-led referendum campaign would scupper any chance of leaving the EU in his lifetime. A young journalist later spied Carswell and Banks in a corridor of the venue at daggers drawn and apparently ready to descend into fisticuffs. Later that day, Banks publicly labelled the MP 'borderline autistic'.

As the country moved towards referendum day, UKIP split down the middle. Carswell and like-minded kippers joined with Business for Britain, now rebranded Vote Leave. Farage toured the country with Leave.EU, which had developed into 'Grassroots Out', a cross-party union made up of fringe political figures including the indefatigable leftist George Galloway and Tory jovial oddball Peter Bone.

As the Tate Britain conspirators had predicted, the official 'Remain' campaign tried as hard as possible to place Farage front and centre of the Leave campaign. He continued to pursue his 'shock and aweful' strategy, bemoaning the 'free movement of Kalashnikov rifles' for Islamists, warning that 70 million Turkish people could move to Britain if it remained in the EU and unveiling a poster with a line of middle-eastern migrants to claim that the UK was at 'Breaking Point'.

Carswell staunchly avoided his UKIP colleagues, instead touring the country onboard the Vote Leave battle bus as supporting artist to Tory talisman Boris Johnson and Labour 'Lexiteer' Gisela Stuart. He despaired at the political illiteracy of Farage's antics, noting: 'I do not see how there can have been any electoral logic in doing what he did. In my view it was all about trying to be the centre of attention.'

There is not yet any agreed explanation for why the majority of British people chose to leave the European Union. The vote has been characterised variously as a cry of anguish from the dispossessed, a protest against the Tory government, a rejection of open immigration policy or the result of Labour leader Jeremy Corbyn's lacklustre failure to energise his voters. What it did not represent was a revival of Carswell's brand of libertarianism: the central tenets of the Vote Leave campaign were the expansion of the state by giving £350 million a week to the NHS and the imposition of strong curbs on migration.

Despite being sidelined in the campaign, Farage was happy to take credit for the victory. Positioning himself worldwide as 'Mr Brexit', he declared 23 June 2016 to be the UK's 'Independence Day', before quitting as UKIP leader for the second time in a year. This time there was to be no immediate return. His central political ambition fulfilled, he announced that, having got his country back, he now wanted his life back.

The Brexit vote threw all of Britain's political parties into a state of turmoil, with the Tories and Labour indulging in rounds of recrimination and destructive leadership contests. But the vitriol within UKIP was unmatched by any other party. After figures in the party governance set the leadership election rules to exclude Carswell, Reckless or any prominent ally, the Faragists appeared once more to be in the ascendency. Then, to widespread surprise, their favoured successor, Steven Woolfe, was banned from standing after letting his membership lapse by mistake and submitting his nomination papers minutes after the deadline. The leadership battle became a fight between UKIP figures with lower profiles. Despite failing to stand as an MP in 2015, attending none of the leadership hustings, giving no interviews and not setting out a single policy, Farage ally Diane James emerged victorious.

Her leadership of the party was a disaster. Frustrated by her lack of influence, she resigned after eighteen days and soon quit the party altogether to sit as an independent MEP. Rumours abounded that Farage had instructed her to trigger another ballot so that Woolfe could replace her. Now eligible again, Woolfe was the early favourite to win the second contest in two months, but his bid imploded again, and this time in the most dramatic of circumstances. Following a reported fist fight in the European Parliament with fellow MEP Mike Hookem, he collapsed and was hospitalised with a brain injury. Withdrawing his bid before he was inevitably banned from running, he, like James, quit the party for good.

UKIP eventually turned to Paul Nuttall, a Liverpudlian stalwart with an apparent proclivity for exaggeration. It was soon alleged that Nuttall wrongly claimed on his website that he had friends that died at Hillsborough, was the proud possessor of a PhD and had played professional football for Tranmere Rovers. UKIP had become a laughing stock just as Theresa May's Tories were in the ascendancy. Their voters began to desert them in droves in favour of May's vow to make a success of Brexit.

Enough was enough for Carswell, who realised that his job was done. He announced in March 2017 that he was quitting the party to sit as an independent, saying: 'Like many of you, I switched to UKIP because I desperately wanted us to leave the EU. Now we can be certain that that is going to happen, I have decided that I will be leaving UKIP… amicably, cheerfully and in the knowledge that we won.' Reckless, then sitting as a UKIP member of the Welsh Assembly, soon followed suit, announcing a few weeks later that he would be switching back to the Conservatives. This time neither triggered by-elections, prompting allegations of rank hypocrisy and a bid by Arron Banks to fund a local insurgency against Carswell.

Theresa May called a snap general election less than a month after the pair's departure from UKIP. Unable to run as a Conservative candidate, Carswell decided to leave politics for good and did not re-contest his seat. His parting blow to UKIP was a wholehearted and unconditional endorsement of the Tory candidate.

That general election spelled the end of UKIP as a relevant force, as it scraped under 2 per cent of the vote. Decimated, the party was left without national representation, with limited access to lobby journalists and teetering on the brink of insolvency. Soon to lose its MEPs and the money that came with them, they had to relocate their head office from Westminster to a small business park in Newton Abbot. Three months after the general election, UKIP held another leadership election after Paul Nuttall resigned. This time UKIP members faced a choice between an unknown man who argued that a gay donkey had raped his horse, a fanatical agitator who had dubbed Islam evil and an amiable computer game designer who argued that the UK would thrive post Brexit by mining the asteroid belt after assembling the world's first flying aircraft carrier. The loonies and fruitcakes had returned, and the racists were no longer living in the closet.

Carswell considers himself to be a footnote in political history. Yet if, as he claims, his plan was to destroy UKIP as a toxic force, reduce Farage's influence over the Brexit movement and facilitate the UK's withdrawal, then he and Reckless are rare examples of politicians who bowed out having succeeded in their aims. In claiming that level of foresight, however, Carswell is attempting to rewrite his own history. Nobody predicted the Tory victory in the 2015 general election, and without that astonishing success there would have been no Leave campaign for Farage to spoil. Carswell and Reckless must have joined UKIP with genuine ambitions to transform it into a libertarian insurgency, increasing rather than diminishing its influence. He did not, however, count on the stubborn resistance of Farage, who was willing to scuttle his own party before letting it fall into the hands of the 'Tory posh boys'.

CHAPTER SEVENTEEN

DAMIAN GREEN

Damian Green was not the first Cabinet minister to be felled by allegations involving pornography. That dubious honour was claimed by Jacqui Smith, who quit as Labour's Home Secretary in 2009 after she unwittingly billed the public for two pay-per-view porn films watched by her husband. Although she was largely blameless, the tabloid feeding frenzy that followed left her with no option but to beat an undignified retreat from high office.

As fate would have it, Smith also played a part in the second Cabinet resignation that revolved around pornography, that of the Tory First Secretary of State in December 2017. Green's downfall was a more complex affair. The train of events that led to his departure began with allegations that he had behaved inappropriately towards a young woman. But in the probe into his conduct that followed, that issue was swiftly overshadowed by sensational claims made against him by former Metropolitan Police officers. In that sense, his resignation has more in common with fellow ex-Tory Cabinet minister Andrew Mitchell, who also went head to head with the police and lost.

Green's saga began nearly a decade before his eventual resignation, in early 2008. Smith was then in her first year as the Home Secretary, yet to face her own drama involving pornography allegations. All was not well at the Home Office. Smith could not understand why her Tory opposite numbers, first David Davis and then Dominic Grieve, always seemed to be one step ahead of her. The newspapers were filled with stories about her department's ineptitude and civil servants' errors, including revelations that the Home Office certified 11,000 illegal immigrants to work as security guards and employed another as a cleaner in the House of Commons. Smith had instructed officials to keep both blunders quiet, as there was 'no explanation good enough for press officers or ministers to use'.

Sir David Normington, the Permanent Secretary at the department, grew increasingly concerned by the leaks. The old-fashioned mandarin suspected that one of his department's officials was maliciously sending the material to the Tories. His instincts proved right. The mole was 26-year-old junior staffer Christopher Galley, an employee in Smith's private office. He secretly harboured ambitions to become a Conservative MP, and when he started his job in 2006 he sent a secret missive to the Tories offering his assistance.

Galley was assigned to Damian Green, then a shadow immigration minister. Green soon became Galley's handler, convincing him to stay at the Home Office and to continue leaking adverse stories. Hoping to secure a plum job with the Tories when his mission came to an end, he duly supplied them with information exposing the Home Office's chaotic management of migration.

In June 2007, Galley came into possession of twenty incriminating documents that he handed over to the party, which strategically released them one after the other. Each story was deployed to prompt a statement from Smith that could be rapidly undermined by another embarrassing leak. She was made to look like a fool, as her shadows ran rings around her. It was opposition politics at its best.

As a New Labour Home Secretary, Smith's political life expectancy was roughly comparable to that of a wife of Henry VIII. She was, as a result, desperate to stem the flow of leaks. After an internal inquiry, which failed to unmask Galley, and a series of blazing rows with Normington, Smith deployed her most potent weapon. The leaks were reported to counter-terrorism police for investigation as a national security issue. As none of the documents released were top secret, this was a decision many later considered to be an inappropriate use of a scant resource.

The officer assigned to the case was Bob Quick, then Assistant Commissioner for Special Operations at the Metropolitan Police. Quick was one of the most senior policemen in the UK, and at the time a leading candidate for the vacant position of the Metropolitan Police Commissioner. He spied an opportunity to burnish his reputation with the Home Secretary at an ideal moment, and his team began to monitor every move at the Home Office from the shadows.

It took Quick three weeks to expose the culprit, and only then because Galley made a rudimentary mistake: he slipped the Tories a letter written by Smith to the Prime Minister Gordon Brown warning that crime figures would rise in the imminent recession. This letter was duly released to the press. It had never been sent to Brown, however, and in the outcry following its publication it transpired that very few people had enjoyed access to the draft. Suspicion soon fell on the young functionary, who was taken into custody on 19 November 2008. After seventeen hours of questioning by Britain's leading counter-terrorism specialists, he cracked and confessed that Damian Green had been his contact.

Receiving classified documents is not a criminal offence, but it is illegal to assist another in their commission of a crime. The officers conducting the investigation decided that there was sufficient evidence to arrest Green for aiding and abetting misconduct in public office. Smith was not alerted before the police moved on the shadow minister, despite the political ramifications. On 27 November, Green was arrested without warning in his constituency of Ashford, Kent. At the same time, nine officers arrived unannounced at his family home in west London. The detectives combed the house room by room as his incredulous wife looked on in horror. Private documents were rifled through, sheets were stripped from beds and the couple's intimate love letters were read. The officers even checked his fifteen-year-old daughter's homework.

Green was taken to a police station and questioned at length. On his release, he made a defiant statement outside Parliament, saying:

> I was astonished to have spent more than nine hours today under arrest for doing my job … I emphatically deny I have done anything wrong … I have many times made public information that the government wanted to keep secret – information that the public has a right to know. In a democracy, opposition politicians have a duty to hold the government to account. I was elected to the House of Commons precisely to do that and I certainly intend to continue doing so.

Tory leader David Cameron sprung to his colleague's defence, branding the police actions 'Stalinesque' and demanding that Smith explain herself. Before Green was taken into custody, three police officers had visited Parliament to meet the Serjeant at Arms Jill Pay, the official responsible for security in the Commons. Without disclosing Green's name, the trio told her that they proposed to raid an MP's office. The Serjeant at Arms was under no obligation to permit the police to enter Parliament, but they warned that a warrant would be obtained if she refused. Labouring under the assumption, which she would later learn was false, that the Director of Public Prosecutions had approved the raid, she granted the police permission to return.

The Speaker, former Labour MP Michael Martin, failed to prevent Green's office being scoured by a team of officers. Despite strong protestations from one of David Cameron's advisors, who was summarily ordered to leave, they rummaged through his papers and confiscated his computers.

The raid on Parliament united politicians of all parties. Former Conservative Home Secretary Michael Howard said that the arrest proved Labour's 'contempt for Parliament', invoking the memory of the 1642 Civil War, while veteran leftist Tony Benn was just as incredulous, warning that 'I may sound strangely medieval, but once the police can interfere with Parliament, I tell you, you are into a police state'. For Liberal Democrat leader Nick Clegg, the raid was 'something you might expect from a tin-pot dictatorship, but not a modern democracy'. The Speaker stood accused of turning a blind eye to a constitutional outrage, failing to preserve parliamentary privilege and abrogating his responsibility to defend MPs from an authoritarian government.

Five months later, the Crown Prosecution Service decided that neither Galley nor Green could be prosecuted. There was no real prospect of convicting either of any crime, and it was not in the public interest to try. The police had spent over £5 million of public money on their investigation, and further money was wasted as Green battled to force them to delete his DNA from their database and purge the records of the raid.

Jacqui Smith survived the row because she had not known that the police were planning to move on Green, and, even if she had, could not have interfered in their operation. Bob Quick, however, was less fortunate. The controversy scuppered his chances of securing the top job of Metropolitan Police Commissioner. He was also subjected to embarrassing news stories about his wife's business, for which he blamed Green and his allies.

In a move he later regretted, Quick accused the Tories 'and their press friends' of 'acting in a wholly corrupt way' to try to undermine his investigation – an accusation he later retracted. Soon afterwards, he was forced into retirement after being photographed entering Downing Street mistakenly displaying a document setting out a planned counter-terror operation, in a blunder that inspired an episode of the BBC's political satire *The Thick of It*. According to Jacqui Smith, Quick thought that his axing for this mistake came after a lack of support from London Mayor Boris Johnson that might have been related to the Green incident. It was widely thought that he entered retirement angry at the press, the Tories and Green himself. He came to be known by the moniker 'Bitter Bob', and was said to nurse a consuming thirst for revenge.

By late 2017, Green had ascended the political ladder to sit at the heart of Theresa May's shaky minority administration. May had endured a nightmare year. She had called an election that cost her party its majority, squandered its twenty-point lead in the opinion polls, felled her two principal advisors and rendered her a figure of public ridicule. Politically scuttled, short of allies and at high risk of a coup, she appeared to keep her place only as a human shield to absorb the bullets of Brexit.

Green, an old university contemporary of the Prime Minister, was one of the few frontbenchers who stuck with her throughout her lowest period. With loyalty in short supply, he earned promotion after claiming to be May's closest friend in politics. Appointed First Secretary of State, a role that made him the de facto Deputy Prime Minister, he sat at the apex of government and on nineteen of twenty-one

Cabinet committees. Despite some critics dubbing him 'Peter Mandelson without the power', he came to be viewed as a crucial figure of stability.

His fall from those lofty heights was triggered by a shockwave from the earthquake that was the #MeToo phenomenon, which began with movie mogul Harvey Weinstein in October 2017. After a series of women accused the Hollywood mega-producer of sexual assault and harassment, others all over the world were emboldened to speak up about their own experience of unwanted sexual encounters. That movement soon spread to Westminster, with men of all political parties and rank, from Members of Parliament to junior assistants, accused of inappropriate behaviour, harassment and even rape.

The scandal, dubbed 'Pestminster', escalated at the beginning of November after Kate Maltby, a 31-year-old PhD student and journalist, approached a reporter at the *The Times* with her story. She was a family friend of Green and, having been involved with a centrist Tory think tank, was in two minds about pursuing a career in politics. She said she met up with Green, thirty years her senior, in a bar in Waterloo in 2015 to discuss her potential political career. The pair gossiped about two figures engaging in sexual relations, at which point Green was said to have described his own wife, Alicia Collinson, as 'very understanding'. Maltby claimed that she then felt 'a fleeting hand against my knee – so brief, it was almost deniable'. She said the encounter left her feeling 'angry' and 'professionally compromised'.

Following the disputed encounter, Maltby said she had avoided contacting Green for around a year. In May 2016, she appeared in *The Times* as the author of a feature about corsets, for which she was photographed in one. Green subsequently sent her a text saying, 'Long time no see. But having admired you in a corset in my favourite tabloid I feel impelled to ask if you are free for a drink anytime?' She ignored this missive, she later told the newspaper, but said she dropped him a line several months later to congratulate him after he was made Work and Pensions Secretary.

Their subsequent relationship, as revealed in text messages, appeared to be friendly. She sent him one message betting bottles of wine that he was the source of a story in the press, for example, while in another she suggested they 'catch up when things calm down' – an invitation he welcomed. Maltby herself said in the *Times* article in which she made the allegations about the encounter at the bar: 'Since he joined the Cabinet I have exchanged many texts with him about political gossip. If you had the mobile number of Theresa May's No. 2, wouldn't you?'

Many commentators, including high-profile feminists and Labour politicians, branded the First Secretary's actions plainly inappropriate and began to call for his head. Green disputed Maltby's account of events and denied making sexual advances towards her or touching her knee. In the febrile atmosphere surrounding the Pestminster scandal, the Prime Minister was forced to order an investigation into her deputy and ally. She referred Green's case to Sue Gray, the Director General of the Propriety and Ethics Team in the Cabinet Office, who immediately commenced a probe into the affair.

The issue split opinion in Westminster, with some questioning exactly what Green had done wrong. His supporters argued that Maltby's story, if true, was less serious than many other allegations flying around Parliament. He stood accused of making an unsuccessful advance that was not followed up. They argued that, if true, such an episode was unedifying but not egregious.

The text messages were submitted to the inquiry by both sides and adduced by Green's supporters as exculpatory evidence showing that even if a clumsy pass had been made in the Waterloo bar, Maltby did not appear scarred or upset by it. The most damning verdict on

Maltby appeared a day later in the *Daily Mail*, which portrayed her as an ambitious, manipulative sycophant with a 'flair for self-promotion'. In an open provocation of women's rights campaigners, the article was headlined 'One Very Pushy Lady'.

Green reasoned that his denial, the text message record and Maltby's request for an apology rather than a resignation meant he would not be sacked. There was certainly no risk that he would be charged with a crime. Considering himself safe for the moment, he hoped that the investigation would take some time. He planned to stay out of the news, lie low and wait for the Pestminster scandal to abate.

He did not, however, wager on the timely return of his old enemy. Bob Quick had watched Green ascend through the ranks over the previous nine years. When Green stood accused of sexual harassment, Quick submitted a statement to Gray's inquiry. It revealed that when scouring the hard drives of Green's parliamentary computer in 2008, his team had discovered that the internet search history included pornographic websites. Quick was also in touch with journalists at the *Sunday Times* about his claims, which were launched into the public arena by the newspaper. The paper's story said one of the investigating officers who had viewed the material found on the computer had described it as 'extreme'. The story was later followed up by unsubstantiated whispers from anonymous sources that the porn had been violent.

Green was warned of the story the night before publication. Despite receiving threatening letters from Green's lawyers, the *Sunday Times* decided that, in the context of the sexual harassment allegations, the story was in the public interest and went ahead in publishing it.

As the paper went to print, Green issued a late-night statement via Twitter, which stated:

This story is completely untrue and comes from a tainted and untrustworthy source. I've been aware for some years that the discredited former Assistant Commissioner Bob Quick has tried to cause me political damage by leaking false information about the raid on my Parliamentary Office. No newspaper has printed this story due to the complete lack of any evidence. It is well-known that Quick, who was forced to apologise for alleging that the Conservative Party was trying to undermine him, harbours deep resentment about his press treatment during the time of my investigation. More importantly, the police have never suggested to me that improper material was found on my Parliamentary computer, nor did I have a 'private' computer as has been claimed. The allegations about the material and computer, now 9 years old, are false, disreputable political smears from a discredited police officer acting in flagrant breach of his duty to keep the details of a police investigation confidential, and amount to little more than an unscrupulous character assassination.

The statement was Green's first mistake. It was overly emotional, too complicated and accompanied by private briefing from sources close to him dismissing the whole story as nonsense. Most commentators thought that he had denied both that he had watched the pornography and that he had been told of its discovery. He would have been better advised simply to say that the allegations were denied and, at any rate, were irrelevant to the ongoing investigation into his conduct.

This element of the unfolding saga also divided MPs and commentators. Many noted that watching porn at work would constitute gross misconduct warranting immediate dismissal for employees in most companies. Others, however, were shocked that someone could be attacked publicly by an ex-policeman using material gathered years ago in a fruitless investigation.

Andrew Mitchell, still smarting from his own war with the police, appeared across the airwaves to condemn Quick's behaviour. As he had for Mitchell, the Brexit Secretary David Davis rode into battle for Green, and sources briefed journalists that he would resign from the Cabinet in protest if the First Secretary were sacked. He personally lobbied the Prime Minister in support of Green, and set up a 'war room' in his private office to firefight the allegations. Many shared his sympathy. Jim Waterson, the political editor of BuzzFeed UK, said that 'the headline on this Damian Green story should be "The police don't delete your data when ordered to do so and are liable to leak details of the legal porn they found in order to embarrass you".'

Quick denied any suggestion that he was pursuing a vendetta, or was motivated by revenge, coyly releasing a statement claiming that 'I am in no way motivated politically and bear no malice whatsoever to Damian Green' and saying that he was considering legal action against the First Secretary.

With the assistance of his allies, Green managed to tough out the bad press for the next two weeks and shift the narrative onto Quick's behaviour. His opponents were far from finished. *The Sun* was anonymously briefed that the pornography found on Green's computer included 'violent hardcore images', some of which were 'so extreme that police took advice from the CPS on whether to prosecute'. It was claimed that possession of them would now be illegal. All of this turned out to be untrue, but heaped further pressure on the embattled First Secretary.

After another week of criticism, another retired policeman, Neil Lewis, provided a copy of his police notebook to the BBC. Lewis had worked for Quick on the 2008 investigation. The notebook seemed to contain reference to pornography found on the parliamentary computer. Lewis accompanied the disclosure with an interview, in which he said that he had been 'shocked' by the material, which comprised 'several thousand' images.

He also claimed that Green must be lying when he said that he had not accessed the porn. According to Lewis, 'it was ridiculous to suggest that anybody else' could have viewed the images because 'in between browsing pornography, he was sending emails from his account, his personal account [and] reading documents'. Lewis added to the calls for Green's immediate dismissal, arguing that 'if a police officer does that, or anyone else, you'd be dismissed, you'd be thrown out'.

The intervention of a second former police officer prompted further criticism. Police watchdog Sir Thomas Winsor released a statement indicating that the police had a duty of confidentiality extending beyond retirement. Others noted with heavy irony that Lewis was neither the head of the House of Commons HR department nor the enforcer of its members' IT usage policy. As Lewis's disclosures did not serve any obvious public interest, he was suspected of political motives. That perception increased days later in the wake of revelations that he had 'liked' anti-Tory posts on social media that instructed Michael Gove to 'fuck off' and dubbed George Osborne 'Cunty McCuntface'.

Gray's inquiry was a prolonged one, with its outcome delayed as the Brexit talks stalled and Theresa May lost two other Cabinet ministers in quick succession: Michael Fallon, who was also caught up in the Pestminster scandal and resigned following revelations of inappropriate behaviour towards women; and Priti Patel, who had engaged in personal diplomacy while on holiday in Israel, in a breach of the ministerial code. Losing a third minister could have prompted the collapse of her government.

Perhaps for that reason, May offered tacit support to Green through the investigation. She gave her indirect endorsement by letting him sit next to her in the House of Commons and asking him to stand in at Prime Minister's Questions when she was away. It looked as though her team was testing the waters with private briefings after a selection of journalists reported that Green was expected to survive. This news was met with a muted response, perhaps because the pornography allegations seemed to have been prompted by a vendetta, and the harassment allegations were milder than other incidents that had been reported. By late December, almost nobody expected Green to be sacked, and it appeared neither Quick nor Lewis had any further cards to play.

Gray's verdict was delivered to May on the morning of 18 December. The Prime Minister was experiencing her first upswing in fortune since the general election, after winning plaudits for concluding the first stage of Brexit negotiations. The full report has not been published, but a summary of its conclusions was released. Although Kate Maltby's account of the alleged knee-brushing incident was deemed 'plausible', Gray surmised that it was impossible to know if Green's behaviour had been appropriate. The testimonies provided by Maltby and Green were 'competing and contradictory', the summary conclusions found, and he was not judged to have behaved improperly or broken the ministerial code regarding this episode.

The pornography allegations presented more of a problem. Although Gray reached no verdict on the nature of the material or who had watched it, she found that Green had broken the ministerial code in the wording of his response to the *Sunday Times* story. By claiming that he had not been told by the police that 'indecent' material was found on his computer, she said he had fallen short of the 'honesty requirement' which forms one of the seven principles of public life enshrined in the code. Gray stated that Green had been told about the pornography claims twice before the article was printed, both in 2008 and in 2013.

The verdict likely came as a shock to Theresa May, whose behaviour indicated that, like many others, she assumed Green would be cleared.

Disinclined to forfeit her ally because of his fudged response to allegations made in breach of confidence, she asked for a second opinion. Sir Alex Allan, her independent advisor on ministerial interests, was instructed to give his view. Two days later, however, Allan confirmed that he agreed with Gray's assessment and May reluctantly accepted that there was no alternative but to sack her friend. After a gruelling afternoon of questioning by a select committee during which she maintained a steely poker face, she arranged to meet Green at Downing Street that evening. On his arrival shortly after 6 p.m., she explained that he must quit.

The pair exchanged resignation letters before the news was released late in the evening. In his missive, Green restated that he 'did not download or view pornography on my parliamentary computers' but added:

> I accept that I should have been clear in my press statements that police lawyers talked to my lawyers in 2008 about the pornography on the computers, and that the police raised it with me in a subsequent phone call in 2013. I apologise that my statements were misleading on this point.

He also apologised to Maltby for making her feel uncomfortable, although he reiterated that he did not accept her version of events.

The next morning, Health Secretary Jeremy Hunt was sent on BBC's *Today* programme as the government's representative. He confirmed that Green had 'lied', but said that he had been 'pushed into a situation' where he said something he 'didn't mean to say'.

As Hunt suggested, Green probably did not intend to deny that he was told by the police about the pornography. That would have been a bizarre lie, which served no identifiable purpose and was certain to be exposed. It was also inconsistent with the rest of his own statement, in which he twice admitted that he had been aware of Quick's allegations 'for some years'.

It is possible, however, that Green's statement was misinterpreted. The public summary of Gray's report stated that Green denied he had ever been told 'indecent' material was found on his computer. This misquoted his contentious statement, which had in fact said that he had never been told that 'improper' material was discovered. It is possible that Green's use of the word 'improper' might have been deliberately chosen for its ambiguity, permitting the interpretation that he had been told about the pornography but not the claims that appeared in the press suggesting that it was extreme. While all pornographic material might reasonably be termed 'indecent', it might be argued that only a smaller subset of perverse or illegal pornography is 'improper'. If Green had intended to afford himself this room for manoeuvre, however, it is striking that he never publicly made this argument.

Either way, as with Peter Mandelson's second resignation in 2001, Green compromised his own position with briefing that was slippery at best and dishonest at worst. Certainly the denials, both those made publicly by him and those made privately on his behalf by allies and supporters, were incompetently executed. If he had simply said that he had never watched pornography at work and left it there, he would likely have survived.

Although breaches of the ministerial code do not necessarily compel a minister to resign, in these circumstances May had no option but to sack him. Given her declared intention to be straight with the public, the tortured vacillation of Green's briefings would have been anathema to her. Having campaigned for decades to encourage more women to participate in Tory politics, she may have felt that plausible allegations of harassment against an aspiring candidate could not be ignored. On top of that consideration, she will also have been sensitive to allegations that she was prepared to protect her allies but not her critics, an accusation often levelled at her Labour rival Jeremy Corbyn.

Whatever her thinking, May's third Cabinet dismissal in two months did less damage than had been expected. Green was sacked at the most convenient time – the day before Parliament rose for winter recess. MPs scattered back to their constituencies, and Christmas, which was three days away, loomed large in the minds of politicians, pundits and the public. Without having to face awkward questions in the House, the Prime Minister was left to bask in the glory of the Brexit talks progress, which the opposition leadership felt unable to criticise.

May emerged from the affair as a strengthened figure on her own benches. Within days of Green's departure, her Eurosceptic back-benchers told journalists that the loss of a leading Remain supporter made them less likely to move against her in the near future. Incapable of making significant domestic reforms, shorn of pro-EU allies and committed to a so-called clean Brexit, her administration had become, in a twisted parody of her former election slogan, 'weak and stable'.

An institution with more to fear from Green's downfall was the police, who nervously awaited a backlash over Quick's and Lewis's conduct. For the second time in five years, a cabal linked to the Metropolitan Police was accused of having conspired to destroy a Tory Cabinet minister. Cressida Dick, the Metropolitan Police Commissioner, condemned the actions of her former colleagues and announced that the Information Commissioner was investigating them with a view to pursuing criminal prosecutions. Ken Marsh, the head of Metropolitan Police Federation, said that the affair threatened to poison the relationship between the force and the Tories. Judging by the visceral fury on the government benches, that was an optimistic assessment.

From afar, it might appear that there was nothing particularly unusual about Green's resignation. To many, he was another government minister mired in allegations of sleaze and personal misconduct. His downfall was, of course, precipitated by the allegations of inappropriate behaviour and the rethink of sexual politics prompted by the Pestminster scandal, but it was also caused by his ten-year-old battle with the authorities. Green tried hard to fight them off, but demonstrated, as Andrew Mitchell had before him, that picking a fight with a policeman is a quick route to the political scrapheap.

DAMIAN GREEN TO THERESA MAY

Dear Prime Minister,

I regret that I've been asked to resign from the government following breaches of the Ministerial Code, for which I apologise. It has been a privilege to serve in your government both as Secretary of State for Work and Pensions and as First Secretary of State and Minister for the Cabinet Office.

It was also a great pleasure to work with you in the Home Office both as Minister for Immigration and as Minister for Policing, Criminal Justice and Victims. Your years as Home Secretary were a model of reforming institutions in the interests of the wider public.

I share and support your vision of a country that works for everyone, using Conservative policies to help those who have for too long been disadvantaged. In particular I am pleased to have published the Race Disparity Audit and to have started the government on a road to a reformed social care system.

From the outset I have been clear that I did not download or view pornography on my Parliamentary computers. I accept that I should have been clear in my press statements that police lawyers talked to my lawyers in 2008 about the pornography on the computers, and that the police raised it with me in a subsequent phone call in 2013. I apologise that my statements were misleading on this point. The unfounded and deeply hurtful allegations that were being levelled at me were distressing both to me and my family and it is right that these are being investigated by the Metropolitan Police's professional standards department.

I am grateful that the Cabinet Secretary has concluded that my conduct as a minister has generally been both professional and proper. I deeply regret the distress caused to Kate Maltby following her article about me and the reaction to it. I do not recognise the events she described in her article, but I clearly made her feel uncomfortable and for this I apologise.

Finally I would like to give heartfelt thanks to my Parliamentary colleagues and my Ashford constituents for the huge support they have shown me in recent weeks. I will continue to argue for the modernising conservatism I have always believed in.

Yours,

Damian

THERESA MAY TO DAMIAN GREEN

Dear Damian,

I am extremely sad to be writing this letter. We have been friends and colleagues throughout our whole political lives – from our early days at university, entering the House of Commons at the same election, and serving alongside each other both in Opposition and in Government. As Secretary of State for Work and Pensions, and as First Secretary of State, you have brought great wisdom, good sense, and a commitment to helping the most vulnerable to my Cabinets in this Parliament and the last. I have greatly appreciated your hard work and the contribution you have made to my team, just as I did at the Home Office, where you served as Immigration Minister and Minister for Policing and Criminal Justice, helping to drive through important but often difficult reforms.

Like you, I know the vast majority of our police to be diligent and honourable public servants, working hard to protect the public and maintain law and order. But I shared the concerns raised from across the political spectrum when your Parliamentary office was raided in 2008 when you were a Shadow Home Office Minister holding the then Labour Government to account. And I share the concerns, raised once again from across the political spectrum, at the comments made by a former officer involved in that case in recent weeks. I am glad that the Commissioner of the Metropolitan Police has condemned that, made clear that police officers' duty of confidentiality endures after they leave the force, and that the Metropolitan Police's professional standards department are reviewing the comments which have been made.

When allegations were raised about your personal conduct, I asked the Cabinet Secretary to establish as far as possible the facts of the case and provide advice on whether or not there had been a breach of the

Ministerial Code. He has produced a thorough report which concludes that your conduct as a Minister has generally been both professional and proper.

You have expressed your regret for the distress caused to Ms Maltby following her article about you and the reaction to it. I appreciate that you do not recognise the events Ms Maltby described in the article, but you do recognise that you made her feel uncomfortable and it is right that you have apologised.

I know that you share my determination to ensure that everyone who wants to play their part in our political life should feel able to do so — without fear or harassment, and knowing they can speak out if they need to. Equally, it is right that those who put themselves forward to serve the public should also be accorded the respect of a private life within the law.

I have also carefully considered the report's conclusions in relation to two statements you made on 4 and 11 November which you now accept were inaccurate and misleading. This falls short of the Seven Principles of Public Life and is a breach of the Ministerial Code — a conclusion which has been endorsed by Sir Alex Allan, the Independent Adviser on Ministers' Interests. While I can understand the considerable distress caused to you by some of the allegations which have been made in recent weeks, I know that you share my commitment to maintaining the high standards which the public demands of Ministers of the Crown.

It is therefore with deep regret, and enduring gratitude for the contribution you have made over many years, that I asked you to resign from the Government and have accepted your resignation.

Yours ever,

Theresa

CHAPTER EIGHTEEN

DAVID DAVIS AND
BORIS JOHNSON

'It's a big turd.'

That was the Foreign Secretary's response to his Prime Minister's painstakingly developed plan for Britain's future after Brexit.

The intervention was made during what a colleague later called a 'six-minute moan' at the now-infamous Chequers summit in July 2018. Boris Johnson's close colleague and fellow Brexiteer David Davis was also critical. Although both initially pledged support to Theresa May, within days they had staged resignations and called for rebellion against her plans. Davis quit because his own plans were rejected and his position as Brexit Secretary undermined. Johnson resigned reluctantly, and only because he thought that he had no other option. The twin departures set the scene for a year of open Conservative Party warfare over Europe – which at the time of writing still has no end in sight.

Most commentators had expected resignations over Brexit from the moment Theresa May ascended to the post of Prime Minister in 2016 in the wake of the vote to leave the EU. After securing the top job, she immediately plucked key Leave campaigners David Davis and Boris Johnson from the back benches to fill two key Cabinet positions. Davis became Secretary of State for Exiting the European Union, responsible for negotiating the terms of the nation's departure from the bloc. Johnson – for many the star of the Brexit campaign – became the Foreign Secretary, tasked with laying the foundations for a post-Brexit foreign policy.

For a year May's position was strong – as an overwhelmingly popular Prime Minister, few dared criticise her approach.

That all changed in June 2017. May had triggered a general election to 'strengthen her hand' in the Brexit negotiations, but returned shorn of her parliamentary majority and dependent on the Democratic Unionist Party, a small band of Northern Irish MPs who would not tolerate any divergence between Northern Ireland and the rest of the UK.

From then on, three central facts governed the intricate Brexit talks. First, the only deals that were on offer from the EU were a close relationship with continued enforceable legal alignment or a loose free trade agreement with hard borders and tariffs. Second, the parliamentary arithmetic indicated that only the former was deliverable. Third, many Brexiteers – including Johnson and Davis – did not consider that to be Brexit at all.

Theresa May had an apparently impossible job on her hands.

The Brexit vote had rapidly morphed into a proxy battle for the nation's future. Former Remainers mobilised to ensure that the UK stayed as close to EU membership as possible. Most former Brexit campaigners sought the freedom for the UK to deregulate and strike free trade deals across the world. One intransigent issue underpinning the negotiations was the question of Ireland – any divergence in regulations would, the EU argued, necessitate either a hard border between Northern Ireland and the Republic of Ireland or one between Northern Ireland and the rest of the UK. Neither was politically acceptable to the Tories.

Although an array of possible proposals was mooted, Britain's political debate had been poisoned by a lack of trust. Former Remainers suspected Brexiteers of wanting to turn Britain into a low-tax, low-welfare Thatcherite dystopia. Brexiteers, in turn, were convinced that the Remainers would collude with the civil service to keep the nation in the EU in all but name.

Out of this chaos emerged two proposals for the UK's negotiating position. The first came to be known as 'Norway minus' – staying within the institutions of the EU but without having to accept unlimited migration of EU citizens. The alternative was dubbed 'Canada plus plus' – a bare free trade deal which would lead to the increasing divergence that the Brexiteers always sought. Although nominally credible, the former was not acceptable to the EU and the latter would not solve the 'Ireland problem'.

Crippled by the failed election, the Prime Minister repeatedly deferred making any decision on her proposals for the future, letting David Davis's department prepare one plan and having her civil servants work on another.

But by July 2018, she could delay no longer. Before going to the European Union with the UK's proposals, they needed to be squared with her Cabinet. With her party and the country at large more polarised than ever, this was no easy task. A day-long summit was convened at Chequers, her sixteenth-century Buckinghamshire retreat, to settle on a policy.

The meeting was intended to reconcile the warring parties and put the Prime Minister back on the front foot. The rules of the day were carefully contrived to make it as hard as possible for members of the Cabinet to stage an effective protest. The twenty-nine ministers who were invited attended without political advisors and were forced to hand in their mobile phones on the way in. Without any advice and unable to brief the press, each one had to decide their position for themselves. The choice was to accept the Prime Minister's plan or resign.

Her aides sent journalists extraordinarily bullish briefings before the meeting. One text read:

All set for Chequers. Totally focused and confident of delivering a successful day for PM. Collective responsibility will be asserted at the end of the day. Taxi cards for Aston's taxis the local cab firm are in the foyer for those who decide they can't face making the right decision for the country but it will be a long walk as it is a mile long driveway. A select number of narcissistic, leadership dominated Cabinet ministers need to support the PM in the best interests of the UK or their spots will be taken by a talented new generation of MPs who will sweep them away.

Mutinous members of the Cabinet unsuccessfully attempted to co-ordinate in advance. Boris Johnson invited seven other long-time Brexit supporters to his office, along with recent converts Gavin Williamson, the Defence Secretary, and Sajid Javid, the Home Secretary. His plan was for them to join together and force an alternative proposal on the Prime Minister.

Javid refused to turn up. Transport Secretary and long-time Brexiteer Chris Grayling was uncomfortable with the suggestion of insurrection. David Davis argued that the time was not right for such an open attack, prompting a Johnson ally to tell Tim Shipman, the political editor of the *Sunday Times*, that Davis had 'bottled it'. With the meeting breaking up without agreement, pro-Brexit ministers duly arrived at Chequers with no unified plan.

The Cabinet assembled at the countryside retreat early on Friday 6 July. Plenary sessions were held covering a variety of less controversial aspects of No. 10's proposals, with much bluster but little meaningful debate.

After a casual lunch outside in the summer sun, the Prime Minister reassembled the Cabinet and announced the key elements of her proposal, which was, as the Brexiteers had feared, to stay closely aligned to the EU's rulebook in return for largely unencumbered trade, while theoretically retaining the option to diverge.

May forcefully argued that there was no viable alternative. The Canada-style free trade deal favoured by the Brexiteers would break up the union by separating Northern Ireland from the rest of the UK, and would be vetoed by the Tories' Northern Irish allies. The only other possibility – a no-deal Brexit – would be, she argued, economically catastrophic.

Her proposal was far more like the Norway minus model than Canada plus – it suggested a continued alignment, without the supposed prize of buccaneering free trade deals. Deregulation would be hard to achieve and European laws would continue to be enforced within the UK, albeit indirectly. In short, No. 10 had proposed to play it safe and May had called the Brexiteers' bluff.

The room was tense, with all assembled waiting to see how the key players would respond. The critical moment arrived at 3.15 p.m. Michael Gove, the Environment Secretary who had played a crucial role for Leave in the 2016 referendum, began to speak. He explained that while his preference was for a Canada-style free trade deal, he felt that 'we should all back the Prime Minister and support her in her efforts to make this work'.

Another key Brexit campaigner, Leader of the House of Commons Andrea Leadsom, then admitted that she was uncomfortable with the policy, but concluded that she would support Theresa May no matter what decision she took.

Boris Johnson also agreed to accept it, although he did reportedly demand and win two minor concessions. David Davis was more openly critical, but said that he would support the majority view. Eventually he firmly backed the Prime Minister and discussed how the EU could be made to agree to her terms. Although others were critical, none pledged defiance.

By late afternoon, Theresa May summed up the mood of the meeting. She said that she had achieved an overwhelming majority in favour of her plans and stressed that anyone who failed to support them from that point on would be immediately sacked.

Presented with the choice between accepting No. 10's plan or quitting in protest, all the Brexiteers bottled it. None of them chose to resign, leaving a nominally united Cabinet and May triumphant.

All twenty-nine ministers present celebrated with a toast of Pol Roger champagne, proposed by Boris Johnson, who reportedly said, 'If only people could see how united we are now.'

He and the other Brexiteers had fallen victim to a cannily planned ambush. May had long known that a so-called 'soft Brexit' was the only realistic option; she thus disregarded the work and preference of Davis's department and worked up her own plan in secret with her chief of staff Gavin Barwell and Europe advisor Oliver Robbins. The details were kept from the Cabinet until the last minute, when they were assembled in a gilded cage at Chequers, without mobile phones to brief journalists or advisors to help them decide what to do.

May used the weekend after Chequers to sell her proposals to the public while David Davis returned home to consider how he might implement them. Although he had expressed muted support for the Prime Minister's proposals at the summit, when he met with his advisors and discussed with friends and family he soon realised his position was untenable. Having asked his department to prepare a negotiating strategy, No. 10 had rejected all the key parts of it and ordered him to return to the EU to negotiate something entirely different. He felt that his authority had been irreparably undermined.

He also found himself unable to accept the Chequers proposal on its merits, telling his friend and LBC radio presenter Iain Dale that the plan was 'like taking back control, but an illusion'.

Davis's disquiet had not been reported in the Sunday papers as he had kept his change of heart to himself. It was not until late on Sunday evening that journalists began to realise that he had made no public comment and had stopped answering his phone. This led Sam Coates of *The Times* to speculate on the BBC's late-night radio show *Westminster Hour* that Davis might be quitting. His bold prediction was proved right half an hour later when the departure was confirmed, with Davis announcing that he was not happy to be a 'reluctant conscript' to May's plans.

Although he was fiercely critical of the newly christened 'Chequers plan', Davis stopped short of open insurrection. Asked on Monday morning whether Theresa May could survive his resignation, he ruled out challenging her, saying, 'I like Theresa May, I think she is a good Prime Minister. If I wanted to bring down Theresa May, now is not the time.'

Whatever his intentions, Davis's departure had one more dangerous consequence for the Prime Minister: it was immediately followed by the resignation of his junior minister, Steve Baker. Before he was a minister, Baker was a furiously organised backbench agitator, leading the European Research Group (ERG) of Eurosceptic Tory MPs into the unified pressure group that did so much to destabilise David Cameron and later Theresa May. On quitting in protest against the Chequers plan, he made it clear that he intended to return to his previous role and defeat the policy. He was immediately re-added to the ERG's WhatsApp group and went on the *Daily Politics* programme at 12 p.m. to say that he was 'absolutely furious' about No. 10's handling of the summit, exclaiming 'I could almost have resigned over the childishness of their briefing [alone].'

Having led the toast in support of the Prime Minister at the end of the Chequers summit, Boris Johnson had not been planning to resign. Right up until the Sunday night, he took the view that the 'pragmatic, sensible' path would be to stay in the Cabinet so he could challenge May's softening of Brexit from a position of influence. But then he started hearing rumours that Davis was considering his position.

Johnson had not had a happy time as Foreign Secretary. He prompt-ed outrage from Tory MPs when reports emerged that his response to briefings against Brexit by top CEOs was to say, 'Fuck business.' Public disdain mounted when he chose to travel abroad on the day of the key vote on a third runway at Heathrow, so he could avoid choosing between his long standing opposition to the scheme and his Cabinet role. He had also been accused of insensitivity abroad, committing several faux pas on his diplomatic tours, notably being rebuked by the British Ambassador to Myanmar for reciting a colonial-era Rudyard Kipling poem in front of local dignitaries. On each occasion colleagues were always ready to brief against him – in part they were jealous of his charisma and universal recognition, but also angry that he never seemed to take his role seriously.

When Davis quit, Johnson panicked. He could not decide whether he had to follow suit. On Monday morning he summoned his key aides to his office and spent the day debating what would be better for his leadership ambitions, and for his Brexit plan. By lunchtime, he had decided he would resign – but still did not tell any outsiders. The team spent three further hours drafting his resignation letter and arranging for a photographer to stage a picture of him signing it – a publicity stunt without historical precedent.

While Johnson was having his picture taken, European Foreign Ministers and dignitaries were waiting for him at a summit he was supposed to be hosting in London. Britain had volunteered to host the meeting of EU and Balkans governments to discuss the future of the region. Ministers from the six western Balkan countries as well as those from Germany, Austria, France and Poland were due to hear Johnson speak at the event and were left wondering where he was. The German Deputy Foreign Minister, Michael Roth, who was at the summit, tweeted: 'We're still waiting for our host.' Exasperated officials were forced to explain to those attending that they did not know why he had not appeared and could not locate him. Even more astonishingly, Johnson later failed to appear at an emergency Cobra meeting concerning the use of a Russian nerve agent in Salisbury.

No. 10 assumed that he had decided to resign, and, after finally hearing from him to confirm, they made the unusual move of announcing the news themselves.

David Davis was in a radio studio when the news of Johnson's resignation broke. Asked for his reaction, he said that he regretted it. In his view there was no need for Boris to resign, because, unlike the DExEU Secretary, the position taken in the Brexit negotiations was not directly relevant to the Foreign Secretary's job. Davis recognised that Johnson's actions were taken for reasons of political expediency, not principle. He said, 'It's a pity, but there we are.'

May survived the departures of Davis and Johnson with little difficulty, replacing them with Dominic Raab and Jeremy Hunt respectively, increasing the number of former Remain supporters at the top table. Although she still faced considerable difficulties in selling the Chequers plan to Parliament, the Tories and the EU, the resignations appeared less totemic in hindsight than at the time. Steve Baker's departure may prove the most important of all, as his organisational abilities in his post at the ERG threaten to scupper any Brexit deal.

Boris Johnson quit as Foreign Secretary on the day that the last Foreign Secretary to resign, Lord Carrington, died. In 1982 Carrington quit with rare honour over the invasion of the Falkland Islands, taking responsibility for others' errors with no thought for his personal career. It is hard to imagine a resignation further removed from Johnson's cack-handed attempt at personal advancement.

Carrington was reportedly whispered the news that Boris had gone, smiled broadly and passed away within an hour – the last of his kind.

DAVID DAVIS TO THERESA MAY

Dear Prime Minister,

As you know there have been a significant number of occasions in the last year or so on which I have disagreed with the Number 10 policy line, ranging from accepting the Commission's sequencing of negotiations through to the language on Northern Ireland in the December Joint Report. At each stage I have accepted collective responsibility because it is part of my task to find workable compromises, and because I considered it was still possible to deliver on the mandate of the referendum, and on our manifesto commitment to leave the Customs Union and the Single Market.

I am afraid that I think the current trend of policy and tactics is making that look less and less likely. Whether it is the progressive dilution of what I thought was a firm Chequers agreement in February on right to diverge, or the unnecessary delays of the start of the White Paper, or the presentation of a backstop proposal that omitted the strict conditions that I requested and believed that we had agreed, the general direction of policy will leave us in at best a weak negotiating position, and possibly an inescapable one.

The Cabinet decision on Friday crystallised this problem. In my view the inevitable consequence of the proposed policies will be to make the supposed control by Parliament illusory rather than real. As I said at Cabinet, the 'common rule book' policy hands control of large swathes of our economy to the EU and is certainly not returning control of our laws in any real sense.

I am also unpersuaded that our negotiating approach will not just lead to further demands for concessions.

Of course this is a complex area of judgement and it is possible that you are right and I am wrong. However, even in that event it seems to me that the national interest requires a Secretary of State in my Department that is an enthusiastic believer in your approach, and not merely a reluctant conscript. While I have been grateful to you for the opportunity to serve, it is with great regret that I tender my resignation from the Cabinet with immediate effect.

Yours ever

David Davis

THERESA MAY TO DAVID DAVIS

Dear David,

Thank you for your letter explaining your decision to resign as Secretary of State for Exiting the European Union.

I am sorry that you have chosen to leave the government when we have already made so much progress towards delivering a smooth and successful Brexit, and when we are only eight months from the date set in law when the United Kingdom will leave the European Union.

At Chequers on Friday, we as the Cabinet agreed a comprehensive and detailed proposal which provides a precise, responsible, and credible basis for progressing our negotiations towards a new relationship between the UK and the EU after we leave in March. We set out how we will deliver on the result of the referendum and the commitments we made in our manifesto for the 2017 general election:

1. *Leaving the EU on 29 March 2019.*
2. *Ending free movement and taking back control of our borders.*
3. *No more sending vast sums of money each year to the EU.*
4. *A new business-friendly customs model with freedom to strike new trade deals around the world.*
5. *A UK-EU free trade area with a common rulebook for industrial goods and agricultural products which will be good for jobs.*
6. *A commitment to maintain high standards on consumer and employment rights and the environment.*
7. *A Parliamentary lock on all new rules and regulations.*
8. *Leaving the Common Agricultural Policy and the Common Fisheries Policy.*
9. *Restoring the supremacy of British courts by ending the jurisdiction of the European Court of Justice in the UK.*
10. *No hard border between Northern Ireland and Ireland, or between Northern Ireland and Great Britain.*
11. *Continued, close co-operation on security to keep our people safe.*
12. *An independent foreign and defence policy, working closely with the EU and other allies.*

This is consistent with the mandate of the referendum and with the commitments we laid out in our general election manifesto: leaving the single market and the customs union but seeking a deep and special partnership including a comprehensive free trade and customs agreement; ending the vast annual contributions to the EU; and pursuing fair, orderly negotiations, minimising disruption and giving as much certainty as possible so both sides benefit.

As we said in our manifesto, we believe it is necessary to agree the terms of our future partnership alongside our withdrawal, reaching agreement on both within the two years allowed by Article 50. I have always agreed with you that these two must go alongside one another, but if we are to get sufficient detail about our future partnership, we need to act now. We have made a significant move: it is for the EU now to respond in the same spirit.

I do not agree with your characterisation of the policy we agreed at Cabinet on Friday. Parliament will decide whether or not to back the deal the Government negotiates, but that deal will undoubtedly mean the returning of powers from Brussels to the United Kingdom. The direct effect of EU law will end when we leave the EU. Where the UK chooses to apply a common rulebook, each rule will have to be agreed by Parliament. Choosing not to sign up to certain rules would lead to consequences for market access, security co-operation or the frictionless border, but that decision will rest with our sovereign Parliament, which will have a lock on whether to incorporate those rules into the UK legal order.

I am sorry that the government will not have the benefit of your continued expertise and counsel as we secure this deal and complete the process of leaving the EU, but I would like to thank you warmly for everything you have done over the past two years as Secretary of State to shape our departure from the EU, and the new role the UK will forge on the world stage as an independent, self-governing nation once again.

You returned to government after nineteen years to lead an entirely new Department responsible for a vital, complex, and unprecedented task. You have helped to steer through Parliament some of the most important legislation for generations, including the European Union (Notification of Withdrawal) Act 2017 and the European Union (Withdrawal) Act 2018, which received Royal Assent last week. These landmark Acts, and what they will do, stand as testament to your work and our commitment to honouring the result of the referendum.

Yours sincerely
Theresa May

BORIS JOHNSON TO THERESA MAY

Dear Theresa

It is more than two years since the British people voted to leave the European Union on an unambiguous and categorical promise that if they did so they would be taking back control of their democracy.

They were told that they would be able to manage their own immigration policy, repatriate the sums of UK cash currently spent by the EU, and, above all, that they would be able to pass laws independently and in the interests of the people of this country.

Brexit should be about opportunity and hope. It should be a chance to do things differently, to be more nimble and dynamic, and to maximise the particular advantages of the UK as an open, outward-looking global economy.

That dream is dying, suffocated by needless self-doubt.

We have postponed crucial decisions – including the preparations for no deal, as I argued in my letter to you of last November – with the result that we appear to be heading for a semi-Brexit, with large parts of the economy still locked in the EU system, but with no UK control over that system.

It now seems that the opening bid of our negotiations involves accepting that we are not actually going to be able to make our own laws. Indeed we seem to have gone backwards since the last Chequers meeting in February, when I described my frustrations, as Mayor of London, in trying to protect cyclists from juggernauts. We had wanted to lower the cabin windows to improve visibility; and even though such designs were already on the market, and even though there had been a horrific spate of deaths, mainly of female cyclists, we were told that we had to wait for the EU to legislate on the matter.

So at the previous Chequers session we thrashed out an elaborate procedure for divergence from EU rules. But even that now seems to have been taken off the table, and there is in fact no easy UK right of initiative. Yet if Brexit is to mean anything, it must surely give ministers and Parliament the chance to do things differently to protect the public. If a country cannot pass a law to save the lives of female cyclists – when that proposal is supported at every level of UK government – then I don't see how that country can truly be called independent.

Conversely, the British government has spent decades arguing against this or that EU directive, on the grounds that it was too burdensome or ill-thought out. We are now in the ludicrous position of asserting that we must accept huge amounts of precisely such EU law, without changing an iota, because it is essential for our economic health – and when we no longer have any ability to influence these laws as they are made.

In that respect we are truly headed for the status of colony – and many will struggle to see the economic or political advantages of that particular arrangement.

It is also clear that by surrendering control over our rulebook for goods and agrifoods (and much else besides) we will make it much more difficult to do free trade deals. And then there is the further impediment of having to argue for an impractical and undeliverable customs arrangement unlike any other in existence.

What is even more disturbing is that this is our opening bid. This is already how we see the end state for the UK – before the other side has made its counter-offer. It is as though we are sending our vanguard into battle with the white flags fluttering above them. Indeed, I was concerned, looking at Friday's document, that there might be further concessions on immigration, or that we might end up effectively paying for access to the single market.

On Friday I acknowledged that my side of the argument were too few to prevail, and congratulated you on at least reaching a cabinet decision on the way forward. As I said then, the government now has a song to sing. The trouble is that I have practised the words over the weekend and find that they stick in the throat. We must have collective responsibility. Since I cannot in all conscience champion these proposals, I have sadly concluded that I must go.

I am proud to have served as Foreign Secretary in your government. As I step down, I would like first to thank the patient officers of the Metropolitan Police who have looked after me and my family, at times in demanding circumstances. I am proud too of the extraordinary men and women of our diplomatic service. Over the last few months they have shown how many friends this country has around the world, as 28 governments expelled Russian spies in an unprecedented protest at the attempted assassination of the Skripals. They have organised a highly successful Commonwealth summit and secured record international support for this government's campaign for 12 years of quality education for every girl, and much more besides. As I leave office, the FCO now has the largest and by far the most effective diplomatic network of any country in Europe – a continent which we will never leave.

The Rt Hon. Boris Johnson MP

THERESA MAY TO BORIS JOHNSON

Dear Boris,

Thank you for your letter relinquishing the office of Secretary of State for Foreign and Commonwealth Affairs.

I am sorry – and a little surprised – to receive it after the productive discussions we had at Chequers on Friday, and the comprehensive and detailed proposal which we agreed as a Cabinet. It is a proposal which will honour the result of the referendum and the commitments we made in our general election manifesto to leave the single market and the customs union. It will mean that we take back control of our borders, our laws, and our money – ending the freedom of movement, ending the jurisdiction of the European Court of Justice in the United Kingdom, and ending the days of sending vast sums of taxpayers' money to the European Union. We will be able to spend that money on our priorities instead – such as the £20 billion increase we have announced for the NHS budget, which means that we will soon be spending an extra £394 million a week on our National Health Service.

As I outlined at Chequers, the agreement we reached requires the full, collective support of Her Majesty's Government. During the EU referendum campaign, collective responsibility on EU policy was temporarily suspended. As we developed our policy on Brexit, I have allowed Cabinet colleagues considerable latitude to express their individual views. But the agreement we reached on Friday marks the point where that is no longer the case, and if you are not able to provide the support we need to secure this deal in the interests of the United Kingdom, it is right that you should step down.

As you do so, I would like to place on record my appreciation of the service you have given to our country, and to the Conservative Party, as Mayor of London and as Foreign Secretary – not least for the passion that you have demonstrated in promoting a Global Britain to the world as we leave the European Union.

Yours ever,
Theresa May

CHAPTER NINETEEN

DOMINIC RAAB AND
ESTHER MCVEY

For some they were wreckers. Others insist they are heroes. The one thing that cannot be disputed about the two Tory Brexiteers who stormed out of Theresa May's Cabinet on 15 November 2018, however, is the ruthlessness with which they pursued their ends.

In sparking open insurrection against the Prime Minister they tore up the rulebook on political attack resignations. Before then, even the most aggressive of quitters had retained a veneer of respect for the government they had left.

Their resignations were sparked by the publication of the draft withdrawal agreement that Theresa May had negotiated with Brussels. Totalling 585 pages, the hefty tome was just the first stage of the complex series of treaties required to extract the UK from the bloc. While the Chequers plan concerned the negotiations on the long-term future partnership with the EU that were to follow, it was the withdrawal agreement that set the parameters for those talks.

In an attempt to maintain a balance between former Remainers, devout Brexiteers, business interests and her Northern Irish Democratic Unionist Party partners, May agreed to a deal that ultimately seemed to satisfy nobody. MPs, who had been promised a vote to approve or disapprove the withdrawal deal, attacked two key aspects of the draft in particular.

Most contentious was the protocol on Northern Ireland, dubbed the 'Irish backstop' – this was the insurance plan to avoid a hard border between Northern Ireland and the Republic of Ireland. If no other solution could be agreed, the UK would remain in the EU's customs union, and Northern Ireland would have to closely mirror EU goods regulations. Many MPs saw this as a trap that would keep the UK shackled to the bloc.

Almost as controversial was the £39 billion divorce bill, covering pension liabilities and other legal obligations. Opponents argued that there was no need to pay a penny.

The deal was loathed by Brexiteers and Remainers alike. Among May's backbenchers, the European Research Group (ERG) of Tory MPs provided the most fervent opposition. As the country polarised further and further over Europe, many members of the ERG considered the deal to be worse than remaining in the EU. Led by Brexiteer talisman Jacob Rees-Mogg – dubbed the 'honourable member for the eighteenth century', owing to his antiquated values and plummy accent – the ERG pivoted to advocate a clean break, or 'no-deal Brexit', with an almost evangelical fervour.

Much like the Chequers proposal in July 2018, Theresa May had kept details of the agreed withdrawal deal secret until the last minute. She first presented it to the Cabinet in a late-night meeting on 14 November and, as with Chequers, gave them the option to agree or face the sack. Despite stubborn resistance, May managed to reach a consensus of agreement in Cabinet, strongly rejecting attempts to force a one-by-one vote around the table. Anonymous briefings recounted tense scenes, in which Cabinet members were shouted down by the Cabinet Secretary. When the five-hour meeting finally came to an end, May went into Downing Street to tell the country that she had backing for her deal.

But behind the closed doors of No. 10, trouble was brewing. Brexit Secretary Dominic Raab had, like his predecessor David Davis, been overruled – he had argued for looser alignment and a bare free trade deal, which was discounted by the withdrawal agreement. Specifically, the Irish backstop envisaged an unending customs union unless an as-yet-unspecified method to prevent a customs border was found. This, in Raab's opinion, would trap the UK into perpetual alignment with EU law but without influence. To him, it was the worst deal possible – making the UK a 'vassal state'. Having twice been overruled on critical negotiations, the position of Brexit Secretary was so undermined as to be almost ceremonial – with its occupant reduced to acting as minister for disaster planning.

After the meeting, Raab approached Gavin Barwell, May's chief of staff, and Julian Smith, her Chief Whip. He told them that he could not accept the deal and would be resigning in protest. Barwell and Smith persuaded Raab to sleep on his decision, to make sure he was certain and to give them time to prepare. Knowing in advance that Raab was likely to be the first of many, Barwell and Smith, unlike most journalists and commentators, were prepared for 15 November 2018 to be the year's most frenzied day in politics – they knew that the long-awaited Brexiteer coup was upon them.

The next morning began with a surprise for everyone, however – Raab's was not the first resignation over the deal. This honour was taken by obscure junior minister Shailesh Vara, who quit at 7.32 a.m. by tweeting his resignation letter, declaring, 'It is a sad day when we are reduced to obeying rules set by other countries who have shown they do not have our best interests at heart.'

Not wishing to be outshone by his junior colleague, Raab then quit at 9 a.m., also via Twitter. Soon afterwards, he declared that 'I don't want to submit to the blackmail of my country.' Careful not to call for her head, he nevertheless delivered the ominous prediction that 'this might be the day [that] it all comes tumbling down' for her.

Westminster went into overdrive, with lobby correspondents wildly speculating on what might come next and hack packs staking out the homes of all Cabinet members susp ected to be teetering on the edge.

The minister that most expected to follow Raab was Work and Pensions Secretary Esther McVey. The former *GMTV* presenter and tough Liverpudlian was renowned in the Tory Party as a ruthless operator. Her political upbringing had been shaped by Brexiteers, with her early mentors Chris Grayling and Iain Duncan Smith among the most influential Leave supporters.

Often suspected to have one eye on a future leadership bid, McVey managed a meteoric rise to the Cabinet, tempered only slightly by the loss of her Wirral West seat in 2015. Having campaigned strongly to leave the EU from outside Parliament, she returned in 2017 as MP for Tatton – George Osborne's old seat – and soon took a seat at the Cabinet table. By January 2018 she had established herself as one of the strongest pro-Brexit voices in government.

McVey had also become a public enemy for Labour supporters, having been described as a 'stain of inhumanity' by shadow Chancellor John McDonnell, and had borne the brunt of many a social media monstering for her role in reforming the disability benefit system. Having toughed out almost constant criticism and abuse since 2013, McVey was in no mood to be steamrollered over Europe.

As many had predicted, she announced her departure from the Cabinet within an hour of Dominic Raab and, in a similar vein, her resignation letter was also published on Twitter before Downing Street could reply. However, McVey's was far more bullish than Raab's, representing a clear challenge to the Prime Minister's authority.

By mid-morning, junior Brexit minister Suella Braverman had also packed her bags. The news of this last departure was shared on WhatsApp by Jacob Rees-Mogg's deputy and key Brexiteer organiser Steve Baker – indicating that it was not simply a principled departure, but part of an externally co-ordinated attack. The pressure on May ratcheted up another notch.

By the time the Prime Minister arrived in Parliament to sell the withdrawal agreement to MPs, she was greeted with shouts of 'RESIGN!' from some of her own backbenchers. The Brexiteers had decided that, after months of restraint, it was now necessary to change the personnel in order to change the policy.

The resignations and accompanying leadership challenge looked suspiciously like an ambush. When Jacob Rees-Mogg appeared outside the Palace of Westminster to deny that Brexiteers were staging a coup, it appeared that, to the contrary, this was his precise aim. The departing ministers did not condemn him.

As if on cue, backbench Brexiteers then took to social media to post pictures of letters they had sent to 1922 Committee chairman Graham Brady, demanding the Prime Minister's removal. No. 10 was under so much strain that it failed to observe the traditional niceties – there were no published replies to the resignation letters of the four quitters.

From then on, the two questions on everyone's lips were whether the Brexiteers would secure the forty-eight letters they needed to challenge May, and whether other leading figures would follow. Giddy reports sprang up suggesting that five further Cabinet ministers were teetering on the edge, and none of them would confirm they were staying in government. Most were watching Michael Gove, the most strategically significant figure of the five, to see whether he would walk. After war-gaming all scenarios with his wife and aides and rejecting an offer from May to take up the poisoned chalice of Brexit Secretary, he stepped back from the brink – for the time being.

That day will live long in the Conservative Party's institutional memory as the moment decorum and unity were sacrificed on the altar of hard Brexit. It was the first mass political ambush to be executed entirely through social media. The ERG directed activities via WhatsApp for maximum impact and briefed journalists throughout the day. News of each departure and the contents of the respective resignation letters were released on Twitter before No. 10 could react, inviting expressions of support from allies and preventing pre-emptive intervention by May's team.

But, despite its unprecedented ferocity, the coup failed. Raab and McVey were replaced promptly and Rees-Mogg's Brexiteer rebellion fizzled out. Steve Baker, who had previously bullishly briefed that he had eighty MPs on his side, was soon dubbed an overexcited blowhard as the ERG backbenchers folded in on themselves. It has even been reported that several MPs actually withdrew their letters of no confidence.

The closest comparable effort was the exodus of twelve of Jeremy Corbyn's shadow Cabinet in one day in 2016, followed by a cascade of other, more junior shadow ministers. The savageness of that attack, as with the ERG's, proved counterproductive, encouraging Corbyn's allies to rally around him. Shielded by the party's leadership election rules, which prioritise members over MPs, the Labour leader faced down the would-be political assassins and tightened his grip over his party.

Theresa May proved every bit as stubborn as Corbyn, and the Tories' leadership election rules also worked in her favour. The Brexiteers needed forty-eight MPs to submit letters asking for a vote of no confidence and then 150 MPs to vote against the Prime Minister. Despite their public protestations and carefully cultivated image as rabble-rousers, they never got near either figure.

That is why, despite the mass resignations, veteran Tory Remainer Ken Clarke perceptively observed that May is 'doomed to carry on leading us through this mess'. At the time of writing, she still battles on, a remarkably resilient figure of continuity among her trigger-happy colleagues.

Although Raab's and McVey's departures were the catalyst for 2018's most frenetic political day, they were ultimately ineffective. May stayed in post, pushing her withdrawal deal to a vote without amendment and heading for a bloody House of Commons clash.

As with David Davis and Boris Johnson in July 2018, both Cabinet ministers failed to make the most of their most potent weapon – their resignation. Had they secured the support of other leading colleagues – in particular Michael Gove – they could have had a greater impact, forcing May to change course or even quit. Instead, they join the long list of ministers who have met a sticky end over disputes about Europe – a forty-year trend that shows no sign of abating.

DOMINIC RAAB TO THERESA MAY

Dear Prime Minister,

It has been an honour to serve in your government as Justice Minister, Housing Minister and Brexit Secretary.

I regret to say that, following the Cabinet meeting yesterday on the Brexit deal, I must resign. I understand why you have chosen to pursue the deal with the EU on the terms proposed, and I respect the different views held in good faith by all of our colleagues.

For my part, I cannot support the proposed deal for two reasons. First, I believe that the regulatory regime proposed for Northern Ireland presents a very real threat to the integrity of the United Kingdom.

Second, I cannot support an indefinite backstop arrangement, where the EU holds a veto over our ability to exit. The terms of the backstop amount to a hybrid of the EU Customs Union and Single Market obligations. No democratic nation has ever signed up to be bound by such an extensive regime, imposed externally without any democratic control over the laws to be applied, nor the ability to decide to exit the arrangement. That arrangement is now also taken as the starting point for negotiating the Future Economic Partnership. If we accept that, it will severely prejudice the second phase of negotiations against the UK.

Above all, I cannot reconcile the terms of the proposed deal with the promises we made to the country in our manifesto at the last election. This is, at its heart, a matter of public trust.

I appreciate that you disagree with my judgment on these issues. I have weighed very carefully the alternative courses of action which the government could take, on which I have previously advised. Ultimately, you deserve a Brexit Secretary who can make the case for the deal you are pursuing with conviction. I am only sorry, in good conscience, that I cannot.

My respect for you, and the fortitude you have shown in difficult times, remains undimmed.

Yours sincerely,
Dominic Raab

ESTHER MCVEY TO THERESA MAY

Dear Prime Minister,

There is no more important task for this Government than delivering on the United Kingdom's decision to leave the European Union. This is a matter of trust. It is about the future of our country and the integrity of our democracy.

The deal you put before the Cabinet yesterday does not honour the result of the referendum. Indeed, it doesn't meet the tests you set from the outset of your premiership.

Repeatedly you have said that we must regain control of our money, our borders and our laws and develop our own independent trade policy. I have always supported you to deliver on those objectives. Even after Chequers when you knew I shared the concerns of a very significant number of colleagues, I believed that we could still work collectively to honour the will of the British people and secure the right outcome for the future of our country. This deal fails to do this.

The proposals put before Cabinet, which will soon be judged by the entire country, means handing over around £39bn to the EU without anything in return. It will trap us in a customs union, despite you specifically promising the British people we would not be. It will bind the hands of not only this, but future Governments in pursuing genuine free trade policies. We wouldn't be taking back control, we would be handing over control to the EU and even to a third country for arbitration.

It also threatens the integrity of the United Kingdom, which as a Unionist is a risk I cannot be party to.

The British people have always been ahead of politicians on this issue, and it will be no good trying to pretend to them that this deal honours the result of the referendum when it is obvious to everyone it doesn't.

We have gone from no deal is better than a bad deal, to any deal is better than no deal.

I cannot defend this, and I cannot vote for this deal. I could not look my constituents in the eye were I to do that. I therefore have no alternative but to resign from the Government.

It has been a huge honour to serve as Secretary of State for Work & Pensions, and I am immensely proud of the part I have played in the record levels of employment we have seen in all parts of the U.K. Youth unemployment has halved since 2010, and we now have record number of women and BAME in work and since 2013, 973,000 more disabled people in work.

With employment over 3.3 million more than in 2010 we have helped 1,000 more people into work each and every day since we took office.

I am extremely grateful to you for appointing me to the role, and for the support you have given to me, not least in the run up to the budget, ensuring Universal Credit got a much needed injection of £4.5billion. That has made my decision a greater wrench.

However, in politics you have to be true to the public and also true to yourself. Had I stayed in the Government and supported this deal with the EU I wouldn't be doing that.

Yours sincerely,
Esther McVey

SHAILESH VARA TO THERESA MAY

Dear Prime Minister,

I write to offer my resignation as a Minister in your Government. I do so with sadness but I cannot support the Withdrawal Agreement that has been agreed with the European Union.

The EU Referendum offered a simple choice – to either stay in or leave the EU.

The result was decisive with the UK public voting to leave and that is what we, their elected representatives, must deliver.

The Agreement put forward however, does not do that as it leaves the UK in a half-way house with no time limit on when we will finally be a sovereign nation.

Given the past performance of the EU, there is every possibility that the UK–EU trade deal that we seek will take years to conclude. We will be locked in a Customs Arrangement indefinitely, bound by rules determined by the EU over which we have no say. Worse, we will not be free to leave the Customs Arrangement unilaterally if we wish to do so. Northern Ireland in the meantime will be subject to a different relationship with the EU from the rest of the UK and whilst I agree there should be no hard border between Northern Ireland and Ireland, the economic and constitutional integrity of the United Kingdom must be respected.

With respect Prime Minister, this Agreement does not provide for the United Kingdom being a sovereign, independent country leaving the shackles of the EU, however it is worded.

We are a proud nation and it is a sad day when we are reduced to obeying rules made by other countries who have shown that they do not have our best interests at heart. We can and must do better than this. The people of the UK deserve better. That is why I cannot support this Agreement.

It has been an honour and privilege to serve as a Minister in the Northern Ireland Office and I leave with the fondest of memories.

Yours,

Shailesh Vara

SUELLA BRAVERMAN TO THERESA MAY

Dear Prime Minister,

This is a difficult letter to write. One which I never expected to compose. It has been an immense honour to support you in delivering the historic opportunity of leaving the EU as a Parliamentary Under Secretary of State at the Department for Exiting the European Union. It has, in many ways, been a dream job which I have enjoyed tremendously. However, despite my strenuous attempts, I now find myself unable to sincerely support the deal agreed yesterday by Cabinet. It is therefore with deep regret that I tender my resignation.

My reasons are simple. Firstly, the proposed Northern Ireland Backstop is not Brexit. It is not what the British people – or my constituents – voted for in 2016. It prevents an unequivocal exit from a customs union with the EU. This robs the UK of the main competitive advantages from Brexit. Without a unilateral right to terminate or a definite time limit to the Backstop, our numerous promises to leave the customs union will not be honoured. 17.4 million people voted for the UK to leave the EU in our own sovereign way and at a time of our choosing. The Backstop renders this impossible and generations of people will see this as betrayal.

Secondly, the Backstop proposals set out different regulatory regimes for Northern Ireland and Great Britain threatening to break up our precious Union. I am confident – having met with customs professionals in my role at the Department – that this could have been avoided.

Throughout this process, I have compromised. I have put pragmatism ahead of idealism and understand that concessions are necessary in a negotiation. I have kept faith in the ultimate destination to justify an uncomfortable journey. However I have reached a point where I feel that these concessions do not respect the will of the people – the people who put us here and whom we humbly serve. We must not let them down.

I thoroughly enjoyed working at the Department and have been supported by excellent civil servants. To them, I am grateful.

Thank you for the opportunity. I have immense respect for the way in which you have conducted yourself during these very difficult times. I know how extremely hard you have worked to serve our national interest.

I look forward to working to deliver Brexit in the best possible way from the Backbenches.

Yours sincerely,
Suella Braverman

JACOB REES-MOGG TO GRAHAM BRADY

Dear Sir Graham,

A few weeks ago in a conversation with the Chief Whip I expressed my concern that the Prime Minister, Mrs. Theresa May, was losing the confidence of Conservative Members of Parliament and that it would be in the interest of the Party and the country if she were to stand aside. I have wanted to avoid the disagreeable nature of a formal Vote of No Confidence with all the ill will that this risks engendering.

Regrettably, the draft Withdrawal Agreement presented to Parliament today has turned out to be worse than anticipated and fails to meet the promises given to the nation by the Prime Minister, either on her own account or on behalf of us all in the Conservative Party Manifesto.

That the Conservative and Unionist Party is proposing a Protocol which would create a different regulatory environment for an integral part of our country stands in contradistinction to our long-held principles. It is in opposition to the Prime Minister's clear statements that this was something that no Prime Minister would ever do and raises questions in relation to Scotland that are open to exploitation by the Scottish National Party.

The 2017 Election Manifesto said that the United Kingdom would leave the Customs Union. It did not qualify this statement by saying that we could stay in it via a backstop while Annex 2, Article 3 explicitly says that we would have no authority to set our own tariffs. It is also harder to leave this backstop than it is to leave the EU, there is no provision equivalent to Article 50 of the Lisbon Treaty.

The Prime Minister also promised an implementation period which was the reason for paying £39 billion. As was made clear by a House of Lords report in March 2017, there is no legal obligation to pay anything. This has now become an extended period of negotiation which is a different matter.

The situation as regards the European Court of Justice appears to have wandered from the clear statement that we are taking back control of our laws. Article 174 makes this clear as does Article 89 in conjunction with Article 4.

It is of considerable importance that politicians stick to their commitments or do not make such commitments in the first place. Regrettably, this is not the situation, therefore, in accordance with the relevant rules and procedures of the Conservative Party and the 1922 Committee, this is a formal letter of No Confidence in the Leader of the Party, the Rt. Hon. Theresa May.

I am copying this letter to the Prime Minister and the Chief Whip and although I understand that it is possible for the correspondence to remain confidential I shall be making it public.

Yours sincerely,
Jacob Rees-Mogg

AFTERWORD

THE NEVER-ENDING
SCANDAL

This book opened with Lord Macaulay's description of the British propensity to suffer periodic 'fits of morality', in which the private lives of politicians are closely scrutinised by a baying public. It has proved an enduring observation. The most notorious fit of morality remains the Profumo Affair, the scandal that all others are measured against. The shaming of Christine Keeler, the frantic search for the Duchess of Argyll's mysterious fellatee and Lord Denning's lofty inquisition into the nation's morals marked a high point for British priggishness. But, as many of the stories recounted in this book demonstrate, it was far from the last time the public was outraged by an elite apparently riddled with sleaze.

When this book first went to press, our politicians were once again facing an outbreak of revelations about their sex lives. This time the scandal was triggered by allegations against a film industry mogul living halfway across the globe. After scores of women accused Harvey Weinstein of sexual assault, others were emboldened to tell their tales. Using the hashtag #MeToo, those who had experienced harassment by men in positions of power began to tell their tales.

Britain's political press leapt at the chance to get in on the act. Within a week, ten years' worth of otherwise unpublishable rumours about Westminster's elite had been leaked, shared online and followed up in the papers. The feeding frenzy climaxed with the release of a secret table laying out the alleged vices of an assortment of Tory MPs. In one memorable entry, it was claimed that an MP appeared in a sex video in which he was urinated on by three other men. Other allegations ranged from descriptions of major sexual offences to suggestions of affairs, the use of a dating website and, in one case, a relationship between two unmarried MPs. Simple gossip was relayed alongside allegations of serious crimes, while the accuracy of the accusations varied wildly. This elision of inaccurate hearsay with serious allegations of criminal activity both defamed some of those accused and diminished the prominence of the allegations against real offenders. The scandal was not restricted to the Conservative Party: Labour faced an allegation of rape made against a party worker by an activist, claims that several MPs were guilty of sexual assault, and the suicide of two party members accused of inappropriate behaviour.

After a couple of weeks, however, the Pestminster scandal had largely died down. In the social media age, outrage seems to abate as suddenly as it appears. Despite the scandal having been widely predicted to bring down the government, there were only two major resignations. The first was the Defence Secretary, Michael Fallon, who quit soon after allegations that he had inappropriately touched the knee of one journalist and tried to kiss another following a professional lunch. Although there was no suggestion of criminal wrongdoing, Fallon accepted that he had failed to meet the standards expected of the British Army, telling the BBC that 'the culture has changed over the years. What might have been acceptable ten or fifteen years ago is clearly not acceptable now.' Rumours abounded that other allegations lurked under the surface, alongside whispers that, as a former 'Remain' supporter, he had been knifed by Brexit-backing colleagues. The second was another key Remainer, Damian Green, to whom a chapter of this book is devoted. Although he stood accused of an inappropriate sexual advance, his resignation was more the result of incompetent briefing during a subsequent battle with one of his oldest political enemies.

Nonetheless, as Lord Macaulay predicted back in 1851, British politicians have periodically been caught out for 'immoral behaviour'. The Westminster lifestyle lends itself to liaisons between those in divergent positions of power. British political life remains male dominated, alcohol-fuelled, characterised by late nights, high-pressure decisions and ill-advised risk-taking. Additionally, many leading politicians harbour egos that are both oversized and fragile, with the weakest of them desperate for approval and easily flattered by the admiration bestowed upon them by junior staffers. As the Westminster village is also home to the parliamentary lobby, an organised cadre of professional gossips, news of indiscretions tends to travel fast.

MPs and ministers are, quite rightly, more likely than ever before to be called out on their inappropriate behaviour – and they know it. Although there will be more sex scandals to come, they are unlikely to match those that have gone before.

SELECTED BIBLIOGRAPHY

Christopher Andrew, *The Defence of the Realm: The Authorised History of MI5* (London: Penguin, 2010)

Norman Baker, *Against the Grain* (London: Biteback, 2015)

Ed Balls, *Speaking Out* (London: Hutchinson, 2016)

Arron Banks, *The Bad Boys of Brexit* (London: Biteback, 2016)

Tony Benn, *The Benn Diaries* (London: Hutchinson, 2017)

Owen Bennett, *Following Farage* (London: Biteback, 2015)

—, *The Brexit Club* (London: Biteback, 2016)

Tony Blair, *A Journey* (London: Arrow, 2011)

Michael Bloch, *Closet Queens* (London: Little, Brown, 2015)

—, *Jeremy Thorpe* (London: Abacus, 2016)

Tom Bower, *Gordon Brown: Prime Minister* (London: Harper Perennial, 2007)

—, *Broken Vows* (London: Faber & Faber, 2016)

Alastair Campbell, *Diaries Vol 1: Prelude to Power 1994–1997* (London: Hutchinson, 2010)

—, *Diaries Vol 2: Power and the People* (London: Hutchinson, 2011)

—, *Diaries Vol 3: Power and Responsibility* (London: Arrow, 2012)

—, *Diaries Vol 4: The Burden of Power, Countdown to Iraq* (London: Hutchinson, 2012)

—, *Diaries Vol. 5: Outside, Inside, 2003–2005* (London: Biteback, 2016)

Douglas Carswell and Daniel Hannan, *The Plan: Twelve Months to Renew Britian* (London, 2008)

Douglas Carswell, *Rebel: How to Overthrow the Emerging Oligarchy* (London: Head of Zeus, 2017)

Peter Catterall (ed.), *The Macmillan Diaries: The Cabinet Years 1950–57* (London: Macmillan 2012)

Alan Clark, *The Last Diaries: In and Out of the Wilderness* (London: Orion, 2002)

—, *Into Politics 1972–1982* (London: Phoenix, 2003)

—, *In Power 1983–1992* (London: Phoenix, 2003)

Ken Clarke, *Kind of Blue* (London: Macmillan, 2016)

Nick Clegg, *Politics: Between the Extremes* (London: Vintage, 2017)

Robin Cook, *The Point of Departure* (London: Simon & Schuster, 2004)

Ian Crawford, *The Profumo Affair: A Crisis in Contemporary Society* (White Lodge, 1963)

Michael Crick, *Michael Heseltine: A Biography* (London: Penguin, 1997)

Edwina Currie, *Diaries 1987–1992* (London: Biteback, 2012)

—, *Diaries: Vol. 2 1992–1997* (London: Biteback, 2012)

Alistair Darling, *Back from the Brink* (London: Atlantic, 2011)

Richard Davenport-Hines, *An English Affair: Sex, Class and Power in the Age of Profumo* (London: William Collins, 2013)

W. F. Deedes, *Dear Bill* (London: Pan, 2006)

Bernard Donoughue, *Downing Street Diary: With Harold Wilson in No. 10* (London: Pimlico, 2006)

—, *Downing Street Diary Vol. 2: With James Callaghan in No. 10* (London: Vintage, 2009)

Francis Elliott and James Hanning, *Cameron: The Rise of the New Conservative* (London: Fourth Estate, 2007)

Nigel Farage, *The Purple Revolution* (London: Biteback, 2015)

Robert Ford and Matthew Goodwin, *Revolt on the Right* (Oxford: Routledge, 2014)

Janan Ganesh, *George Osborne: The Austerity Chancellor* (London: Biteback, 2012)

John Golding, *Hammer of the Left* (London: Biteback, 2016)

Matthew Goodwin and Caitlin Milazzo, *UKIP: Inside the Campaign to Redraw the Map of British Politics* (Oxford: Oxford University Press, 2015)

Philip Gould, *The Unfinished Revolution* (London: Abacus, 2011)

Peter Hain, *Outside In* (London: Biteback, 2012)

Robin Harris, *The Conservatives: A History* (London: Corgi, 2013)

Diane Hayter, *Fightback! Labour's Traditional Right in the 1970s and 1980s* (Manchester: Manchester University Press, 2005)

Simon Heffer, *Like the Roman: The Life of Enoch Powell* (London: Faber & Faber, 2008)

Michael Heseltine, *Life in the Jungle* (London: Coronet, 2001)

Geoffrey Howe, *Conflict of Loyalty* (London: Pan, 1995)

Christine Keeler, *Secrets and Lies* (London: John Blake, 2012)

Victor Khadem and Alan Petford, *Mapping Saddleworth, Vol. 1: Printed Maps of the Parish, 1771–1894* (Saddleworth: Saddleworth Historical Society, 2007)

David Laws, *Coalition* (London: Biteback, 2016)

Nigel Lawson, *The View from No. 11* (London: Bantam Press, 1992)

Magnus Linklater and David Leigh, *Not With Honour: The Inside Story of the Westland Scandal* (London: Sphere, 1986)

Damian McBride, *Power Trip* (London: Biteback, 2014)

Donald Macintyre, *Mandelson: The Biography* (London: HarperCollins, 2000)

John Major, *The Autobiography* (London: HarperCollins, 2010)

Peter Mandelson, *The Third Man* (London: HarperPress, 2010)

Kevin Marsh, *Stumbling Over Truth* (London: Biteback, 2012)

Bob Marshall-Andrews, *Off Message* (London: Profile, 2012)

Seumas Milne, *The Enemy Within* (London: Verso, 2004)

Charles Moore, *Margaret Thatcher: The Authorised Biography, Vol. 1: Not for Turning* (London: Allen Lane, 2013)

—, *Margaret Thatcher: The Authorised Biography, Vol. 2: Everything She Wants* (London: Penguin, 2016)

Chris Mullin, *A View from the Foothills* (London: Profile, 2009)

—, *A Walk-On Part* (London: Profile, 2011)

—, *Hinterland* (London: Profile, 2016)

Andrew Neil, *Full Disclosure* (London: Macmillan, 1996)

Peter Oborne, *The Rise of Political Lying* (London: Simon & Schuster, 2005)

Matthew Parris, *Great Parliamentary Scandals* (London: Robson Books, 1995)

Chris Patten, *First Confession: A Sort of Memoir* (London: Allen Lane, 2017)

Jeremy Paxman, *The Political Animal* (London: Michael Joseph, 2002)

Mark Peel, *Shirley Williams: The Biography* (London: Biteback, 2013)

Ben Pimlott, *Harold Wilson* (London: HarperCollins, 1993)

Matt Potter, *The Last Goodbye: A History of the World in Resignation Letters* (London: Constable, 2015)

John Prescott, *Docks to Downing Street* (London: Headline, 2009)

John Preston, *A Very English Scandal: Sex, Lies and a Murder Plot at the Heart of the Establishment* (London: Viking, 2016)

David Profumo, *Bringing the House Down: A Family Memoir* (London: John Murray, 2006)

Andrew Rawnsley, *Servants of the People* (London: Penguin, 2001)

—, *The End of the Party* (London: Penguin, 2010)

Geoffrey Robertson, *The Justice Game* (London: Vintage, 1999)

—, *Stephen Ward Was Innocent, OK* (London: Biteback, 2013)

Nick Robinson, *Live from Downing Street* (London: Transworld, 2012)

David Runciman, *Political Hypocrisy* (London: Princeton University Press, 2010)

Dominic Sandbrook, *Seasons in the Sun* (London: Allen Lane, 2012)

Anthony Seldon (ed.), *The Blair Effect* (London: Little, Brown, 2001)

— (ed.), *Blair's Britain, 1997–2007* (Cambridge: Cambridge University Press, 2007)

— and Guy Lodge, *Brown at 10* (London: Biteback, 2011)

— and Mike Finn (eds.), *The Coalition Effect 2010–2015* (Cambridge: Cambridge University Press, 2015)

— and Peter Snowdon, *Cameron at 10: The Inside Story* (London: William Collins, 2015)

Tim Shipman, *All Out War* (London: William Collins, 2016)

Clare Short, *An Honourable Deception: New Labour, Iraq and the Misuse of Power* (London: Simon & Schuster, 2005)

John Stonehouse, *My Trial* (Star, 1976)

—, *Death of an Idealist* (London: W. H. Allen, 1975)

Peter Stothard, *30 Days: A Month at the Heart of Blair's War* (London: HarperCollins, 2003)

Jack Straw, *Last Man Standing* (London: Pan, 2013)

Anthony Summers and Stephen Dorril, *The Secret World of Stephen Ward* (London: Headline, 2013)

Margaret Thatcher, *The Path to Power* (London: HarperCollins, 1995)

—, *The Completed Speeches* (London: HarperCollins, 1999)

—, *The Downing Street Years* (London: HarperPress, 2012)

Andrew Thorpe, *A History of the British Labour Party* (Basingstoke: Palgrave Macmillan, 2015)

William Waldegrave, *A Different Kind of Weather* (London: Constable, 2015)

Alan Watkins, *A Conservative Coup: The Fall of Margaret Thatcher* (London: Duckworth, 1991)

Philip Webster, *Inside Story: Politics, Intrigue and Treachery from Thatcher to Brexit* (London: William Collins, 2016)

Harold Wilson, *Labour Government: The Final Term* (London: Michael Joseph, 1979)

Rob Wilson, *The Eye of the Storm* (London: Biteback, 2014)

Diana Woodhouse, *Ministers and Parliament: Accountability in Theory and Practice* (Oxford: Oxford University Press, 1994)

Peter Wright, *Spycatcher* (London: Viking, 1987)

INDEX